Gardening
with
Native Wild Flowers

Gardening
with
Native Wild Flowers

Samuel B. Jones, Jr.
and
Leonard E. Foote

TIMBER PRESS
Portland, Oregon

ISBN 0-88192-175-0
Printed in Singapore

Timber Press, Inc.
9999 S.W. Wilshire
Portland, Oregon 97225

Library of Congress Cataloging-in-Publication Data

Jones, Samuel B., 1933-
    Gardening with native wild flowers / Samuel B. Jones, Jr., Leonard
  E. Foote.
        p.   cm.
    Includes bibliographical references.
    ISBN 0-88192-175-0
    1. Wild flower gardening. 2. Wild flower gardening--United
  States.   I. Foote, Leonard E.   II. Title.
  SB439.J66   1990
  635.9'5173--dc20   90-33273
                                                             CIP

Contents

Color photographs follow page 64.

Dedication

This book is dedicated to the memory of Leonard E. Foote. Len died at age 70, just as the first draft of *Gardening with Native Wild Flowers* was to be sent to Timber Press. Len was an extraordinary person, the sort of outstanding individual and friend one rarely encounters along the path of life. It was a marvelous experience to work with Len, one that I will treasure for the rest of my life.

Samuel B. Jones, Jr.

Acknowledgments

The preparation of any book discussing over 1000 species is dependent upon the works and experiences of many persons. Such contributions have made this volume possible because much of the included information has come from dedicated individuals who have grown and studied plants since the time of Linnaeus.

Much inspiration for this project has come from our associations with professional coworkers, with members of various wild flower societies, from the staffs of gardens and perennial plant nurseries, and from members of the Perennial Plant Association. We are especially indebted to Harriett DiGioia, Bert Weertz, Margarita and Eugene Cline, Fred Galle, Ben Pace, Leo Collins, Fred and Mary Ann McGourty, André Viette, Pierre Bennerup, and Richard Simon. We are grateful to all who have shared information and experiences. We are appreciative of photographs from Nancy Arrington, Nicky Staunton, Darrel Morrison, Nancy Ross Hugo, Jim Manhart, F. M. Mooberry, Jeff Rettig, Beth Anderson, Wildseed, Inc., Michigan Department of Transportation, Texas State Department of Highways and Public Transportation, Lilypons Water Gardens and the National Wildflower Research Center.

The staff of the University of Georgia Department of Botany and of the Herbarium were helpful in every way. We are especially grateful to Nancy Coile who identified many voucher specimens and read some of the text, to Ann Baker who assisted with making copies and refiling specimens, to the Botany Office staff and especially to those associated with the senior author when he directed the University Botanical Garden during the development of a wildflower garden, including: Maureen O,Brien, Jim Manhart, Lynn Hill, Usher Thomason, Betsy Arrington-Tsao, Kay Kirkman, Mike Moore, and Danella Lee.

The facilities of the University of Georgia Library were extended to us most cooperatively by Arlene E. Luchsinger.

We appreciate the editorial assistance and the thoughtful suggestions for direction and emphasis we received from Richard Abel. Other members of the Timber press staff made the steps from manuscript to published volume most congenial: their artistic creativity has been invaluable.

We are grateful for the help and companionship of our wives, Carleen Jones and Grace Foote, who helped with field collections,photograph selection, editorial suggestions and proof reading. Carleen has largely been responsible for development of their display garden at Piccadilly Farm in Bishop, Georgia, where many native wildflowers and ferns are grown.

Samuel B. Jones, Jr.
Leonard E. Foote

CHAPTER 1

An Introduction To Native Wild Flowers

If you are interested in gardening with herbaceous plants native to eastern and midwestern North America, or using these plants in the landscape, this book is written for you. It is especially designed to provide practical advice for people who are interested in landscape settings that include our desirable and useful native wild flowers and hardy ferns. We hope to discredit the erroneous notion that the cultivation of wild flowers is a complicated and difficult process, or that natives are scraggly and unattractive. The intense competition prevailing in the wild for space, light, nutrients and moisture may cause some wild flowers in their natural habitat to appear less attractive than the introduced exotics which are grown in a garden situation. But when given the room to develop in an uncrowded and congenial location, well supplied with adequate light, moisture, and nutrients, many wild-flowers become compact and shapely, and produce more, larger and better flowers than do their wilding counterparts.

SCOPE

The chapters of this book provide information on which native perennials to use and how to use them in the perennial or wildflower garden. The book also provides useful information on how to propagate native perennial plants. It describes specific groups of native herbaceous perennials for both sun and shade, aquatic and wetland plants, grass-like plants, ferns, and meadow plantings. Recommended for the latter are some introduced or exotic plants such as Queen Anne's Lace (*Daucus carota*). For other plantings, only species occuring naturally in the eastern two-thirds of North America are recommended. Suggestions are made about those species which make good garden plants: species with superior aesthetic and cultural attributes, with desirable form, foliage, flower and fruits, and which are easy to propagate and grow.

DEFINITIONS

To adequately communicate with the reader, it is necessary to establish some working definitions. For the purposes of this book, a *native plant* is a grass, herb, shrub or tree which grows naturally east of the Great Plains or grasslands, and north of subtropical Florida. An *indigenous* or *endemic* plant is found in a specific geographic or habitat area. An *introduced* or *exotic species* has been introduced or brought into an area through intentional or accidental human activity. Some exotics may escape from cultivation or spread from the point of accidental intro-duction and become established, successfully reproducing themselves and surviving normal climatic fluctuations. These exotics are said to be *naturalized*. They literally become part of the *flora* or the plant life of the region. Many of our most troublesome weeds are naturalized exotics.

For our purposes, a *wild flower* is defined as a native, herbaceous flowering plant and includes grasses, and grass-like plants, as well as many aquatic plants. It should be remembered that the term wild flower is a paradox; for example a species tulip growing in a meadow in Turkey or southern Russia is a wild flower there, but all tulips are exotics to North Americans. *Herbaceous* means the stems are not woody and usually die back to the ground during the winter season. The native ferns, and other plants which reproduce by spores rather than seed, are not technically considered to be wild flowers, but due to their usefulness and desirable garden qualities are included in this book. A *wild flower garden* may be defined as a place where herbaceous native plants are grown under conditions suggesting their natural habitats.

A wild flower garden may vary in size from a small bed 3 × 8 ft. in size to a large woodland or sunny border covering many hundreds of square feet (Fig. 1-1 & 1-2). The use of wild flowers and hardy native ferns is not limited to placement in wild flower gardens. Native plants can be valuable sources of plant materials for all developed landscapes (Fig. 1-3, 1-4, & 1-5). One of the purposes of this book is to encourage gardeners and professional designers to incorporate herbaceous native plant material together with exotics into their designs and gardens.

Some additional terms should be clarified. An *annual* is a plant which germinates, lives, flowers and sets seed during one growing season then dies during or at the end of that growing season. A *winter annual* germinates in the fall, overwinters, flowers and produces seed in the spring and then dies. A *biennial* is a plant which germinates during the first growing season, overwinters, and then flowers during the second year. Biennials die the second season immediately after producing seed. *Herbaceous perennials* are non-woody plants living in one place for three or more years; the shoot system dies back to the ground each winter. In horticulture, herbaceous perennials are referred to simply as *perennials*. Living from year to year, perennials annually send forth new shoots from a bulb, a rhizome, or some other type of rootstock. Mature perennials form the mainstay of a wild flower garden. A plant growing where it is not wanted is called a *weed*. The word weed frequently implies an aggressive and often unsightly plant of disturbed or cultivated habitats. An *invasive weed* is a plant that is displacing native plants. *Noxious weeds* are plants legally determined to threaten human health or agricultural practices.

WHY GROW NATIVE WILD FLOWERS?

Why would anyone wish to grow native perennial wild flowers, ferns, and grasses when the seed catologs and garden centers are full of lovely, bright, colorful exotic annuals and perennials? By contrast, native wild flowers are often unavailable in the nursery trade and are often difficult to locate. Many well trained professional horticulturists, sales people, and landscape architects are unfamilar with native plants and have not been informed about their potential. Thus, assistance is not readily available. In short, the recognition and cultivation of natives are not as well established in the commercial nursery trade as that of exotics.

There are several reasons for growing native wild flowers. One is the intellectual reward that is somehow missing when one grows only petunias or coleus. There is the aesthetic experience of sharing an appreciation of natural beauty. With the cultivation of native wild flowers, one enters a new field, limited only by knowledge, imagination and originality, and providing much pleasure from the beauty of nature. The British and other Europeans have imported our wild flowers and have grown them as garden flowers for almost 300 years. Clearly, this demonstrates the merit of wildflowers. By examining wild or natural landscapes, it becomes apparent that the perennial wild flowers and ferns hold the scene together. They embellish the landscape by leading the eye from garden to shrubs to trees, completing the landscape picture.

We can learn much from the natives in our gardens. By observing native plants, the gardener gains a more profound insight into seasonal rhythms and life cycles. This, in turn, assists in developing a sense of identity with nature and the natural environment. There is that marvelous sense of satisfaction resulting from encouraging rare species of plants, or perhaps reestablishing species which might once have been abundant in the wild and may have previously grown in nearby areas. As eastern North America becomes more crowded, many of our native species of plants will survive only through cultivation in gardens.

One simple approach is to use native wild flowers and ferns in existing gardens to complement and enhance exotic annuals and perennials. Keep in mind that one does not have to start on a grand scale or in vast spaces with wild flowers. Marvelous wild flower gardens have been established in a small bed at the side of a house or in a perennial border in a space no larger than 3 × 8 ft. In fact, so as not to become over-extended, begin gardening with natives on a small scale.

The rewards of using natives are endless when they are provided with comfortable quarters in which soil moisture, sun and shade, and other environmental factors duplicate those of their natural haunts. Many species excel when placed in the well-cared-for perennial border. To insure bloom and attractive foliage, keep out weeds, and prevent overcrowding by occasionally dividing the native plants and by properly spacing them. Information is provided in this book to make gardening with natives successful.

CONSERVATION

In our efforts to establish wild flowers in gardens, we should be mindful of good conservation practices. *Conservation* may be defined as the protection of native plants and their natural habitats by wise land management, the establishment of wilderness areas, the preservation of natural areas, and careful development to protect the flora. Avoid digging plants from their natural habitats unless a site is about to be destroyed for development. In this case, a rescue mission can be organized with permission of the landowner. Otherwise buy only nursery propagated and grown material from reputable suppliers. Purchase plants from nearby sources so they are adapted to local growing conditions. Attempt to propagate plants from field or garden collected seed. This book provides suggestions for conservation practices and encourages a positive approach of action rather than a negative approach of telling the reader no! Cooperate with local and national organizations dedicated to protection and enhancement of wild flowers, particularly those which are endangered or threatened.

MEADOWS

Growing wild flower meadows is another exciting form of gardening, currently receiving much attention in popular horticultural and conservation publications. A *wild flower meadow* is defined as an open, sunny grassland with numerous species of colorful perennial flowers. Such a meadow can be somewhat reminiscent of an undisturbed prairie or grassland, the numerous and diverse herbaceous perennial flowering plants dominated by grasses. A meadow can occupy

11

a space as small as a treeless backyard or as large as an open field of several acres. The meadow concept is often employed along highway right-of-ways with varying degrees of success. The chapter on meadows explores the question, "Can wildflower meadows be the answer to gardeners' dreams?"

NOMENCLATURE

The assignment of names to plants is called *nomenclature*. It relies upon principles governed by rules formally listed in the *International Code of Botanical Nomenclature*. The oldest botanical plant names we now use were once the common names used in ancient Greece and Rome. Today, the scientific or botanical names of plants have a Latinized spelling or are treated as Latin regardless of their origin. This custom originates from medieval scholarship and from the use of Latin in most botanical publications until the middle of the 19th century. The assignment of names to plants was relatively unstructured until the middle of the 17th century when the number of plants known to Western botanists began to increase greatly, resulting in the need for a more precise naming system. Our system of nomenclature has its roots in the publication of Linnaeus' *Species Plantarum* in 1753.

Prior to 1753, plant names were usually composed of three or more Latin words comprising a descriptive phrase called a *polynomial*. This complex name-description system was not useful because it was cumbersome and not readily expandable. Linnaeus provided us with a two word format that made names more convenient to use and provided a readily expandable system. It is called the *binomial system* because the botanical name consists of two words: the generic name and the specific epithet. The binomial brings together the generic name and the specific epithet to form the species name. The term "species name" is often erroneouly used to refer to the specific epithet alone, but properly the species name consists of both the generic name and the specific epithet. For example, the scientific species name for Virginia Bluebells is *Mertensia virginica,* the generic name is *Mertensia,* the specific epithet is *virginica*. The reason scientific names are underlined or placed in italics is that they are foreign words, in this case Latin. As mentioned earlier, the binomial system is said to be expandable because additional specific epithets can be added as new species are discovered and placed within an existing genus.

Latinized scientific names often appear formidable to the beginning gardener. There is a natural and understandable tendency to avoid words with unfamiliar and seemingly difficult pronunciations. Why then do botanists and horticulturists use Latin scientific names instead of common names? Common names present a number of problems.

Common or vernacular names are not universal and may be applied only in a single language. Scientific names, on the other hand, are universal and are recognized throughout the world. Some plants may have a dozen or more common names in several different languages. For example, the introduced wild flower *Chrysanthemum leucanthemum* in English is called Daisy, White Daisy, Ox-eye Daisy, Shasta Daisy, or White Weed; the naturalized Eurasian *Centaurea cyanus* is variously known as Cornflower, Bluebottle, Bachelor's Button, or Raggedy Robin. Two or more plants may have the same common name and some species lack common names altogether. The informational content of scientific names is much greater since they indicate relationships at the generic level. Common names are provided in this book for each recommended species. These common names should not be regarded as "official" because there are no standardized or official common names of plants.

Scientific names can provide a great deal of information about a species once the Latin is understood. For example, *Campanula lactiflora* literally means "milky bell flower," which tells the reader that the plant produces a milky juice when injured and has flowers shaped like a bell. Although scientific names seem difficult to pronounce, one should attempt them and not worry about pronunciations that may differ slightly from the accepted. The important thing is to learn and to use scientific names and to communicate even if the pronunciation is variable. It is the fear of mispronouncing the botanical name that holds many back. Take the botanical name to your tongue and don't worry! The bastardized Latin used in botany makes professors of Classics shudder, so botanical Latin can hardly afford to put on airs.

The *International Code of Nomenclature for Cultivated Plants* deals with nomenclature for plants developed under cultivation. A plant brought in from the wild and cultivated retains the scientific name applied to that species in its native habitat. Horticultural plants produced in cultivation through selection, hybridization, or other processes are the only forms to receive cultivar names. The term *cultivar* is derived from the term *cultivated variety*. It should be noted that a cultivar is not analogous to a *botanical variety*, which is a category of the botanical naming system below that of the rank of species. The use of the term variety to refer to cultivars is improper and is incorrect in plant circles. Cultivar names are written with an initial capital letter and are either preceded by the abbreviation "cv" or placed within single quotes. For example, *Coreopsis verticillata* cv. Moonbeam or *Coreopsis verticillata* 'Moonbeam' are the two ways to denote that this plant is a cultivar. In some instances, the names of desirable cultivars are mentioned in this book under the discussion of recommended native species if these cultivars are known to be available.

Purists may wish to use only the species in their garden. Others may disagree, and grow selections from the natives representing various cultivars with outstanding attributes. However, if one wishes to refuse to acknowledge a cultivar with better flowers or growth habits, that is surely acceptable. Gardening can be one of life's finest pleasures and personal opinions should not be permitted to interfere with the enjoyment of gardening.

CLASSIFICATION OF PLANTS

To group related plants, and to communicate with others, botanists name plants as individuals but also arrange them into a *hierarchy of categories*. This work of arranging plants into related groups is called *taxonomy*. The *categories* of *variety, subspecies, species, genus, family,* and so on are the ranks assigned to plants. The hierarchy is an orderly array of categories, each category in the above sequence being more inclusive than the previous one. The classification system is based upon the fundamental and basic category of the species. Species may include subdvisions of their natural populations such as subspecies or varieties. Related species are grouped into genera and in turn related genera are grouped into families. This book provides the family name for each species described and the species are alphabetically grouped by genus and family.

A logical question: What is normally meant by these categories, or, what do botanists mean when they use a term such as species? In the practice of plant classification, a group of plants which is fundamentally alike is generally treated as a *species*. Ideally, a species should be separated by distinct, heritable, morphological differences from other closely related species. In developing concepts of species, individual plants should be regarded as samples of living, reproducing populations of plants growing in natural environments and having genetic variability. They are populations of plants that differ from all others in their reproductive biology and habitat requirement. Species cannot be defined in exact terms and by rigid, inelastic definitions. The word "species" is both the singular and the plural form. To manage and organize the natural variability often manifested within a species, the categories of *subspecies* and *variety* are utilized. For the most part, only one infraspecfic category will be utilized within a species, either subspecies or variety. In actual taxonomic practice, the terms are often used interchangeably even though subspecies is a higher ranking category. As used in this book, *hybrids* refer to plants produced from crosses between two distinct but closely related species.

The concept of *genus* (plural *genera*) is an important category in plant classification. It serves to bring aggregates of closely related species together. The genus might be loosely defined as a category whose species have more in common with each other than with the species of other genera within the same family. A more inclusive category is that of *family*, serving to group related genera. Plant families can be quite diverse or relatively homogeneous depending upon how many millenia they have existed and their evolutionary history. Some families contain only one species and hence only one genus, while others, such as the Sunflower family, may contain 20,000 species. Families are delimited based upon the overall similarities of the included species and genera. The names of most families end in—*aceae*; however, eight families have two absolutely correct family names. For example, the Mint family may properly be called either the Labiatae or the Lamiaceae; the Sunflower family is known as either the Compositae or the Asteraceae. In order to avoid confusion, this book provides both family names.

CHAPTER 2

Developing a Wild Flower Garden

At long last a growing number of North Americans have begun to appreciate things of lasting value such as perennial wild flowers. A garden of perennial, native wild flowers provides enduring joy and pleasure, something permanent in a world of impermanence. The growing of natives is no longer the exclusive concern of a handful of sophisticated, dedicated plantsmen. The popularity of our native treasures is a logical extension of the concern to preserve America's natural landscape features. As a consequence, landscape architects, designers, landscape contractors, nurserymen, and amateur gardeners are planting natives in increasing quantities. Leading trade publications such as the *American Nurseryman* now advocate the use of native plant material.

This chapter is intended to provide guidance on how native, perennial wild flowers can be used in the home landscape. It is our hope that it will also help to dispose of the notion of the difficulty of growing natives that has slowed their acceptance. Most native plants succeed quite well in any good garden soil if reasonable attention is given to their growing conditions of moisture, sun or shade, exposure, soil pH and nutrients. If a gardener is conscientious in selecting species which match the garden environment, and in planning a suitable landscape layout, a beautiful garden can be made with North American wild flowers. Although native perennials do not necessarily out-perform exotics, as some have claimed, many are of such garden quality that they merit use in our landscapes.

APPROACHES TO GARDENING WITH WILD FLOWERS

Numerous approaches may be taken in using native flowers to create a wild flower garden. One extreme is a hands-off, *laissez-faire* method. Carried to the extreme, such a garden is a long term project which simply calls for permitting the site to grow whatever species happen to appear, more or less following the orderly stages of natural plant succession. This technique was successfully used by the junior author and his wife at their place in the upper Piedmont of Georgia. The site was largely an old field pine community, which had evolved over 20–25 years following row crop cultivation. A thick duff of pine needles covered much of the area when the land was acquired. Only three Pink Lady's Slippers, *Cypripedium acaule*, were present at the time, yet some 15 years later, large colonies of this orchid have formed drifts in numerous locations under the pines (Fig. 2-1). All of this happened simply by following a hands-off approach and allowing nature to take its course. As the old field pine community continues toward an oak-hickory climax forest, it is likely the Pink Lady's Slippers will decline, but other wild flowers will invade and take their place.

On the other hand, a managed approach involves deliberate planning and site manipulation to develop a garden which capitalizes on the assets of native wild flowers. With this approach, wild flowers may be used in a variety of distinct ways. They may be incorporated into a traditional perennial border or into an island bed. Here little thought need be given to the ethics of mixing native and exotic perennials. The emphasis is on design, the effectiveness of the species, and the desires of

15

the designer or gardener. Beautiful combinations of native and exotics are grown with nary a twinge of conscience as to their intermixture. If desirable cultivars of native perennials are available, they might well be included rather than the original species. This is the approach the senior author and his wife have used in developing their garden.

Others, following the dictates of personal preference, consistently and faithfully use only perennials native to North America, excluding not only all exotics but cultivars as well. Only plants of the wild species are used. The most rigorous proponents of this approach may decide to restrict the plant list to species found in the local area or to include those native somewhere in eastern North America. For example, one must decide whether Virginia Blue Bells (*Mertensia virginica*) from limestone areas of the Ridge and Valley and Appalachian Plateau are appropriate in a garden on the acid soils of Piedmont, North Carolina or in the eastern parts of New England. Alternatively, one might select the most desirable wild flower species hardy in the local area. Here garden value is the most important consideration, the plant material used might well be a combination of native local plants and other wild flowers of interest and beauty. Basically, this approach turns on the principle of selecting plant material which is most appropriate to the design, be it for a formal and traditional perennial border or a woodland shade garden.

In other instances, the objective might be to restore a natural plant community by using only those native species growing prior to European settlement in the local area. Since much of eastern North America was originally forested, this approach is typically employed in a woodland setting. Restoration has the disadvantage of limiting the choice of wild flowers, but it has the distinct advantage of giving a regional signature to the garden. Such a garden's plant list is quite selective; the native species found in most wild flower gardens will not be used. The selected species might be incorporated in a designed approach, but more probably a naturalistic approach would be taken, the natives displayed in drifts. With this approach, it is essential that the designer be familiar with the flora of the area and the composition of similar local plant communities. Such knowledge is best gained by getting into the woods and learning from nature. Where possible, nature's designs should be emulated. This might also be labeled a purist's approach.

A garden of wild flowers, or for that matter one of exotics, should always reflect a personal interest and use regardless of the opinions of others.. There is no right or wrong approach as long as the garden produced is pleasing to the owner (Fig. 2-2). A garden should reflect the owner's preferences in color, form, style, and plant materials. Gardening is a very personal undertaking and the garden should display the vision of its creator. Although the hodgepodge of wild flowers in a collector's garden is not pleasing to all, it brings happiness and joy to the collector and so be it (Fig. 2-3).

The full enjoyment of gardening depends critically upon the reading of good gardening books. Here may future projects be envisioned or sound directions found for the taking of those immediate actions so often required to handle an unforeseen problem or opportunity in the garden. There are many ways of achieving some expertise, taste, and ability in gardening, but it is difficult to describe how one should start. Clearly, the beginner should not attempt too much all at once. Years can be spent learning how to use plants effectively, but one of the best ways to begin is by visiting the gardens of others. Visits to nearby gardens,

16

both private and public, and to nurseries always provide ideas. For the moment, study catalogs, delve into some of the better gardening magazines, and build up and regularly use a good personal library.

WHY MAKE A PLAN?

Good gardens begin with design, not with plants! Basic design and planning are the framework upon which everything else depends. Good garden design brings order and beauty to the whole scene. Whether it is a large formal affair or a tiny, informal, charming place, a garden of good design gives pleasure to all who see it. Planning is probably the most difficult part of gardening. A plan on durable paper can be a constant spur toward accomplishment. It can ensure that spaces are used to best advantage so that unpleasant views are screened off and vistas of more desirable ones provided.

Winter is a good time to start gardening with native wild flowers by reading and planning. These joint activities help to ensure that the garden is laid out to best advantage. One must begin somewhere—so don't be afraid to start. Study cures ignorance. Aided by books, friendly gardeners, magazine articles, and flower shows, any reasonably intelligent person can plan and lay out a decent garden or redesign an old one. The beginning gardener may feel utterly lost and wonder how it is humanly possible to retain so many details, plant names, and what have you. However, one learns what makes a good garden by practice, trial and error, making mistakes, and trying again.

With first plantings, the inexperienced gardener is apt to have a wonderfully delightful and trustful feeling that all is going to stay and grow as planned—each plant coming up in its given place year after year—with nothing to do but a bit of weeding and watering now and then. What really happens is something quite different. The first year the individual plants look small and somewhat disappointing, with too much space in the bed. The next season the garden is much better, the clumps have thickened and there is more flowering. By the third year the garden is lovely. Unfortunately, it will not stand still. Clumps of perennials keep growing, some aggressively. Others self-sow, providing plants for neighbors or becoming weeds. Some plants never do well and either disappear or struggle along barely alive in that wonderful spot that seemed so right. So one moves plants about, attempting to find a happy place for them, divides the more aggressive sorts, and replaces others. A garden never crystallizes into some supreme moment of great beauty but changes and evolves through time.

Plants and gardens are like our children, they grow and change and may even produce grandchildren. Despite the best of plans, gardens are not eternal: they need to be reworked when they become unkempt. Before reworking a wild flower garden, it is time again to plan improvements in the design, rework the soil, change widths of the beds, make new arrangements of plants, and add new species. The design and plan must be updated periodically. Notes and photographs are helpful to understand the changes as a garden goes through the seasons. This never ending change is one of the things that make gardening particularly interesting and challenging.

HOW TO DEVELOP A PLAN

Many of us have yearned to have a garden using native wild flowers but have felt some degree of insecurity about our abilities to make one. It is only natural to feel timid about making a plan. Anyone can design if they go slowly and learn by looking at what others have done. While it is true that some lovely gardens seem to simply appear and to grow and develop beautifully with only a mental plan in the owner's head, it is best for most to work with an actual plan drawn to scale on graph paper. It is much cheaper and easier to move a group of plants around on paper than after they are planted. Mistakes are easily removed with an eraser. Most successful garden lay-outs take shape on a drawing board. Planning on paper helps to crystallize thoughts and a base plan aids in setting down goals. A good plan often solves difficulties; a pleasing design attracts the eye and gives a good effect (Figs. 2-4 & 2-5).

The materials needed are relatively simple: a 50–100-ft. tape measure; a ruler or straight edge of some sort; some large sheets of tracing paper and graph paper, the latter marked off in grid squares; and a few pencils and erasers. The first step is the development of a base map on the grid paper so that the tracing paper can later be placed over it repeatedly to make the working drawings.

In many instances, the survey attached to the property deed can aid in establishing an outline of the boundaries. Next, establish an easy to use scale to convert measurements into grids on the base map. With these steps accomplished, insert the outline of the house, outbuildings, existing trees, shrubs, and other prominent features in their proper location on the base map. The idea is to first concentrate on measuring and recording all existing features so an accurate bird's-eye view of the property and proposed garden can be seen. A base map aids in getting a detailed and critical view, and it becomes easier to plan with a fresh view looking down on the scene from above. Once the base map is finished, it is time to use the tracing paper to outline initial thoughts about the site and later the final layout.

Take the time for a careful look at the property using a sheet of tracing paper to record observations. Plot characteristics of the land, including drainage, vegetation, and topographic features. Mark major lines of views, both good and bad, as well as true north. Determine sun and shade areas to later help decide upon the plant species to be used. Record problem areas such as wet or dry spots. View the grounds from inside the house to facilitate enjoyment of the garden from indoors. At this stage, still other sheets of tracing paper can be used to sketch various ideas and to experiment with the lay-out of the garden. Since overlays are used, any number of ideas may be tested without disturbing the base map.

No plant, be it tree, shrub, or wild flower, exists by itself; therefore, all elements in the design must relate to each other and to the whole garden. For example, a garden should not be laid out in a series of disconnected beds surrounded by paths serving no purpose. A garden is made up of many elements; paths, benches, walls, streams, terraces, rocks, and plants. Relate the garden to the topography. Woodland gardens, for example, might follow the course of a stream. Consider the location and proximity of water lines, driveways, patios, and decks. Give consideration to probable uses of the garden and how it is to be placed and connected to the house. No two sites present the same problems or opportunites so only generalities can be given here.

In planning a garden, follow personal tastes and preferences, bearing in mind certain ground rules. The relationship of the garden to the house should be obvious in any plan. Relate the garden to some important feature of the house. While the shape and type of lay-out of a flower garden is a matter of personal taste, much of what is done is determined by the configuration and character of the site, the style of the house, the available space, and last but not least, the life style of the owners. Wild flowers are suitable for formal and geometric gardens, planted alongside walks, or in front of hedges or walls. They may be used in island beds that allow freer and more informal designs arranged for viewing from all sides. A garden site with trees suggests the use of woodland wild flowers and ferns. Uneven ground, perhaps with a ravine or stream, or rock outcrops, is just waiting for a gardener with imagination. All are perfect spaces for native plants.

A most important consideration is personal dedication. Is gardening an all-absorbing interest or simply a pleasant adjunct to life? Be realistic about the time required for gardening and avoid planning an area larger than can be maintained.

PLACEMENT OF PLANTS IN THE GARDEN

At this point, the placement of the plants in the beds must be decided. This is done by making an overlay of the proposed beds on tracing paper. To use plants to their best advantage, their approximate height and spread, habit of growth, form of foliage, season of flower, and color, must be known. Large wild flowers look best when grown in wide, rectangular perennial borders against a background of shrubs or a vine-covered wall or fence. Some gardeners may choose to use them in front of a woodland border with a natural background of native shrubs and small trees. Still another possibility is to use the plants in randomly shaped island beds in a central open area. Island beds provide an opportunity to view the plants from all angles. In a shady, informal, woodland garden, the plant bed will likely be a random thing meandering along paths. A border against a background of shrubs needs a root barrier and a 3–4-ft. margin between the hedge and the perennial border. Stepping stones placed in beds can aid in weeding.

The next step in planning is the preparation of a list of plants desired in the garden. Keep in mind that environmental conditions dictate which species can be successfully grown. The plants selected must be appropriate for minimum temperatures, available light, moisture, pH, etc. conditions. The environmental factors of the garden must be considered: how much sunshine or shade during what part of the day; is the site wet, dry or mesic; how fertile is the soil; is water available for irrigation?

A proper balance can be obtained by distributing the plants relative to their heights. Place the tall growing ones at the back (such as *Baptisia australis*), the medium sized ones near the center (e.g. *Amsonia tabernaemontana*), and the low ones at the front (e.g. *Oenothera fruticosa* or *Stokesia laevis*), but don't carry this principle out to the point of monotony. Occasionally bring a tall group, such as Upland Sea Oats (*Chasmanthium latifolium*), to the foreground of the bed for accent. Also, plan some good groups of color, such as Butterfly Weed (*Asclepias tuberosa*), for the front of the bed for additional accent. John Williamson's book, *Perennial Gardens*, provides some good suggestions for combinations using native plants (Figs. 2-6, 2-7, 2-8, & 2-9).

Combinations of flower colors are a very personal matter; who is to say one color is better than another? Perhaps one of the best practical discussions on the use of color in the garden can be found in Graham Stuart Thomas' book, *The Art of Planting*. Color use does not necessarily mean some startling vision, but the rather deliberate intention of creating a desired effect. Color in a garden is often taken to mean any color other than green. However, green is a color too, indeed the most important color in many gardens. The possibility of the cooling effects of green on a hot summer's day is too often overlooked. A few practical suggestions regarding color:

1) Flowers of the same color can be planted together;
2) Blues and mauves provide contrast;
3) White is useful next to strong reds;
4) Gray foliage blends well with both strong colors and cooler shades;
5) Strong yellows are best with orange or reddish shades;
6) Crimson is a good accent for deep purple or violet;
7) Do not mix blue with orange or purple, or cherry reds with blues and oranges, unless that is your taste;
8) With perennials, time of flowering is all-important in working out color combinations. That is, color harmonies or contrasts are only meaningful if the plants flower at roughly the same time.

Categorize the desired plants by height, season of bloom, flower color, texture, and growth habit. Special thought should be given to blooming season. Overlays can be prepared indicating those plants which flower each month. By using colored pencils to shade in groups with the appropriate flower color, one can more easily evaluate the monthly color combinations. In much of the eastern United States, it is difficult to have continuous color and it may be necessary to select plants flowering at the principal times the garden is used. Consider integrating native wild flowers with some of the attractive exotic perennials or even a few annuals in order to extend the season of color. It is important to remember that the foliage of many plants, such as *Baptisia* and *Amsonia*, has value and provides intrinsic interest in the garden.

Wild flowers in woodland gardens usually bloom in April and May with pastel colors which show up well in light shade. Summer in the woodland garden brings on the refreshing cool green of ferns. The sunny garden begins to flower in May and peaks in June and July with Stokes' Aster (*Stokesia laevis*), Butterfly Weed (*Asclepias tuberosa*), Purple Cone Flower (*Echinacea purpurea*), Spiderwort (*Tradescantia* spp.), Bee Balm (*Monarda* spp.) and Black-eyed Susan (*Rudbeckia hirta*). In September, color and interest returns with various Asters (*Aster* spp.) and Goldenrods (*Solidago* spp.), *Boltonia*, Sunflower (*Helianthus* spp.) and the seed heads of grasses. One should aim to use plants with complementary colors and bloom periods that overlap.

As a rough working rule, perennials should be spaced half their height apart, i.e., if they grow 3 ft. tall, space them 1.5 ft. apart. Of course, the more one works with plants, the greater the awareness that some plants need more room than others. The size of the groups of one kind of plant is governed by the size of the bed. Plants can be effectively grouped singly or in groups of threes, fives, or sevens or more. If their ultimate size is small, more individuals are needed to make a statement. Repeating a plant or a grouping is an effective technique in any garden where there is sufficient room. Remember, a plan is only a guide; undoubtedly some parts will be changed once the plants start to grow. Placement can be adjusted by moving the plants.

WOODLAND GARDENS

Successful woodland gardens depend on the sympathetic interpretation of the site's possibilities and an awareness of appropriate plant associations. Woodland gardens using natives can be a whole ecological world apart from the formal perennial border of exotics. Here native wild flowers are encouraged to spread and seed themselves and to form natural drifts. Simplicity, rather than ostentation, is the keyword in a woodland garden. Allow woodland garden paths to melt imperceptibly into the setting. Natural features, such as contours of the ground, streams, springs, and indigenous trees and shrubs, are enhanced by shade-tolerant wild flowers to create a delightful picture.

The creation of a woodland garden requires a comprehensive working plan, and a fairly definite program of successive steps is essential. As in the case of a perennial garden, an outline base map drawn to scale, together with overlays is essential for planning. Locate on the base map springs, streams, rock outcrops, open glades, boulders, evergreen trees, and individual trees of size and beauty. Learn about the growth habits of trees, shrubs, wild flowers, and ferns that are already present. Determine which species are worthy of being preserved. Identify areas in the woodland in need of plants. Free and easy access to the woodland is a matter of prime importance. Roads and trails provide access but they also lead to, or connect with, points of special interest. Paths do not have to go the most direct route, but can ramble about with unexpected twists and turns. The paths should invite the visitor to continue forward by providing interest and mystery ahead. Stepping stones and bridges over streams or boggy sections are essential. Combine informality and comfortable progress by respecting the contours of the ground. Boulders can be given an aged appearance by grinding moss plants in a blender and applying the material to the surface of boulders. The ground plant material will regenerate moss plants. Rock crevices provide footholds for some species of plants, especially the tiny ferns.

If possible, paths should be wide enough to allow access by garden equipment used during landscape construction, tree removal, installation of water lines, and soil preparation. Remove undesirable trees, such as Red Maples, which provide excessive competition, as well as spindly or dead trees. If not dangerous, however, the latter can be left in place for wild life. Eliminate weeds such as Poison Ivy, Japanese Honeysuckle, and Privet. Remove the stumps of woody plants to prevent sprouting. Trees should be "limbed up" to provide high shade. The removal of less desirable trees opens up the woodland and provides a variety of light situations. Many shade plants are at their best when given as much light as possible without causing burning of the foliage, and flowering can be enhanced by judicious overstory thinning. Thus, wide paths not only provide access but also have the advantage of opening up the garden and creating a variety of habitats. Free spaces, glade-like in appearance, should be encouraged along the paths and roads.

Some areas may be left natural, such as wood-shrub borders, thickets, and inaccessible interior areas that cannot be clearly seen. Such areas add mystery and excitement. Areas of dense growth provide cover for wildlife and natural erosion protection for the site. Borders of the woods should be planted with low growing trees and shrubs because such ecotones between clearings and forests attract birds. They also provide windbreaks for the delicate wild flowers of the woodland garden. Many berry bushes, vines, creepers, and sun-loving herbaceous perennials are ideal for wildlife. A group of fruiting shrubs or a clump of dogwoods provides food for birds thereby giving pleasure to both the gardener and the birds.

SOME NOTES ON DESIGN CONSIDERATIONS

Planning involves not only the selection and placement of plants but also the design and construction of the physical site. Consider features such as walks, patios, and garden furnishings. Again, read extensively (see the bibliography for sources) and visit other gardens for ideas. Mistakes will be made, but these can usually be corrected. Proper planning prior to construction and planting helps to minimize errors. The goal is to make the garden both visually pleasing and functional.

Some considerations for planning include:

1) While planning, study the site from all perspectives including from inside the house and from the street. Consider how the garden will be viewed from these areas and take advantage of these views to maximize the effect of the plantings.

2) The landscape plan should suit the site. Consider factors that should be worked into the design such as drainage and topography, utilities and irrigation, existing vegetation, sun and wind directions, and soil types; take note of any outstanding site features such as streams or attractive rock outcroppings that could be developed into focal points for the garden; use the plan to bring out the assets of the site. With native plant material, be attentive to the ways plants arrange themselves and select plants that coexist harmoniously with the site. Be led by mother nature, never oppose her.

3) Determine the layout and materials for the garden features and furnishings to be used. To do this, plan the functional as well as the aesthetic features of the design; lay out pathways to connect the garden areas and paths to facilitate viewing and maintenance; plan seating areas, and outdoor living areas if desired. It is important to keep all of these elements in scale with the area and each other; larger features look better in a large garden and smaller detailed items are ideal for the small garden.

4) Create focal points within the landscape. Determine which areas need accenting or emphasis such as the entrance from the street, the walkway to the front door, or the central feature adjacent to a seating area. Highlight these areas with special plantings of native perennials using a variety of colors and textures, a piece of statuary, or different paving patterns; lighting and site furnishings can also add interest.

5) Allow room for the ultimate growth of the plantings—do not over-plant to achieve immediate effect. Plants grow better and to a more natural, mature shape if not crowded into a situation where they must compete for light, moisture, and nutrients. Over-planting is also more costly than correctly spacing the plants initially. The height as well as the width of the plants should be considered; if a tall plant is used in front of a low-growing plant, the lower plant will not be seen. If not sure of the ultimate size of a particular species, ask a nurseryman or consult this book and other reference materials on the subject.

6) Keep the garden simple and restrained. A simple design with emphasis placed on the good features of the site is more likely to work than an overly complex plan. To avoid a "hodgepodge" look, use fewer species in massed groupings. Color enriches the beauty of a garden scene, but can be distracting if used improperly; do not crowd too many colors together into one planting, and be sure the colors used complement, rather than clash with one another. Site furnishings and other constructed items should reflect the style of the garden; for example, a modernistic bench would be out of style in a natural woodland garden. Select a style or theme and use it throughout the garden; be sure that this style is also one that suits the architectural motif of any buildings on the site. Above all, never make the garden larger than can be cared for; a small well-kept garden is much more effective than one that is too large and suffers from neglect.

7) Planning is crucial to the success of a garden. Put together the plants and other elements of the scene to make a pleasing combination of masses, forms, lines, colors, and textures. Prior to installing plants, measure the site and prepare a sketch plan of your design to determine the materials needed. Lay out the plan on the ground using string or other markings, and position plants in containers to balance spacing and to make sure the design works before beginning construction and planting. If uncomfortable with the plan, consult with a qualified design professional such as a landscape architect or experienced designer who has worked with native plants.

CHAPTER 3

Preparation and Management
of the Wild Flower Garden

Few plants provide the excitement, joy, and intellectual fulfillment of perennial wild flowers. No matter where the reader lives, or under what conditions he or she must garden, whether it be sun or shade, city or country, there are native wild flower species that can be grown. The aim of this chapter is to help you get started. The keys to success with perennial wild flowers are preparing and planning, choosing the correct species for the garden situation, and making a garden of manageable size. But to begin, one must get started! When one does so, the rewards are endless!

Before starting to grow wild flowers, learn as much about them as possible. Visit a good library or buy a few, good books on the subject. Take a course on the local flora at a nearby college, nature center, or botanical garden. Join a local or state botanical club and visit gardens which feature native plants. Learn to identify wild flowers, where they grow, their growth requirements, when they bloom, and when they mature seed. For many species, the best clues for success are right at hand.

The practiced eye can observe the native plant in its natural setting, which is not the case with exotics from some distant corner of the earth. Thus the environmental conditions which best suit that species are immediately obvious. The serious gardener regularly studies native plants in their respective habitats in order to understand their ecological requirements. Field study must always be coupled with meticulous study of printed sources on the local flora and in the event field study is impossible, the printed sources must be studied even more carefully. The best practice, however, is first hand observation gathered in the fields and woods. Start nearby to examine local wild flowers as they occur in nature, noting how they distribute themselves, and where they grow. Take notes on how they relate to shade and sun, soil moisture, soil depth, and the soil type (sand, clay, etc.), and then study the plant itself. Does it have corms, rhizomes, tubers, basal offsets; is it invasive, can it be divided? Does it grow in colonies, or does it prefer to be solitary?

In nature, plants typically are associated in various ecological habitat groupings. Botanists call these groupings *plant communities*. Each distinct plant community has its own combination of temperature, moisture, light, soil, terrain and other factors determining the species of plants inhabiting it. Some species have wide ranging ecological tolerances and may be found in several very different plant communities; others have very strict requirements and are found in only one specific community type. In an abandoned, formerly cultivated field, one may find Asters (*Aster* spp.), Daisies (*Chrysanthemum leucanthemum*), Goldenrods (*Solidago* spp.), Broomsedge (*Andropogon* spp.), and Wild Carrots (*Daucus carota*). In a maturing old-field pine community one encounters Christmas Ferns (*Polystichum acrostichoides*), Pink Lady's Slippers (*Cypripedium acaule*), and Pipsissewa (*Chimaphila maculata*). Herbaceous plants of a mature, undisturbed deciduous woodland would likely include Broad Beech Ferns (*Thelypteris hexagonoptera*), Wild Geraniums (*Geranium maculatum*), Trilliums (*Trillium* spp.), and Hepaticas (*Hepatica* spp.). The ecological conditions of each of these communities differ as reflected by their species composition.

Most gardens have a variety of exposures providing microhabitats where many different native wild flowers can grow. To make gardening with wild flowers an enjoyable undertaking, one must learn to work with nature and to make use of the conditions prevailing in one's garden. With experience, the eye begins to look over the site and inventory its qualities. Is the garden site wet or dry? Drain spouts or splash from pools may provide moisture for the plants requiring extra water. If too wet, it may be necessary to drain the area or use only bog plants. What is the condition of the soil? Is it a good loam or is it sandy or a clay subsoil? How much sunshine or shade is available? Are trees or large shrubs needed to frame the garden or to provide background or windbreaks? If the garden is in the woods, plan to develop a shade garden, since sun plants are unlikely to be successful. Examine the type of shade; are the trees evergreen or deciduous? Is the shade light or heavy? What kind of deciduous trees are present? For example, maples and beeches typically provide too much shade and make for fierce root competition. Trees may need to be removed to build a successful shade garden. Is tree removable acceptable? A successful shade garden may require the sacrifice of a few trees! A wild flower garden requires study, planning, funding, and hard work. Perhaps the best advice is: start small and do not plant more than can be maintained.

SOIL PREPARATION

With adequate mechanical preparation of the soil, the addition of plenty of organic matter (humus), sand where needed, sufficient nutrients, and water during droughts, plantings of native perennials will thrive. Extra time, energy, and money invested in soil preparation pays significant dividends in the long run. Soils must usually be prepared and amended prior to planting. The extra effort will be worthwhile since perennial wild flowers live for many years in the same spot. The addition of sand or very fine gravel may be necessary to improve drainage. Organic matter invariably improves the structure of the soil—basically how the soil particles relate to one another—by increasing the ability of sandy soils to hold nutrients and moisture and by improving drainage and texture in heavy soils.

Developing good garden soils from undesirable soils may seem to pose a real problem, but with patience, energy and planning, wonders can be accomplished: red clay cotton fields, gravely glacial soils, sandy hillsides, woodlands, and even sites scraped bare by the developer's bulldozer can successfully be improved and conditioned. Start by improving one small area and persevere in management and improvement. Probably the most important key to developing a good garden soil is *organic matter*. In most instances it is impossible to add too much organic matter during soil preparation. Before preparing the soil have a soil test made to determine the needed nutrients. Soil tests are usually available through the state extension service. With the results in hand, the needed nutrients or pH factors may be added to the soil in an intelligent way.

Few absolute fixed rules governing soil preparation can be given due not only to the numerous and widely variable local conditions prevailing, but also to the fact that the same species grow under different conditions in different parts of the country. Peat moss, for example, decomposes rapidly in the hot humid south but less rapidly in the cooler north. So peat moss is an excellent source of organic matter in the Northeast but one's money is better spent on ground pine bark in the Southeast. Some plants need shade and moisture in the Southeast but can grow in more sun and with less soil moisture in New England. Thus, not only do garden conditions vary in different localities but plants grow differently as well.

Plants are generally bothered less by dry spells when plenty of organic matter has been added because the organic matter enables the soil to hold additional moisture. With adequate and deep mechanical preparation of the soil, the roots are able to penetrate it, making most plants respond with greater productivity. There are no sites where it is impossible to improve the soil, and if the budget allows, few sites where it would be impossible to grow perennial wild flowers. Even on a New York City rooftop, in containers or window boxes, above a parking garage in Washington, DC, or on a bare tract lot of a subdivision, beautiful plants can reward the well-informed gardener.

Almost as important as humus is soil drainage. Even some of the so-called bog plants actually grow on hummocks raised above the level of the bog and hence are better drained than might be imagined at first glance. Penstemons (*Penstemon* spp.) and Butterfly Weed (*Asclepias tuberosa*) always require well drained soil and do poorly in soils high in organic matter. Keep in mind that under garden conditions, natives often thrive in drier soil or in more sun than they do in nature because much of the competition from other plants is eliminated.

When establishing a native perennial wildflower garden, the gardener will likely encounter one of several typical situations. The first is the revitalization of an *existing garden*. In this case in particular, the soil should be tested for available nutrients and pH with the assistance of an extension agent. Soil testing should be done in all situations, but it is especially critical in older gardens where the past use of high analysis fertilizers may have led to a build-up of phosphorus which can cause problems. Too much phosphorus binds other nutrients, such as iron, leading to their unavailablity. Furthermore, if the garden had in the past received regular applications of lime and potassium, additional amounts of these two nutrients may not be needed, thus saving money that could better be spent on plants or organic matter. Continue to obtain soil tests on an annual basis for your garden to maintain favorable levels of nutrients.

Next the bed should be tilled or dug by hand as deeply as possible. This should be done only when moisture conditions are suitable. If the soil is too dry, it will be too hard to prepare; if too wet, digging or tilling causes clods to form especially in heavy clay soils. If the area is not too large the English method of "double digging" (18–30 in. deep) might be used. But quite frankly, most wild flower perennials grow nicely if the soil is prepared to a depth of 8 in. Another possibility is to rent a heavy duty roto-tiller. If the area is accessible and of sufficient size, it is worthwhile to rent a tractor with a heavy roto-tiller. A subsoiler attachment on a tractor can be used to break up the soil to a depth of 18–24 in. and to eliminate any *hardpan* (a layer of hard, impermeable, compacted clay that often develops below the normal tillage zone in gardens). Once the soil is mechanically prepared, 3–4 in. of organic matter should be incorporated into the bed by spading or roto tilling it in, together with the fertilizer and lime in the amounts determined by the soil test.

The organic matter used will likely depend upon what is available in the local area, e.g., ground pine bark, weed-free manure, composted leaves, peat moss, composted and approved sewage sludge (some caution needed here), decayed sawdust (10–15 years old), etc. Basically organic matter acts likes a sponge permitting the soil to hold more water and nutrients and to allow the ready exchange of gasses passing to and from the roots. Organic matter also encourages the growth of microorganisms which promote, in various ways, plant growth. Heavy clay soils also benefit from the addition of sand to improve drainage, and *perlite* (expanded volcanic material) or gypsum to improve aeration. Once the organic matter, nutrients, and other amendments have been throughly worked into the top 6–8 in. of the bed, the bed is ready for planting.

A second common situation is the plot of ground located around a new home in a subdivision *scraped bare* by the developer, and the existing subsoil further compacted by the vehicles of the construction workers and heavy concrete trucks. Graded and leveled off by a so-called landscaper, the site is probably well drained, hence dry in summer, and lacks good soil and organic matter. Don't give up, miracles can and will happen even on this seemingly poor site.

The first step in this case is to purchase good, weed-free, herbicide-free loamy top soil to cover the entire area to a depth of 3–4 in. Once the top soil has been spread, mark out the beds. Mechanically prepare the beds by digging or roto-tilling as in the first situation. Then add 3–4 in. of organic matter, sand, and recommended nutrients based on a soil test made before preparing the bed. The senior author did just as recommended above on a perennial bed located on hard-packed Georgia red clay with excellent results.

Thirdly, the gardener may wish to develop a planting of perennial wild flowers on an existing *lawn*. In this case outline the bed with a garden hose if a curved bed is wanted or with a string if the beds are to be rectangular. Spray the entire bed area with an environmentally safe herbicide which the extension service can recommend, to kill most existing green weeds and grasses. Allow one week for the herbicide to kill the grass and weeds, then mechanically prepare the bed as in the first situation, add organic matter, sand if needed, and nutrients as indicated by the soil test. The bed is now ready to plant.

Many wild flower perennials require shade, so the next two situations discuss soil preparation for *shade gardening*. In eastern North America many established home sites have large, mature trees growing on them and casting a thin to dense shade. In a garden situation, most native shade perennials perform best in dappled or mottled shade, so some trees may have to be removed prior to establishing a shade garden. Beech, maple, and some conifers commonly produce too much shade as well as excessive root competition, so as a general rule, shade gardens are less than satisfactory if under such species. In most instances, professional assistance is required to take down large trees and to grind the stumps because such work and the equipment required is beyond the capability of most homeowners.

Once the selected trees and their stumps have been removed, the beds should be prepared as recommended for other types of sites. It may be necessary to add some extra humus to the site, especially if it had been in a shady lawn. Tree roots will undoubtedly be encountered during preparation of the beds. Normally, these roots are removed in order to reduce competition for moisture and nutrients with the newly transplanted wildflowers. Loss of a few roots does not usually harm trees, providing the trees were healthy prior to preparing the beds, and assuming only a few of the roots are severed in the process. Nearby trees typically benefit from gardening activities such as the addition of nutrients and water, and the mechanical preparation of the beds.

If the objective is to develop a naturalistic woodland garden in *existing woods*, much of the process is the same as that described above. In a natural forest situation, paths must be planned and developed; trees and brush must be cleared both from the planned beds and the paths. Excessive or undesirable trees should be removed during the construction process, while the area is accessible to heavy equipment and prior to planting. Even though it may seem too wide at the time, a width of about 18 ft. is required to establish the trail system and planting areas. Roughly 6 ft. are required to maneuver machinery (tractor, stump grinder, roto-tiller, and ditching machine for irrigation lines) and to establish the path or walkway through the woods. About 6 ft. on either side of the path is needed for the planting beds.

By clearing a wide swath through the woods, the dappled sun-shade situation required by many shade loving woodland plants is provided, as is the space for shrubs used to form a background for the native perennials. The remaining trees will grow rather quickly, casting more and more shade once water and fertilizer are added to the woodland system. It is easier and cheaper to remove trees before planting rather than later. This lesson was learned in the senior author's woodland garden at Piccadilly Farm, where the tree clearing was not done initially as thoroughly as it should have been. In less than 10 years additional trees had to be removed, resulting in damage to some of the plantings. Additionally, opening the canopy may be needed periodically to induce or increase flowering of both background shrubs and the native perennials.

The final general situation is an *urban site* where one wishes to grow native perennial wild flowers upon *concrete, asphalt,* or *hard packed soil.* Provided the site is drainable and free of chemicals that might kill the plants, it is possible to develop a native perennial wild flower garden in what might seem to the suburban gardener a most unpromising location. Bring in sufficient soil and humus to provide at least 8 in. of soil when settled and compacted. Allow at least 20% extra soil and humus, that is, 2 in. more, for settling and compaction. This mixture should be spread over a 1 in. bed of pea gravel to provide drainage. Used railroad ties or concrete blocks are placed to retain the soil. Mounding of the material may be done to give additional soil depth for background shrubs. The mounds are held in place by any of our several native plants that are suitable for use as ground covers. Of course, additional fertilizer and water must be provided in addition to the soil materials.

Native perennials can also be grown in *containers,* such as pots or halves of whiskey barrels, rather than beds. The commercial peat-lite mixtures are usually unsatisfactory for container gardening as they settle or dry out too quickly. Certain of the commercial potting soils based on composted pine bark are much better for this purpose. If preparing a soil mix for containers, one recommended recipe consists of:

6 parts ground pine bark,
1 part sand,
1 part weed free woods soil, and
1 part perlite.

For each construction-sized wheelbarrow of the above mixture, add a 4 in. pot each of dolomitic limestone, superphosphate, 10-10-10 fertilizer and 14-14-14 slow release fertilizer.

SOIL pH

Soils of eastern North America tend to be acid or sour unless they are above a calcareous bed rock such as limestone. This does not mean they taste sour, but that they are more acid than pure water. Acidity or alkalinity is based on a scale of 0–14 called the *pH scale*. Pure water which is neither acid or alkaline has a pH of 7 as does a neutral soil. Alkaline soils have a pH reading above 7 and acidic soils have a pH of less than 7. The pH scale is negatively logarithmic, therefore a pH of 6 is 10 times more acid than the pH 7 of pure water, pH 5 is 100 times more acid, and so on. Agricultural limestone (calcium carbonate) is used to raise the pH or sweeten the soil while sulphur corrects alkaline soil by lowering the pH. The level of pH is important because it affects the availability of nutrients to plants. In very acid or very alkaline soil, the nutrients are locked in and are unavailable to plants. The optimum pH range for most wild flowers is pH 5.5–6.5.

Soils become acid due to the removal of basic elements, especially calcium, by the leaching action of rainfall. Decomposing organic matter also lowers the pH by producing carbon dioxide which combines with soil moisture to form carbonic acid. Many areas east of the Mississippi have regular rainfall the year around, causing the leaching of calcium and producing acid soils. West of the Mississippi where normal rainfall is light, and where alkalinity is a problem, sulphur must be added to the soil. Soil pH can be checked by means of an easy-to-use pH kit or through a soil test provided by the extension service. Two to six pounds of ground limestone are needed per 100 square feet to raise the pH level 1 unit and several months will be needed for the liming to be effective. For the same 100 square feet, 1/2–2 pounds of sulphur lower the pH 1 unit. The pH should be checked from time to time as the addition of organic matter and other amendments may alter the pH level. With wild flowers in place, amendments to alter the pH can be added in small amounts. Most commercial fertilizers are designed to be neutral to slightly alkaline. Some acid-loving plants may benefit from acid, commercial fertilizers such as those formulated for Azaleas and Rhododendrons.

NUTRIENTS

Amounts of available soil nutrients and elements essential for plant growth affect the growth of native plants in the same way they do exotics. Generally speaking, most natives require lower levels of soil fertility than needed in a vegetable garden. There is no reason to conclude, however, that native wild flowers should never be fertilized.

Agencies such as extension services and experiment stations usually provide soil testing services. A paper container (available from the agency) holding about a pint of dry soil is sent to the soil testing service. To obtain a true evaluation, several samples should be taken at depths of 2–6 in. from the whole area to be planted. The samples should be mixed throughly in a clean plastic pail, the sample container filled, and your name and address, and a statement of the proposed use enclosed. In due time, a report giving recommendations for liming and the use of fertilizers will be received and should be followed in preparing the planting site.

Some gardeners are firm believers in purely *organic gardening* and employ no chemical fertilizers to supply nutrients. This is fine but it should be understood that humus derived from organic matter may not supply enough nitrogen or phosphorus, two of the most important elements essential for plant growth.

Without a test of the organic matter it is impossible to determine the level of nutrients. Well-rotted cow manure, for example, has less than 1% available nitrogen and so another nitrogen source such as blood meal must also be used.

Every container of commercial *chemical fertilizer* bears a numerical figure such as 6-8-6 indicating the percentage in alphabetical order of nitrogen (6%), phosphorus (8%), and potassium (6%). The remainder of the contents is inert matter. Perennial wild flowers tend to need more phosphorus and potassium than nitrogen. Phosphorus is essential for good root growth and potassium for floral development. Plants also require small amounts of other elements known as minor or trace elements. Some of the more expensive fertilizers contain trace elements; if so, they are listed on the label. Some commercial fertilizers release their nutrients very quickly once added to the soil. Other, so-called *slow release fertilizers,* release nutrients over a longer period. The latter are more expensive but are particularly effective in the wild flower or perennial garden.

When preparing a bed in new soil, in the absence of a soil test, use 3–4 pounds of chemical fertilizer, such as 10-10-10 per 100 square feet of bed. If the bed is on new ground, 3–4 pounds of super-phosphate should be added as phosphorus is often in low supply in new soils. Unless otherwise noted, most wild flowers also benefit from the addition of a small amount of ground dolomitic limestone which supplies not only calcium but also magnesium, a trace element in short supply in many soils.

To maintain fertility, apply 2 pounds of 14-14-14 slow release fertilizer per 100 square feet of bed each spring prior to the appearance of the wild flowers. Such fertilizers release nutrients slowly over several months and eliminate the danger of over-fertilization. Alternately, a complete fertilizer, such as 10-10-10, may be broadcast, at the rate of 3 pounds per 100 square feet, over the area in early spring prior to emergence of the wild flowers.

PLANTING

Several factors determine the best time for planting perennial wild flowers. The first is the region. From New England through the upper Midwest spring is the best time for planting bare-rooted plants. But, further south, fall is the better time for planting. One advantage of fall planting is that it allows root development during the winter months prior to the commencement of the spring growth cycle.

The second factor is the time at which native perennial plants are available. Some growers offer them only at certain seasons, usually governed by the life cycle of the plant, or by when they may successfully be moved. Also to be considered is the form in which the plants are bought. With bare-root, it is generally easier to see the buds in the spring than in the fall. If plants have been grown in containers, they can be set out at almost any time the soil can be worked with virtually no risk of loss. An increasing number of growers are producing quality container-grown natives which can be obtained at local nurseries or through mail order.

How planted is as important as when planted. If planting a new bed, set the plants on the ground according to the design and groupings. But do not hesitate to move them around until satisfied with the arrangement. If the new bed has been properly prepared, it is easy to scoop holes large enough for the roots. When planting *bare root* material, spread the roots outwards and downwards. If the bare root plant has a large mass of roots, build up a firm mound in the center of the hole and place the crown of the plant on the mound. Spread the roots down around the mound to provide good root-soil contact and eliminate air spaces.

Depth of planting is extremely important for all perennials and woody materials; planting too deeply or too shallowly causes problems. With bare-rooted material, determine from the crown or old stems the depth at which they were previously growing. If in containers, plant them at the same depth at which they grow in the container. If the plants happen to be extremely pot bound, break the ball and spread out some of the roots. It is desirable to break up the ball on those plants grown in artificial peat-lite mixtures, since they are slow to send their roots into native soil. Once planted, firm the soil around the plants with feet or hands. Avoid excessive walking on the bed; it leads to compaction of the soil.

Some native perennials have aggressively spreading rhizomes and tend to be invasive, thereby discouraging their use. A bottomless, 3 gallon, plastic nursery container buried in the soil of the bed can be used to enclose those aggressive rhizomes and allow the growing and enjoyment of some native wild flowers that otherwise are better avoided.

If working with *an existing bed*, spade the area, add organic matter and nutrients and dig the area again. Finish by raking the soil and laying out the plants. When satisfied with their positioning, plant as suggested above. If you are planting in hot, open sun, some plants may benefit from being shaded for a day or so. If you are using small transplants grown from seed, be sure to harden the plants by gradual exposure to the elements prior to transplanting.

Once they are planted, water the plants well using a water breaker attachment (a device to break the water into a soft stream like the nozzle of a sprinkling can), or use a watering can. Soak each plant throughly and deeply. If the weather is especially hot or very dry, arrange a sprinkler to stay in place for a week or two, permitting regular watering until the plants become established and produce new growth.

One final word on planting; mark or label each plant in some way. Memory will fail, so what was planted (and where) will be forgotten and be likely to be hoed down as weeds or overlooked if slow starters. Mark each group of plants installed with a 10 in. redwood stake. Place a plastic label marked with water proof ink on the stake. Also consider burying one or more plastic labels marked with the name since children and dogs seem to enjoy removing labels!

MULCHING

Most wild flowers benefit from a mulch that conserves moisture, discourages weeds, and moderates temperatures. Many organic materials can be used but the one selected is determined by cost, availability, durability, appearance, and freedom from weed seeds. Among the preferred materials are decayed wood chips, pine straw, partially decayed leaves, cotton seed hulls, peanut hulls, or other agricultural products. To prevent crown rot neither the base of the plant nor the offshoots should be covered by mulch. Use the mulch to cover the soil between the plants to a depth of 1–2 in. Mulch should normally be applied in the spring after the plants have appeared and after the application of fertilizer. In the south, heavy mulching in the fall can cause perennials that require well drained soil, such as Butterfly Weed (*Asclepias tuberosa*) and others to rot.

WEEDING

Weeding is the never-ending, unexciting companion to gardening. Mulches assist in keeping weeds in check but never eliminate all weeds. Pull weeds while they are young and never, never allow a weed to go to seed. Some may ask: Why not use a *pre-emergence herbicide,* a chemical preventing the germination of seeds? In a wild flower garden one grows many genera and species of minor economic importance that have not been tested for herbicide tolerance. Herbicides might damage them even though safely developed for economically important crop plants. Furthermore, a pre-emergent herbicide may prevent self-sowing of desirable species. Understanding this precaution, the gardener may still wish to use a pre-emergence herbicide in which case the advice of an extension agent should be sought. In most wild flower gardens, the best thing is to pull the weeds by hand.

MOISTURE AND WATERING

While mulch helps to conserve moisture in wild flower plantings, mulch alone will not do the job. With several plants growing vigorously side by side, tremendous quantities of water are required to sustain plantings. This is even true of the shade garden in which trees are greedy consumers of moisture. Watering should be done during periods of drought, soaking the soil deeply each time. Newly planted wild flowers require extra water daily when it is hot and windy as do all plantings during periods of drought. As we have already urged, do not over-extend to the point that water cannot be supplied to the wild flower garden. Plantings should not be attempted if water is unavailable or may be in short supply. Adequate water supply has become even more critical in the face of recent droughts and increased populational demands.

Each of the many ways to water a garden has its own advantages and disadvantages. Electronically controlled irrigation systems have recently become cheaper and more widely available. Such systems must be properly designed and laid out to adequately water a garden. Thus careful attention to design is necessary, as some perennial wild flowers go dormant in summer and need little water while others make growth to the extent that they quickly block sprinkler heads. Hand watering with a hose is usually unsatisfactory because few gardeners have the time and patience for deep soaking. Drip irrigation conserves water but produces a maze of hoses, the outlets of which often become clogged if the water is not carefully filtered. Perhaps the best choice is a manually operated sprinkler system—provided the layout is satisfactory. The senior author waters a 3 acre perennial and wild flower display garden and production nursery using conventional hose bibs, garden hoses, and sprinklers on stands. The hoses and sprinklers stay in place during the growing season so that nothing has to be moved from place to place. I have a large number of hoses and sprinklers to turn on and off, but it works!

Where allowed by zoning and planning commissions, plan on developing an on-site water supply source such as a stream, spring, lake or well. Wells adequate to supply water for an irrigation system can be drilled relatively inexpensively in many parts of the country.

Whatever system is used, plan very carefully to supply moisture as needed to plantings of native wild flowers: learn to feel and observe the soil and to recognize symptoms of wilting; try neither to overwater nor underwater; take extra care in watering newly planted material; and be willing to spend the time and money to get water to the plants. If gardening in an area where water is in short supply or has become expensive, become acquainted with drought-tolerant wild flowers. Native plants have evolved under a wide variety of moisture conditions ranging from wet to dry, with some even adapted to growing on continually wet soil. Variation in soil moisture results from topographic characteristics of the terrain (flat or sloping), different rates of drainage, and differing soil types. Sandy soils drain rapidly, clay soils drain poorly. Most native perennial wild flowers do best on soils with free drainage that are neither water-logged nor excessively dry, but have moisture levels typical of good garden soils. For best results, match the optimal requirements of the species selected with conditions naturally present in the garden. A word to the wise: under favorable garden conditions, plants often do well at moisture levels differing slightly from those in nature.

LIGHT

All green plants need light, but they differ in the amount they need. Some require full sun, and so dwindle away in the shade, others require shade and their leaves burn if placed in full sun. Our native species of herbaceous perennial wild flowers have evolved to survive in a wide range of light conditions, from dense shade to full sun. This wide variation in light requirements actually provides an opportunity to select species appropriate to the light conditions in a particular garden setting. Wild flowers from the forest floor are shade tolerant, natives from open places demand full sun. However, even when a particular species is found in full sun or full shade, it frequently does not need sun or shade for the entire day.

During the heat of summers, a bit of shade may be helpful to some sun perennials. Conversely, many shade perennials often tolerate morning sun but do poorly in afternoon sun. Actually, few shade perennial species do well in heavy, deep shade but are very happy in a dappled shade which moves with the sun. A rule of thumb: give shade perennials as much sun as they can stand without developing leaf burn. Move them if they burn! Alternatively, if too much shade is provided by trees, remove some of the lower limbs or eliminate some of the trees.

If plants are well watered, whether they be sun or shade types, they can handle more intense sunlight. Thus, time of day, the type of sun or shade, and soil moisture are equally important considerations in understanding, and providing for, the reaction of plants to light intensity. Together with soil and moisture, light conditions are one of the major keys in choosing the right native species for successful cultivation.

TEMPERATURE

Temperature is the environmental factor which most markedly influences the natural distribution of our native plants. Cold winter temperatures limit the northern distribution of a species and hot summer temperatures limit the southern distribution. Some wild flowers may require cold winters to break dormancy in spring, or winter chilling of their seeds for germination. But, in our gardens, we can often provide growing conditions sufficiently favorable to grow natives outside their normal range. For example, Wild Bleeding Heart (*Dicentra eximia*) is easily grown in Georgia 100 miles south of its natural range and *Coreopsis auriculata* is marvelous in New England several hundred miles north of its range.

Within the broad limits of a regional climate, particular localities depart from the norms with exceptional warmth or cold depending upon topography, elevation, direction of slope, wind breaks, soil, ground cover, and man-made structures. A 100-ft. rise in elevation lowers the temperature and delays spring flowering by one day. Spring progresses northward about 20 miles per day. This is provided for in the plant descriptions by giving the range of flowering dates reflecting the northward movement of spring.

Within a region, and indeed within the 17-acre farm of the senior author, differences in temperature and other environmental factors occur that are called *microhabitats*. By careful observation and the employment of good old common sense, the gardener can use microhabitats to advantage by putting a particular species in a place where it is perfectly happy. Even on a level garden site, the terrain can be remade into pleasing irregularities which provide the additional advantages of specific microhabitats. Man-made mounds, depressions, masonry walls, and pools provide a diversity of microhabitats in any garden. Those fortunate enough to have a natural array of slopes, rock outcrops, and wet depressions, have before them endless opportunities for exploiting these environments.

PLANT BIOLOGY AND INTERACTIONS

Many years of experimental work on the nature of plant species have clearly proved that local populations of flowering plant species are genetically highly variable. This variation may be in external appearance, in habitat adaptations as well as in many cryptic, genetically controlled characteristics. Such local populations are called ecotypes. For our purposes, an *ecotype* can be defined as a local population or a series of populations adapted to particular climatic and soil conditions and other environmental factors.

Ecotypes develop in response to the forces of *natural selection;* that is, populations of plants have, through geological time, become genetically adapted to their local environment. Hepaticas and Trilliums collected in the south tend to flower earlier than plants of the same species collected in the north when grown in the same bed. It can be seen from this example that plants from different areas of the range of a species have become genetically adapted to flower at times favorable for their reproductive success. Other examples could be cited for adaptation to prevailing soil and moisture conditions. The lesson to be learned from this botanical knowledge is that native plant material in a garden should be obtained from nursery sources in the immediate area, because the local plant material is better adapted to local growing conditions.

From many years of observations of plants growing in nature, it is clear that the interactions of plants affect the growth and development of other species. *Competition* for light, moisture, nutrients, and space may, following hardiness, be the most important limiting factor determining where a plant grows. Certainly, it is easy to see how the effect of an overtopping native shrub or tree, or an invasive perennial or an aggressive weed adversely affects a planting. Equally evident is the way tree roots remove immense quantities of water from shade garden beds. Initial root competition during establishment of perennials can be eliminated by good soil preparation. Careful planning, soil preparation, spacing, lifting, and pruning, can, if not eliminate, reduce competition in our native wild flower gardens.

Lastly in this consideration of plant biology, as it affects plants existing in nature, mention should be made of *allelopathy*. Many native species are known to produce inhibitory chemicals which, under experimental conditions, inhibit the growth of other plants. The classic example is *Juglans nigra* (Black Walnut) which produces a chemical inhibiting the growth of other species. This affect is known as allelopathy, and is defined as the adverse effect of one plant's chemistry on another plant's growth. Allelopathy can be viewed as a type of chemical warfare by which a species reduces competition. This type of plant-to-plant interaction must be taken into account at the time of planning a native flora garden.

SUMMARY

The whole objective of gardening with native wild flowers is pleasure and enjoyment. Before starting to grow natives, learn as much about them as you can in order to prevent grievous errors, and eliminate needless experimenting. Beg, buy or borrow a few good books to aid with identifications. Find out where native wild flowers grow, what conditions they like, and whether they are suitable for garden conditions. Start nearby by studying plants in the woods, fields, and meadows, visit gardens and nurseries featuring native species, and join native plant societies. For an enjoyable and fascinating wild garden using natives keep the following in mind:

1) Become acquainted with the local flora.
2) Delve into reference material both botanical and horticultural.
3) Give careful attention to the details of soil and site preparation, including soil tests, mechanical preparation, and the addition of organic matter and nutrients.
4) Select the proper species for the microhabitats of the garden.
5) Give reasonable care to the all important matters of planting, fertilization, mulching, and irrigation, that is to say, practice good horticulture.
6) Be aware that all gardeners must cope with both mistakes and successes.
7) Do not be overly ambitious as it is much better to care well for a few species than to have a great many and not adequately provide for their needs.

CHAPTER 4

Propagation of Perennial Wild Flowers

Almost everyone sufficiently interested in wildflowers to garden with them will ultimately undertake to propagate at least some of these plants. Many species of wild flowers native to eastern North America thrive under almost any set of gardening conditions, and are also easily propagated if given reasonable care. So it is not difficult to obtain plants, seeds, or plant parts for propagating most of the commonly grown native wild flowers. In addition to purchase from several commercial sources, there are other sources of propagation material. Perhaps a friend has plants that are ready to be divided or large enough to obtain cuttings. Wild flowers can occasionally be salvaged from a tract about to be bull-dozed, or seed from natural populations can be collected at the proper time. However one proceeds, the important issue is to get started and begin to enjoy this wonderful and engaging enterprise. By following the directions in this chapter, even the rankest tyro should be able to propagate most species.

Some nurseries sell plants collected from the wild. This practice is thoroughly undesirable from a conservation standpoint. Often these plants are collected illegally from public or private lands, some from populations of species already endangered by over-collecting or habitat destruction. Plants such as Trilliums (*Trillium* spp.), Bloodroots (*Sanguinaria canadensis*) and our native Lilies (*Lilium* spp.) fit into this category. Actually, until very recently most of the perennial wild flowers commercially available were collected from the wild in amazingly large numbers. If the plants are priced very cheaply, they were probably collected rather than nursery grown. An advertisement in a recent wholesale trade journal lists ferns, Blood Root, and Trilliums for 35 cents each, suggesting that collected, not nursery, material is being offered. Plants simply cannot be propagated commercially that inexpensively. Other nurseries, possibly of more devious inclination, collect plants from the wild, place them in beds for one year, and then call the plants "nursery grown." The key word is "nursery propagated"; insist upon *nursery propagated* material only and do not support nurseries decimating wild populations.

Thanks to the conservation movement and the growing interest in native plants, an increasing number of nurseries are offering nursery propagated, native species. Nursery propagated, container grown stock is more likely to live and to grow than bare rooted, collected material. As with any purchase, it is advantageous to obtain quality material; although the nursery propagated plants may seem expensive, their survival rate is higher than that of stock collected in the wild. But this consideration, while clearly advantageous to the buyer, is surely of lesser importance than the preservation of wild populations.

Another method of acquiring plants is surplus plants from friends and neighbors. Many perennial wild flowers multiply rapidly, and as with puppies and kittens, their owners are eager to find a good home for them. Members of a botanical garden or garden interest group often sponsor surplus plant sales to raise money for some project. Surplus plant sales are ideal for gardeners to stock up at low cost and at the same time assist a worthy cause. Many such sales feature unusual wild flower species that do particularly well in the local area. These sales also help gardeners to become aware of many unfamiliar and fascinating native species that can be propagated with great ease.

Propagating native perennials leads to an active involvement in plant societies and aids the botanic garden conservation movement. Indeed, this approach offers the opportunity to participate in efforts to conserve the native flora, as well as the pleasure and joy of learning more about native plants. Wild flowers bring other pleasures as well, such as the memories of childhood and the anticipation of days to come. They provide sentimental pictures to delight the eye; they intoxicate the senses with fragrance and beauty. They become intimate companions in the garden. And, last but not least, wild flower propagation stems their extermination and increases their chances of survival as part of our natural heritage.

METHODS OF PROPAGATION

Perennial wild flowers may be propagated by several methods. First and most obviously, they can be *propagated by seeds* gathered or purchased. Seeds are produced in fruits that develop from flowers. *Seeds* result from the sexual union of eggs located in the developing fruit of the mother plant and sperm from the pollen source plant. The features of the seedling are a blend of the genetic makeup of the parental plants. Many wild flowers within the same species vary greatly in appearance. They may vary in flower or foliage color, in height or habit of growth, or in the size and form of the flowers. If seeds are sown from individual plants which vary in these features, there is no assurance that the resulting seedlings will be identical to the parental plant.

All the other methods of propagation are *asexual* (vegetative propagation); that is, new plants are produced from pieces taken from various parts of the original plant. Asexual propagation results in plants having all of the traits identical to the original plant. Vegetatively propagated plants precisely duplicate the growth form, size and flower color, etc. of the mother plant. Plants are propagated vegetatively by division, by stem cuttings and root cuttings, and commercially by tissue culture. Because each of these methods assures identical copies of parental material, and generally is very easy and practical, we discuss them first. Reproduction by seeds will be discussed later in this chapter.

DIVISION: Most herbaceous perennials can be divided and this is often the simplest and quickest method of propagation (Fig. 4-1). Dividing perennial wild flowers not only provides additional plants but also usually rejuvenates older plants that have become stunted and overcrowded. Indeed, plants which form large crowns or clumps, such as *Monarda*, decline in vigor if not separated periodically. Furthermore, divisions are often stronger and come into flower sooner than seedlings. Although perennial wild flower species vary in the form of vegetative reproductive parts produced, the majority depend upon the development of buds or immature branches called eyes, shoots, or offsets.

Propagation by division involves the separation of parts of the plants having eyes (growth buds), offsets, shoots, or plantlets. Each such vegetative part is capable of growing into a mature independent plant. The method of division used by the gardener is largely determined by the growth form of the species being propagated. *Division* is a simple method which requires little in the way of equipment or supplies. A heavy, very sharp knife and a stout spade-type shovel or fork are needed to dig and lift the plants and later to cut the clump apart.

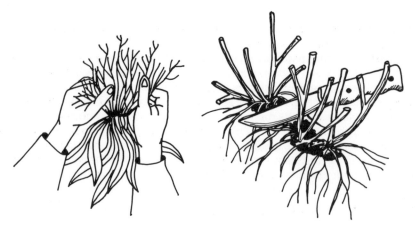

Fig. 4-1. Some perennial wild flowers are easy to divide simply by pulling the segments apart. Other species are sufficiently tough to call for a sharp knife to cut the rootstock into pieces. Be sure that each separate piece has one or more growth buds.

The best *time to divide* is when the plants are in a semi-dormant growth phase, either late summer and early fall, or very early spring. Avoid disturbing the plants in hot weather when they are liable to wilt and when rots are more common. For early blooming plants, such as Blood Root (*Sanguinaria canadensis*) and Blue Woodland Phlox (*Phlox divaricata*), divide in late summer in the north, or early fall in the south. Divide the Monardas (*Monarda* spp.), which flower in summer, in very early spring. In colder regions, spring division of perennial wild flowers allows them a chance to establish a root system prior to the onset of cold weather. In northern regions, fall divisions must be mulched with salt marsh hay or evergreen boughs so that frost will not heave them out of the ground. But in the south, mulching in the fall causes the divisions to rot. Those plants that go dormant early, such as Virginia Bluebells (*Mertensia virginica*), must be marked with a stake so the rootstocks can be located for division in the fall or early spring.

Pie-shaped wedges are cut and lifted from clumps of plants that should not be disturbed, such as *Galax* or *Shortia*. Fill the resulting hole with a humic, rich soil mixture and the missing wedge will soon grow back. Some wild flowers such as Bleeding Heart (*Dicentra eximia*) and Columbine (*Aquilegia canadensis*) tolerate little abuse or rough handling. Others are easily divided. Clumps of plants which may be disturbed must be dug carefully to avoid injury to the roots at the time of dividing. Then, shake the soil loose from the roots or, if small, wash away the soil to expose the eyes. Strong or matted clumps may have to be pried, or forced apart to get divisions of workable size. The older or central portion of some clumps may be woody and unsuitable for forming new plants, and should be discarded at the time of division. Use only vigorous, healthy plant parts for divisions.

With the plant now in a position to be worked on and the entire plant including the crown visible, use the opportunity to divide and to put pieces of the plant back into good condition. Prune old stems back to the basal foliage and cut away excess foliage. Now bring the knife into play to separate the plant parts to be used into suitable sections to form new plants. Damage as few roots as possible and be sure the knife is sharp and makes clean cuts. Dust the cut surfaces with wetable sulphur powder to help prevent rot in the new plant. The size of the resulting new plants is determined by the size of the divisions. Do not divide too finely unless very tiny plants are desired, or must be tolerated due to the rarity of the species; very small divisions require much more time to become effective garden material.

In the case of rhizomotous plants such as *Iris,* the rhizome branches at or near the soil surface. Simply pull or cut the *rhizomes* apart but make sure that each division has one or more eyes or shoots. Other species such as Eared Coreopsis (*Coreopsis auriculata*), Foamflower (*Tiarella cordifolia*), Green and Gold (*Chrysogonum virginianum*), and Alum Root (*Heuchera americana*), which develop *crowns of several shoots,* are easily divided by teasing the shoots apart. Yet another class of plants such as Stokes Aster (*Stokesia laevis*) produces dense, overlapping *rosettes* which may be divided by cutting and/or forcibly pulling the rosettes apart. Species such as *Monarda* or *Physostegia,* which develop numerous stems and *underground rhizomes,* are simply pulled apart.

Species producing *runners and stolons,* such as *Waldsteinia,* are easily divided by pulling the plants apart. Cut plants growing from *tubers* into pieces, each with one or more eyes, and plant as is done with white or Irish potatoes. Some plants, such as Virginia Bluebells (*Mertensia virginica*), develop intertwined, fleshy rootstocks with several eyes on each root. Pull or cut the roots apart to get independent pieces, each with one or more eyes. Some large, clump-forming species, like the Carolina Bush Pea (*Thermopsis villosa*), have a dense, *woody rootstock* that requires the services of a sharp hatchet.

The small *offsets* that develop on the sides of corms and bulbs are removed and replanted during the dormant season. The *outer scales* of lily bulbs are removed and planted in flats of soil mix or in a bed with plenty of organic matter. Plant them with the tip of the scales pointed upward and just barely cover with soil mix. The cormlike rhizomes of *Trillium* are carefully dug when dormant. The rhizomes are washed and then a u-shaped groove cut around the top of the rhizome, dusted with sulphur and replanted. Small offsets will appear in about one year. The small corms, rhizomes and bulbs of lilies and Trilliums produced by the above methods usually take several years to reach flowering size.

Pot the divisions, however done, in nursery containers, or set out the multiple plant parts in cold frames and nursery beds, or in their permanent positions in the garden. Before placing in nursery garden beds be certain the beds have been properly prepared as discussed in the previous chapter. Shade and protect the newly transplanted plants from the hot sun. Water thoroughly, but be careful not to overwater; wet, over-watered, or poorly drained soils invite root rot problems.

STEM CUTTINGS: The technique of propagating from *stem cuttings* circumvents the need to dig up plants; it is a form of division in which new plants are grown from shoots or portions cut from above-ground stems and rooted in a moist rooting medium (Fig. 4-2). Cuttings, like divisions, result in plants bearing the characteristics of the parental plant. Some species of wild flowers can be propagated quite readily by cutting segments of their stems with leaves attached, and inducing these portions to produce roots. Cuttings are simply vegetative portions of plants lacking roots. The secret of success is creating a rooting environment conducive to root formation. If cuttings are taken carefully, the parent plant is not injured but, on the contrary, benefits by being forced to branch and become stocky; unlike divisions, a native plant clump multiplied by stem cuttings is not harmed in the process.

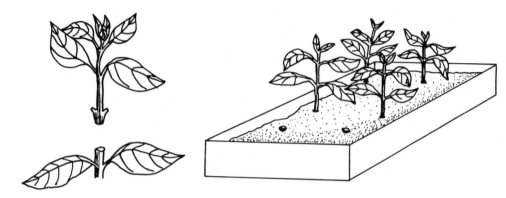

Fig. 4-2. Many native wild flowers can be propagated by stem cuttings. Make the cutting 3–6 in. long, cutting through the stem just below a node; remove the leaves at the base. Place the cuttings upright in the rooting medium. After the cuttings have rooted, they can be removed and potted.

Generally *the best time* for taking cuttings of perennial wild flowers is late spring or early summer. Use a razor-sharp knife or a clean, sharp pair of pruning shears to remove a 3–6-in. segment of a shoot having a minimum of 3 nodes (a *node* is the point where the leaf joins the stem). Make a clean cut just below the node. The typical cutting should be 3–6 in. long, firmly limber and neither as hard as in late summer nor as soft as the first flush of new growth. The leaves of the lowest nodes are removed to facilitate "sticking" the cutting in the rooting medium. Top leaves and tender new growth at the top may be trimmed to reduce the risk of wilting. Flower buds are removed to concentrate the growth activities of the cutting toward the production of roots. Some perennial wild flowers, such as *Rudbeckia fulgida*, produce *basal cuttings* or small divisions without roots. These short, young shoots are cut from the base of the clump and treated as if they are cuttings.

Make sure the plants providing the cuttings are vigorous, free of disease, and well watered. Since cuttings taken from the mother plant wilt quickly, remove the cuttings in the morning when it is coolish and the mother plant most turgid. Place the cuttings in small plastic bags with some moisture to prevent wilting. Do NOT store the cuttings by placing them in a container of water, nor expose plastic bags containing cuttings to direct sunlight. It is a best to drop the bags into an ice chest with a few ice cubes in the bottom.

Sanitation is very important when working with cuttings. Use only a knife or pruning shears that have been disinfected prior to each use. Also be sure that the work area for making and sticking the cuttings is clean. Cover the work surface with clean newspaper and dip shears, knives, flats, and pots into a 10% solution of Chlorox (1 part of Chlorox in 9 parts of water) before each use.

Flower pots with the cuttings covered by a clear plastic cup will do just fine for a few cuttings. In the case of larger numbers, a shallow wooden or plastic box or gardener's flat should be used. The container should be 3–6 in. deep with holes in the bottom to provide drainage. Perfect drainage is absolutely essential to avoid plant diseases causing the cuttings to rot. Fill the container to a depth of 1/4 in. from the top with a 1-to-1 mixture of clean, coarse builder's sand and perlite. A suitable rooting container can also be made of an old styrofoam ice chest with 6 in. of sand and perlite mixture and with holes cut in the bottom for drainage. The rooting medium must be thoroughly wetted before sticking the cuttings.

Many gardeners, and virtually all commercial growers, dip the base of the cutting in a hormone rooting compound prior to sticking the cutting. The rooting hormone increases the number of roots and speeds up the process of rooting. Excessive amounts of the hormone must be shaken off before sticking as too much is harmful. A sterilized putty knife, or similar tool, is used to cut slit-like trenches in the rooting medium into which the cuttings are inserted. If "sticking" just a few cuttings a pencil can be used to make individual holes. The cuttings should be inserted in the open rows at 1–2-in. intervals to a depth of about ½ the stem length. Label the cuttings with their name and date. Avoid over-crowding the cuttings to discourage rots.

Securely arch chicken wire over the flat or box, then cover the arch and the sides with a sheet of plastic. The plastic should not be allowed to touch the cuttings. Seal by tucking the plastic sheet under the flat. This creates a *miniature greenhouse* that will conserve moisture. Place the covered flat in open shade where it does not receive direct sunlight, because in direct sunlight a heat buildup develops which kills the cuttings. Check the cuttings every other day to assure they are moist. Water only sparingly. Watch the cuttings for signs of discoloration or disease and immediately remove any cuttings with symptons of rotting.

Alternatively, one can use a rugged, clear vinyl "Propagation Dome" available at many garden centers and designed to fit on standard commercial plastic "1020 Flats." The domes create just the right micro-environment needed for the successful rooting of cuttings. They are inexpensive and economical.

Rooting normally occurs in 3–5 weeks. As rooting begins, new top growth often appears as well. The cuttings have rooted when they resist a gentle tug. After rooting has occurred, gradually give the cuttings some fresh air to acclimatize the new plants before removal from the rooting medium.

Although the young wildflower plants have roots, they are not yet ready to go directly into the garden. At this stage, they are unable to compete with nearby plants and their watering might be overlooked. Instead, they should be potted and placed in a nursery area. Using an old dinner fork, gently remove the rooted cuttings from the rooting medium. They should have roots ½–2 in. long. Pot the cuttings in nursery containers using a soil mixture similar to that suitable for seedlings (see propagation by seeds).

The containers are in turn placed in a shaded, protected area where they can be checked and watered as needed on a daily basis. Wild flowers normally growing in the sun should be left in the shade for only a week or two and then moved to a spot where they receive sun for at least 3–4 hours each day.

When their roots begin to fill the containers, the plants must be transplanted into the garden. The gardener should aim to have reached the transplanting stage about one month before the first killing frost so that the plants can become established prior to winter. If not, plunge the containers into sand in a cold frame to hold them safely until the following spring. Rooted cuttings can also be transplanted into a well cared for and protected nursery bed.

ROOT CUTTINGS: Another asexual method often used to increase certain species of wild flowers such as summer flowering *Phlox,* Solomon's Seal (*Polygonatum biflorum*), Butterfly Weed (*Asclepias tuberosa*), Shooting Star (*Dodecatheon meadia*), and Stokes Aster (*Stokesia laevis*) is *root cuttings* (Fig. 4-3). These species are able to regenerate new shoots and roots from bits of roots snipped off the parent plant and propagated in a particular way. In order to obtain root cuttings, the plants are dug in the fall in the north, or in February in the south. Thick roots one-tenth in. in diameter or more are cut into 1–3-in. lengths with a sharp knife or pruning shears disinfected with a 10% chlorox solution after each cut. The parent plants are then replanted to grow and produce flowers again. Place the root cuttings horizontally in flats of rooting mix 1 in. apart. Cover the roots with about ½ in. of the rooting mix. Use a rooting mix of equal parts of perlite, coarse builder's sand, peat moss, and ground pine bark. Various other mixes can also be used—even just good clean sand. Water the root cuttings thoroughly and put the flat in a cold frame for the winter. Check the flats from time to time and keep moist,

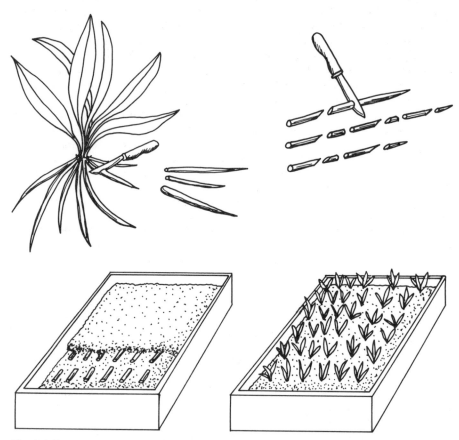

Fig. 4-3. For propagation by root cuttings, cut healthy roots into sections 1–3 in. long; place them horizontally on rooting medium in a flat; cover the root sections to a depth of about ½ in. with the same medium. New plants will eventually appear which are then lifted and potted.

but not wet. Check periodically for rot. In the spring, young shoots appear and new roots develop. Note that the roots of Solomon's Seal may lie dormant for one year prior to sprouting.

When the new shoots have appeared and are about 3 in. high, and after danger of a late spring frost has passed, pot the new plants in a good soil mix. Grow the young plants in a protected and well-watered nursery area until late summer or early fall. After they are established, transplant to their permanent site at least one month prior to the first killing frost.

The advantages of root cuttings lie in the ease with which some species can be propagated, the large number of plants that can be produced, and the fact that tough, old plants can be used during a dormant period without disrupting the flowering by taking stem cuttings.

SEEDS: In growing wild plants from seed, one should follow the same general rules as for growing other hardy perennials from seed. Seeds are often the cheapest and best known, and usually the fastest, method of propagation if large numbers of plants are needed. However, more attention to detail is required than with propagation by division. Although less expensive than nursery propagated plants, seedlings do try the patience, since it may take 2–5 years to bring a plant into flower from seed. The seeds of some perennial wild flowers germinate immediately, others may lie dormant in the seed bed for a year or more. Some wild flower seeds need to be sown immediately after they mature. Others need a cold period or a combination of a cold period and a warm period in order to break dormancy and germinate.

Seeds of some species can be purchased from standard commercial sources or from those who collect in the wild. Seeds of other species may be unavailable for years unless collected by the gardener. Further, since fresh seeds germinate more dependably than do old ones, it may be wise to collect one's own supply, as commercial seeds are at least 6–9 months old by the time they are purchased. If planning to collect in the wild, mark the plants at blooming time with stakes or tags because many species, such as Fire Pink (*Silene virginica*), are less conspicuous after flowering or are hidden by the growth of other plants. Collection of a small amount of seed from natural colonies of perennial wild flowers has little or no effect on those populations or their survival. As a collection of native perennials is developed in one's own garden, a ready source of seeds becomes available to use and to share with friends.

A close watch is needed to collect seeds at the right moment between maturity and shedding. Many plants shed seeds before the gardener realizes they are ready. It takes a bit of experience and a keen eye to recognize when the seeds are set on some species. But above all, harvesting seed requires a sensitive attunement to the rhythms of the plants. In the South, seeds of some of the early March bloomers such as Bloodroot (*Sanguinaria caanadensis*) or Virginia Bluebells (*Mertensia virginica*) will be gone by the end of April, and a month later in New England. Collect the pods just as they begin to turn from a greenish color to a darker color.

Place the unopened pods of a single species in an open kraft paper bag. The fruits will dry and expel their seeds. Never use plastic bags to collect or store seed. Plastic bags retain moisture rather than allowing it to escape. Use only paper sacks in order to prevent molding of the seed or fruit. Drying is followed by cleaning to separate the seed from the chaff. Some species, such as Sundrops (*Oenothera fruticosa*), must have their pods crushed after drying to separate the seeds from the pods. Above all, keep meticulous records as to where and when the seeds were collected, and clearly mark the paper bags used to store the seed.

Dry seeds should be stored in an envelope in a refrigerator set at around 40° F (5° C). Never store seeds in a freezer. Seeds with a fleshy outer covering should be soaked in water for 24 hours after which the pulp should be removed using running water in a kitchen strainer. Seeds produced in fleshy, berry-like structures, such as Jack-in-the-Pulpit, should be stored in the refrigerator in damp sphagnum moss in plastic containers.

Seeds of some legumes such as False Blue Indigo (*Baptisia australis*) have hard seed coats which must be scarified by hand filing or by placing them in an electric rock polisher with sand for a few minutes. Immersion in hot water at 200° F (94° C) for a brief period, followed by an overnight soak in water at room temperature, also softens the seed coats of legumes. The seeds of some species, such as Bleeding Heart (*Dicentra eximia*), must be kept moist and stratified at around 40° F (5° C) for 1–2 months. Store in sphagnum moss in plastic containers in the refrigerator, or plant in ground beds immediately after the seeds are mature and let nature provide its own winter chilling. This is the natural condition under which plants have evolved through geological time.

Unlike many annual bedding plants which are rather tender and require warm temperatures, most perennial wild flowers are best grown from seed in out-of-door beds or in cold frames (Fig. 4-4). Since they do not need frost protection and may even be damaged by warm, indoor temperatures, an out-of-door approach is the simplest way to start natives from seed. Order seed as soon as the catalogs arrive—usually in January. The best time to sow purchased seed is February–May for northern areas, while in the South January–March is best. Seeds of perennial wild flowers sown out-of-doors in cold frames will not germinate until they are ready to face the weather. They will germinate in their own time, usually immediately, but some may require 1–2 years. As a general rule, seeds collected by the gardener should be sown at the time they are ripe, and then nature should be allowed to take its own course. The gardener can be assured that they will germinate when they are ready and virtually always at the proper time.

A cold frame is an outdoor, glass- or plastic-lidded box heated by the sun in winter and shaded by snow fencing or an old window screen in summer (Fig. 4-4). The frame serves to protect the plants from extreme cold in winter and drying winds and excessive sun in summer. It is easily made from pressure treated, decay-resistant wood enclosing an area 3 × 6 or 6 × 6 ft. The back of the box-like frame should be 24–30 in. high and the front 18–20 in. high. The sides should gently slope and connect the front and back with the slope facing towards the south and the frame placed in full sun. The frame is covered with a variety of clear plastic covers or even used window sashes.

An alternative is a rectangular, open-ground bed, 3 ft. wide, surrounded by treated 2 × 6 boards or 6–8-in. diameter logs. The soil level in the bed should be raised about 4 in. above the surrounding soil to ensure good drainage. A crude frame of some sort is needed to support an arrangement for shade. Wild flower seed sown in such a bed do just fine, if watered and protected from the sun while the seeds are germinating, and if care is given until the plants are transplanted. Both beds and cold frames should be placed in well-drained locations close to a water source.

For either an open bed or a frame, the soil must be properly prepared.

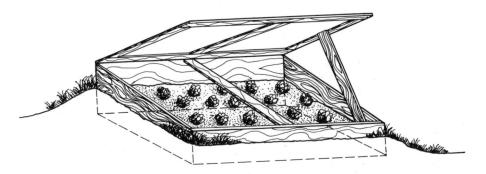

Fig. 4-4. A cold frame with a hinged sash is ideal for germinating seed, rooting cuttings, or over-wintering young plants.

Pulverize the soil to a depth of 6 in. by forking it over 2–3 times and mixing in a 3–4-in. layer of peat moss or ground pine bark. If the soil is sticky clay, a 2-in. layer of coarse builder's sand should also be mixed in. Do not add any fertilizer. The soil should be raked to remove any lumps, stones or debris. Never walk on the bed; if it is a site you must walk on, then place some pieces of board or plywood walkways on it.

Commercial soil mixes such as "Redi Earth," "Metro Mix," "Fafard," or "Pro-Mix" can be used if wild flower seeds are sown in pots. Plunge the pots in sand in the cold frame.

Seeds can be sown directly in the bed or cold frame or in pots plunged in sand in the cold frame. The use of cold frames is preferable because it gives better protection against the elements, the neighbors' pets and trampling by wild deer. Plant the seeds of a single species thinly in a row or in a pot; each row or pot should be labeled with the plant name and the date of sowing. It is often helpful to bury an extra label in the row or pot to guard against accidental loss of the label or weathering. When planting in a bed, use a board to press a shallow furrow into the soil. Sow larger seeds about ¾–1 in. apart in the furrows and cover with about ¼ in. of one of the commercial soil mixes or with vermiculite. For fine seeds, such as Cardinal Flower (*Lobelia cardinalis*), fill the furrows with one of the commercial soil mixes and sow the seeds thinly on top of the soil mix. They will sift down into the mix. Seeds of some species such as Columbine (*Aquilegia canadensis*) should not be covered since light is required for germination. Broadcast Columbine seeds thinly in a 6-in. band across the bed.

When sowing is completed, the bed or frame should be watered with a soft, fine spray and covered to provide protection against the elements. Put the plastic or glass cover of the frame in place, but tilted to allow the entrance of fresh air. For a bed in the open, cover with lath-type snow-fence or an old window screen.

Once planted, the seed bed or cold frame should be examined on a daily basis. Water carefully to keep the soil constantly moist but neither too wet nor too dry. Overheating of the cold frame by leaving the frame closed on hot days, lack of air circulation, too much shade, or overcrowding of seedlings all promote a disease called "Damping-Off." This fungus disease is very destructive of seedlings. If seedlings become discolored and fall over, remove the infected plants. Treat the bed with a mixture of fungicide in water applied to the bed with a sprinkling can.

45

After the seeds have germinated, remove any competing weeds and fertilize the seedlings weekly with a liquid soluble fertilizer at one-third the normal rate. Do not over-fertilize.

Small seedlings transplanted directly into the garden are usually forgotten or overlooked, crowded by neighboring plants, or damaged by cats and dogs. For these reasons, seedlings should either be potted or transplanted to a protected nursery area and grown for a year or more prior to transplanting to their permanent site in the garden. When the seedlings have 3–4 true leaves, they can be potted or reset into a nursery bed, spaced 6–8 in. apart. If potted, the pots must be plunged into sand or soil to provide winter protection for the root mass. In the North, finish transplanting by the end of August and in the South by late September to assure that the plants will survive the winter. If the seedlings should fill their pots with roots the first summer, they can be transplanted to their permanent location a month prior to frost.

For potting, one of the commercial mixes can be used or a soil mix made up. Every gardener seems to have his or her own favorite potting mix and the best advice to experienced gardeners is to use one that seems to work well. The senior author and his wife grow a wide variety of exotic and native perennials at their nursery, Piccadilly Farm in Bishop, Georgia, in the following soil mix.

1 part loamy, weed-free, woods soil
1 part coarse builder's sand
1 part coarse perlite
6 parts ground pine bark

To each construction-size wheelbarrow of the mix add a 4-in. pot of each of the following:

10-10-10 granular fertilizer
super phosphate
ground dolomitic limestone
slow release fertilizer 19-6-12 or 14-14-14

All of the components must be carefully stirred together to produce a uniform mixture.

SELF-SOWN SEEDLINGS: A very simple method of obtaining new plants is to collect self-sown seedlings around parental plants in the garden for some species, such as Bleeding Heart (*Dicentra eximia*), Blue Woodland Phlox (*Phlox divaricata*), and Yellow Wood Poppy (*Stylophorum diphyllum*). We use this method with great success on a commercial scale at Piccadilly Farm. Once certain species have become established in the garden, self-sown seedlings appear and can be removed and potted, or spaced out in a nursery bed. The number of self-sown seedlings can be increased by keeping the area around the parental clumps free of decaying leaves so that the seeds fall on mineral soil. This approach seems to be especially effective when encouraging the self-sowing of Bloodroot (*Sanguinaria canadensis*). Beds overcrowded with mature plants seem to produce fewer self-sown seedlings. This is certainly an easy, trouble-free and very satisfactory method to produce new plants for oneself and for sharing with friends and neighbors.

46

SUGGESTED READING

For specific suggestions on the propagation of many species of perennial wild flowers, the authors urge the reader to consult:

Philips, H. R. 1985. *Growing and Propagating Wild Flowers*. University of North Carolina Press, Chapel Hill, NC.

New England Wild Flower Society. 1986. *Propagation of Wildflowers*. Garden in the Woods, Framingham, MA.

Young, J. A. and C. G. Young. 1986. *Collecting, Processing and Germinating Seeds of Wildland Plants*. Timber Press, Portland, OR.

CHAPTER 5

Wild Flowers for the Shade

A widespread misconception is that sun is needed to garden. Unlike vegetables, which always need full sun, many perennial native plants thrive in shade or partial shade. There are any number of wild flowers which either alone or in conjunction with domestic or exotic bulbs, ferns and perennials, make attractive gardens in a shady situation. In the long, hot days of midsummer, shade is a welcome relief to the gardener and provides habitat for a wider variety of native wild flowers than a sunny garden can. With the possible exception of the northernmost regions, this is true in most of the East and Midwest, so gardeners should come to welcome a shady place rather than deplore it.

If one lives on a wooded site, native perennials, ferns, bulbs, and exotic perennials can be used in combination to create an exciting woodland garden. The soil must be well-prepared with sufficient organic matter and nutrients and enriched with annual top-dressings of fertilizer. In dry weather, thorough watering is required to encourage robust and healthy growth as most shade plants enjoy a cool, somewhat moist soil. Much of the bloom in the woodland garden comes in spring before the canopy of the trees is in full leaf. After that the landscaping emphasis must be on foliage plants such as native ferns and exotics such as Hostas and Hellebores. This chapter, however, offers numerous suggestions of native species that flower in the shade in summer and fall so gardeners should have no difficulty in selecting a large number of species appropriate for providing color in the shady garden throughout the growing season. It should be noted that some woodland natives will be found in other chapters such as the one on groundcovers.

How much shade do the species included in this chapter require? Wild flowers requiring shade do not usually need it all day. Most shade-loving plants do best when there is a bit of light. The ideal exposure for many species of flowering natives is mostly shady but with a portion of the day in sun. Plants suitable for a shade garden can tolerate sun for 1–3 hours with no harm but if the same plants are planted in full sun, burning usually occurs. Species of shade-requiring wild flowers from the South, grown in the northern part of the continent, are often able to tolerate full sun. Also, if a shade plant is kept moist at the roots, it tolerates more sun. In the South during the heat and drought of summer, many sun-preferring native perennials genuinely benefit from a few hours of shade. Shade plants can accept longer exposure to morning sun than to hot, late afternoon sun.

Greedy trees such as maples and beeches project dense shade, permitting little but moss to grow under them. Buildings and walls project shade which varies during the day depending upon their relation to the sun's direction. Evergreen trees project a constant, filtered shade. The higher the tree canopy, the more light reaches the ground. So the gardener must assess the situation at each site: light shade, high shade, dappled shade, full shade, morning shade, afternoon shade, dry shade, moist shade, north-facing or south-facing shade, or artifical shade from overhead lath or shade cloth. Dappled shade formed by a partial tree canopy with openings permitting sunlight to reach the ground below intermittently during the course of the day is undoubtedly the best for the greatest number of shade-loving of native species.

Experienced gardeners move plants around until they find a site where they grow luxuriantly. So each species must be tested until one discovers the amount of shade, exposure, moisture, and so on that is best suited to its needs. For each species of native wild flower there is an optimum balance between shade and sun, the spot where a species thrives and dominates its habitat. To find this balance is the great challenge to the gardener using shade-loving plants.

Manfreda virginica (Agave virginica)   Rattlesnake Master, Aloe
Agavaceae   Agave Family

DESCRIPTION: A succulent perennial arising from a bulb-like rootstock. It bears narrow, fleshy, light green, sometimes spotted, pointed leaves 4–12 in. long, the outermost of which lie prostrate and twisted on the ground. From the center of the rosette rises a scape to 4 ft. tall surmounted by a spike of greenish to brown flowers which are not showy but are fragrant at night.

CULTURE: Grow the plants in poor, well-drained soil (pH 4.5–6), in very light shade to partial sun.

HABITAT AND RANGE: Inhabits dry, sterile soil of thin woodlands or woodland edges from southern Ohio and Missouri southward to North Carolina and Texas.

FLOWER SEASON: June and July.

PROPAGATION: Seeds.

COMMENTS: This species is useful in the rock garden or a Spanish-type landscape. Yuccas and Sedums are excellent companion plants.

Arisaema triphyllum   Jack-in-the-Pulpit, Indian Turnip
(including *A. atrorubens* and *A. quinatum*)
Araceaae   Arum Family

DESCRIPTION: An erect, striking plant 1–3 ft. tall, from a corm. The leaf blades are palmately divided, with 3–5 segments. A cylindrical spadix and a variously-colored, cornucopia-like spathe are borne on an erect scape. When mature, the fruits are in a handsome bright red cluster (Fig. 5–1).

CULTURE: A moist, shaded, woodland garden with an abundance of organic matter and a pH of 4.5–6. Space the plants 12–18 in. apart in clumps of 3–5.

HABITAT AND RANGE: Native to rich, moist woodlands, wooded bottom lands and talus slopes from Nova Scotia to Minnesota south to Florida and Louisiana.

FLOWER SEASON: March–May.

PROPAGATION: Seeds; the plant self-sows readily.

RELATED SPECIES: *Arisaema dracontium*, the Green Dragon, has a whip-like spadix which terminates in a long, thin projection resembling the tongue of a dragon (Fig. 5-2).

COMMENTS: These unusual plants deserve a place in every woodland garden. The hooded spadix is intriguing, especially to children. The berry-like fruit, at first green, becomes scarlet by fall. The peppery bulb is said to be edible after boiling and was a favorite food of the American Indians.

Symplocarpus foetidus   Skunk Cabbage
Araceae   Arum Family

DESCRIPTION: A conspicuous, large-leaved bog plant, 2 ft. tall, arising from a deep rhizome. The leaves have cordate blades and the globular spadix is enclosed by a thick, colored spathe (Fig. 5-3).

CULTURE: Must be grown in a bog garden where there is always abundant moisture. Space the plants 3 ft. apart, as the leaves are rather large.

HABITAT AND RANGE: Found in shaded bogs and grassy swales from Nova Scotia and Minnesota south to North Carolina.

FLOWER SEASON: December–May.

PROPAGATION: Seed or division of the rhizome.

COMMENTS: Useful for the bog garden, this common aroid is interesting for its purple and green hooded spathes that appear in earliest spring, and for its huge, bright green leaves which are handsome all summer. Odor is produced only when the foliage is bruised.

Panax quinquefolium   Ginseng, Sang
Araliaceae   Ginseng Family

DESCRIPTION: A delicate, erect herb, 6–16 in. tall with palmately divided leaves with 5–7 segments, the leaves are whorled and thus borne in a circle. The yellow-green flowers are arranged in a simple umbel; the fruit is a deep ruby-red berry in a small cluster (Fig. 5-4).

CULTURE: Ginseng requires a rich, moist woodland with a soil containing plenty of humus and having a pH of 4.5–6.

HABITAT AND RANGE: A rare plant of rich woods from Quebec to Minnesota south to Georgia and Mississippi.

FLOWER SEASON: April–July.

PROPAGATION: Seeds.

RELATED SPECIES: *Panax trifolium,* Dwarf Ginseng, is a dainty, much prized plant for the woodland garden. It has 3–5 sessile leaflets. It is very rare and considered endangered.

COMMENTS: Ginseng is an interesting conversation plant for the wild garden because its root is exported to China where it is used for folk medicines. The name is a corruption of the Chinese Jin-chen, meaning man-like, from the two legged appearance of the forked root. Because of its commerical value, natural populations are being depleted by collectors and it is often listed as theatened or endangered.

Caulophyllum thalictroides   Blue Cohosh, Papoose Root
Berberidaceae   Barberry Family

DESCRIPTION: A handsome, erect plant, 1–3 ft. tall, arising from a rhizomatous rootstock that has numerous buds. The stem has one thrice-compound leaf with lobed leaflets and a smaller leaf just below the flower cluster. The yellowish green or purplish flowers are rather small and are followed by berry-like blue fruits borne in a loose cluster (Fig. 5-5).

CULTURE: The plants need light shade, and moist, well drained soil, pH 5.5–7, with abundant humus. Space the plants at least 2 ft. apart as they form large clumps.

HABITAT AND RANGE: Found in rich, damp woods from New Brunswick to Manitoba south to Georgia and Alabama.

FLOWER SEASON: April–May.

PROPAGATION: Seeds or by division.

COMMENTS: The glaucous foliage and bright blue fruit provide a striking contrast to the foliage and fruits of other species in the woodland garden.

Diphylleia cymosa   Umbrella Leaf, Pixie Parasol
Berberidaceae   Barberry Family

DESCRIPTION: The striking umbrella form of the leaves of this species are 18–36 in. tall and 12–20 in. wide. The cluster of white flowers and the later blue fruits arise above the leaves (Fig. 5-6).

CULTURE: Must be grown in a cool, shady, very moist spot with plenty of humus and a pH of 4.5–6, it is excellent for wet seepage areas.

HABITAT AND RANGE: Found in rich, moist, often rocky, cool, mountain coves from Virginia south to Georgia.

FLOWER SEASON: May.

PROPAGATION: Seeds or by division.

COMMENTS: Use in the woodland garden with Lady and Cinnamon ferns; excellent in cooler northern gardens but not for the lower South.

Jeffersonia diphylla   Twinleaf, Rheumatism Root
Berberidacease   Barberry Family

DESCRIPTION: Called Twinleaf because of the leaf blade which is divided into two equal halves. A low rhizomatous plant about 8–10 in. tall when in flower, becoming 15–18 in. high in fruit. The flowers are white, single, and about 1 in. broad, with 8 oblong flat petals. They somewhat resemble the Bloodroot blossom (Fig. 5-7).

CULTURE: *Jeffersonia* is easily grown in a soil high in organic matter at a pH near neutral. For best results, add dolomitic limestone if the soil is acid.

HABITAT AND RANGE: Inhabits rich woods, usually on calcareous soil from Ontario and Wisconsin south to Alabama and Georgia.

FLOWER SEASON: March–May.

PROPAGATION: Seeds and division.

COMMENTS: Named after the third president of the United States, Thomas Jefferson, who was an excellent gardener. Twinleaf is a neat plant for the woodland garden and when properly grown can be used as ground cover.

Podophyllum peltatum   May Apple, Mandrake, Ground Lemon
Berberidaceae   Barberry Family

DESCRIPTION: Two light-green, umbrella-shaped leaves are borne at the top of the flowering stem, often measuring 1 ft. in diameter, the plant reaches a height of 12–18 in.; the ill-smelling, white flowers are solitary and nodding, borne below the leaves, typically with 6 petals and twice as many stamens. The nodding fruit is a large, fleshy, lemon-shaped berry (Fig. 5-8).

CULTURE: May Apple grows best in light shade, in moist soil at pH 5–6. Once established, it spreads rapidly by means of long rhizomes, crowding other plants.

It should not be planted in a small garden unless confined within a large buried pot.

HABITAT AND RANGE: Native to moist open woods and clearings from Quebec to Minnesota south to Florida and Texas.

FLOWER SEASON: April–May.

PROPAGATION: Seeds and division.

COMMENTS: Use May Apple to carpet large areas under deciduous trees in moist, open woodlands. Combine with the fine texture of native ferns. The nodding, waxy-white flowers are best seen when the plants are installed on slopes above a path or walk.

Mertensia virginica   Virginia Bluebells, Virginia Cowslip
Boraginaceae   Borage Family

DESCRIPTION: Arching, shining, smooth stems, 1–2 ft. high, bear clusters of pinkish buds that open to rich blue-hued, trumpet-shaped flowers nearly 1 in. long; the leaves are deep green; the stems arise from a thickened or fleshy rootstock (Fig. 5-9).

CULTURE: Virginia Bluebells grow best in shaded, moist, rich soil at pH 6–7. Space the plants on 18 in. centers and they will rapidly fill the area.

HABITAT AND RANGE: Found in rich alluvial woods and along stream banks from New York to Michigan, south to Georgia.

FLOWER SEASON: March–May.

PROPAGATION: Division and seeds.

COMMENTS: Virginia Bluebells are among the first plants to bloom in the spring; however, the plants die back to the ground soon after flowering so should be interplanted with ferns or Wild Ginger to provide interest when the Bluebells go dormant.

Campanula divaricata   Bellflower
Campanulaceae   Bellflower Family

DESCRIPTION: A dainty species with a few spreading to erect stems with scattered lanceolate to elliptic leaves. The blue, bell-shaped flowers are borne in a diffuse, delicate cluster.

CULTURE: Grow in light shade in poor, thin, well-drained soil amongst rocks or on slopes.

HABITAT AND RANGE: Found in rocky woods, along road cuts and on cliffs from Maryland and Kentucky south to Georgia and Alabama.

FLOWER SEASON: July–October.

PROPAGATION: Seeds.

RELATED SPECIES: *Campanula rotundifolia*, the Hairbell, occupies more northerly habitats and is a fine textured, long bloomer, ideal in lightly shaded rock gardens. In the spring the plant displays a tuft of round leaves hence the name *"rotundifolia."* The spring leaves are succeeded by linear leaves and a succession of airy, blue-violet, bell-like flowers.

COMMENTS: The Bellflower is not at all aggressive and should not be crowded by other species.

Silene virginica   Fire Pink
Caryophyllaceae   Pink Family
   DESCRIPTION: The 1–2 ft. tall Fire Pink has a stem with sticky feeling hairs and spatulate to elliptic-lanceolate leaf blades. The flowers are bright crimson and each of the 5 petals has a notched tip (Fig. 5-10).
   CULTURE: This showy-flowered species adapts well to the thinly shaded woodland garden, preferring a well-drained and rather sunny site; the soil should not be too rich, with a pH of 5–6. This is an adventurous species, and so grows well on lightly disturbed ground. For maximum visual impact, Fire Pink should be planted in groups of 3–5 on 18-in. centers.
   HABITAT AND RANGE: Native to rocky, well-drained, thin woodlands, road cuts, and wood edges from New Jersey to Ontario and Oklahoma south to Georgia and Mississippi.
   FLOWER SEASON: May–June.
   PROPAGATION: Seeds and cuttings.
   RELATED SPECIES: *Silene polypetala* bears attractive, large, pink flowers but has proved difficult to maintain in the woodland garden at Piccadilly Farm (Fig. 5-11). Although easily rooted by cuttings, other Silenes are much better adapted for garden culture. *Silene caroliniana* is one of our most beautiful wild flowers. Low in habit, a single plant can produce 50–100 showy, rose-pink flowers. The plants can be successfully grown in a well-drained rock garden with acid soil and some shade. *Silene stellata*, the Starry Campion, has white flowers with fringed petals and is terrific for late summer flowers in a woodland garden. The rare *Silene regia* is a prairie species and should only be grown in full sun.
   COMMENTS: Fire Pink is a must for every woodland garden.

Stellaria pubera   Giant Chickweed
Caryophyllaceae   Pink Family
   DESCRIPTION: Giant Chickweed is a perennial, 6–12 in. tall, forming a semi-erect clump. The leaf blades are arranged opposite each other and are ovate-elliptic in shape. The flowers are white, the 5 petals so deeply notched as to give the appearance of 10 petals (Fig. 5-12).
   CULTURE: Use this clump-former in the shady woodland garden in well-drained soil.
   HABITAT AND RANGE: Native principally in rich mountain and Piedmont woods from New Jersey to Illinois, south to Mississippi and Georgia.
   SEASON: March–May.
   PROPAGATION: Seeds or division.
   COMMENTS: Giant Chickweed is not as aggressive or invasive as the annual and very weedy Common Chickweed, *Stellaria media*. It stays in place and does not become a problem.

Tradescantia virginiana   Spiderwort, Blue Jackets
Commelinaceae   Spiderwort Family
   DESCRIPTION: The plants grow in erect clumps 18–24 in. tall, with mucilaginous, succulent stems and long narrow, green leaves, the leaf bases clasping the stems. The flowers are regular, with three blue petals and last only part of the day (Fig. 5-13).

CULTURE: Spiderwort does well in gardens when provided with light shade and a fertile, well-drained soil, pH 5–6. In late summer, their untidy foliage can be distracting if not cut back to near the ground. They self-sow and spread but pull easily so pose no great problem as a weed.

HABITAT AND RANGE: Found in nature in meadows and open woods, and along roadsides from Maine to Minnesota southward.

FLOWER SEASON: April–August.

PROPAGATION: Transplanting of self-sown plants.

RELATED SPECIES: *Tradescantia virginiana* hybridizes in nature with *T. ohiensis* and others, making it sometimes difficult to assign a species name to an individual plant. Among the cultivars are 'Rubra', 'Snow', and 'Purple Dome'.

COMMENTS: Use Spiderwort in the front of the perennial bed or tucked in here and there in the wild garden. Spiderworts are fine garden plants requiring little effort, and are greatly admired for their blue flowers which are open in the mornings. Long grown in gardens, they are familiar, old-fashioned garden flowers. They have performed well in the recent heat and drought years that have troubled the Southeast.

Coreopsis auriculata — Eared Coreopsis, Dwarf Tickseed
Compositae or Asteraceae — Sunflower Family

DESCRIPTION: An attractive plant bearing small, sunflower-like heads from a leafy rosette. The leaves are lobed or auriculate at the base, hence the name, and the ray flowers are a rich yellow color with the disk flowers also yellow (Fig. 5-14).

CULTURE: *Coreopsis auriculata* grows best in good garden soil, pH 5–6, in partial shade. For best results it needs 3–4 hours of direct sunlight each day.

HABITAT AND RANGE: Found in thin woods or along woodland edges from Virginia and Kentucky south to Georgia and Mississippi.

FLOWER SEASON: April–May with scattered flowers until frost.

PROPAGATION: Division.

RELATED SPECIES: The cultivar 'Nana' seems little different from the species. This is one of the best members of the genus *Coreopsis* for gardens.

COMMENTS: An excellent plant for the front of the perennial border if a bit of shade is available. Its dwarf and compact growth habit and evergreen foliage make it ideal for the lightly shaded woodland garden.

Erigeron pulchellus — Robin's Plantain
Compositae or Asteraceae — Sunflower Family

DESCRIPTION: The soft stems are about 12–18 in. high, and the plants produce rosettes from surface runners, forming large colonies. The paddle-shaped leaves are softly hairy. The lavender-blue to white flowers are borne in clusters of several heads; the disk flowers in the center of the heads are yellow.

CULTURE: Easily grown in any lightly shaded spot in good garden soil. Space the plants 12–18 in. apart in groups of 5 or more and allow the plants to form a large colony.

HABITAT AND RANGE: A common species in woodlands from Maine to Ontario and Minnesota south to Mississippi.

FLOWER SEASON: April–June.

PROPAGATION: Division.

COMMENTS: One of the first members of the family to bloom in the spring, it is a natural choice for the woodland garden. Bees, bumblebees, and butterflies are attracted to the flowers in great numbers.

Eupatorium coelestinum   Mist Flower, Hardy Ageratum, Blue Boneset
Compositae or Asteraceae   Sunflower Family

DESCRIPTION: Mist Flower or Hardy Ageratum, with its heads of precisely the shape and color of the annual Ageratum, but with long slender stems, is a rhizomatous plant 12–30 in. tall with opposite leaves of toothed blades triangular in outline. The flowers are a soft, misty, lavender blue.

CULTURE: This species prefers partial shade to slightly sunny situations where the soil is reasonably fertile, somewhat acid (pH 5–6), and moist.
Hardy Ageratum spreads rapidly and can become a pest. In northern gardens it is often winter killed.

HABITAT AND RANGE: Found naturally along wooded streams and ditches or bottom lands from New Jersey to Kansas south to Florida and Texas.

FLOWER SEASON: August–October.

PROPAGATION: Division.

COMMENTS: The most showy of the Eupatoriums, Hardy Ageratum provides needed color in the early fall. It is best suited for the wild garden as it is aggressive and not easily controlled. It makes a very fine cut flower, especially nice when arranged with lemon-yellow marigolds.

Hieracium venosum   Rattlesnake Weed, Poor Robin's Plantain
Compositae or Asteraceae   Sunflower Family

DESCRIPTION: An early flowering species, with deep yellow flowers closely resembling small dandelions, and generally leafless stems. The light green hairy leaves are dull magenta on the veins, margins, and undersides, forming a basal rosette of attractive leaves. The flowering stalk is 12–18 in. tall and bears ray flowers in small heads.

CULTURE: Grows best in light shade of woodlands on well-drained soil, at a pH of 4.5–6.

HABITAT AND RANGE: Inhabits dry, open woods from New Hampshire and Vermont south to Alabama and Florida. Less common inland to Missouri.

FLOWER SEASON: April–July.

PROPAGATION: Division of off-shoots.

COMMENTS: *Hieracium venosum* is useful in the wild wooded garden in places where the soil is too thin and impoverished to support other wild flowers. The leaves are interesting and the flowers a dainty texture.

Senecio aureus   Golden Ragwort
Compositae or Asteraceae   Sunflower Family

DESCRIPTION: An early blooming perennial with handsome deep golden yellow, daisy-like flowers, 1 in. broad, with 8–12 rays, borne on grooved, brown-streaked stems. A rhizomatous plant 12–30 in. tall with tufted stems and attractive, heart-shaped basal leaves resembling violet leaves, dark green above and purplish beneath. The stem leaves are more or less deeply lobed (Fig. 5-15).

CULTURE: Golden Ragwort flourishes when cultivated in light shade to part sun in moist garden soil, pH 5.5–6.5. Space the plants 18 in. apart in groups of 3–5 or in mass for an attractive and unusual ground cover.

HABITAT AND RANGE: Found in damp, fertile woods from Labrador to Minnesota south to Florida and Arkansas.

FLOWER SEASON: April–June.

PROPAGATION: Division in the spring.

RELATED SPECIES: *Senecio obovatus,* the Obovate Ragwort, is similar but grows in rich soil over calcareous rocks in woodlands. It is a superior garden plant if the soil is given a bit of limestone.

COMMENTS: Although seldom seen in wild flower catalogs, the Golden Ragwort is a marvelous plant for the woodland garden. The large, rounded, basal leaves are handsome and the attractive, deep golden, daisy-like flowers contrast with other spring blossoms. The flowers are long lasting. It is a favorite at Piccadilly Farm.

Sedum ternatum — Wild Stonecrop
Crassulaceae — Orpine Family

DESCRIPTION: A prostrate native Sedum found in shady woods on rocky ledges; it is a light green succulent, 6 in. tall. Its leaves vary, those on sterile shoots whorled near the tips and alternate below; leaves of the flowering branches are smaller and scattered. Flowers are on horizontal, spreading branches, the 5 green sepals and 5 white petals presenting a starry effect.

CULTURE: One of the few Sedums partial to the shade. Grow it on thin soil on rocks in light shade, add a bit of ground limestone to the area.

HABITAT AND RANGE: Found on mossy rocks and ledges on neutral to alkaline soils in shaded woodlands from Connecticut west to Michigan and south to Georgia and Arkansas.

FLOWER SEASON: May–July.

PROPAGATION: Division, cuttings or seeds.

COMMENTS: An ideal plant for moist, rocky woodland or shaded rocks. The junior author has a colony in a north, shaded location receiving sun for part of the day that has been maintained for 10 years by the occasional application of dolomitic limestone.

Dicentra eximia — Wild Bleeding Heart
Fumariaceae — Fumitory Family

DESCRIPTION: A quite bushy perennial with finely cut, fern-like, basal leaves and drooping, narrow, heart-shaped, magenta-pink flowers. The plants are 12–18 in. tall, arising from a short, scaly rhizome. The leaves are dissected into lanceolate or oblong, toothed segments (Fig. 5-16).

CULTURE: Best grown in lightly shaded woodlands, in fertile, moist soil, pH 5–6, with abundant organic matter. Space the plants 18 in. apart in groups of 3–5.

HABITAT AND RANGE: Found in rich mountain woods from New Jersey and Pennsylvania south to Tennessee and North Carolina.

FLOWER SEASON: March–October; it flowers more or less all season making it highly desirable for the shade garden.

PROPAGATION: Seeds; it self-sows, so look for seedlings around the parent plant.

RELATED SPECIES: *Dicentra cucullaria,* Dutchman's Britches, derives its common name from the shape of the flowers, and for this reason is an interesting species (Fig. 5-17). It goes dormant and disappears after flowering and should be interplanted with other later-season natives. Squirrel Corn, *D. canadensis,* is an early-flowering native with small, yellow tubers accounting for the common name; it also goes dormant after blooming (Fig. 5-18).

COMMENTS: Wild Bleeding Heart is a common garden perennial that excels when naturalized in the woodland garden. It forms pleasant natural drifts due to its habit of self-sowing. Its fine-textured foliage blends well with that of other shade perennials such as the coarse-textured foliage of Hostas. It is a favorite woodland native at Piccadilly Farm.

Gentiana saponaria   Soapwort Gentian
Gentianaceae   Gentian Family

DESCRIPTION: Grows to about 8–20 in. tall, having light green, opposite leaves on slender stems; the leaves are commonly ovate lance-shaped, pointed at either end and three-ribbed. The blue-violet or light lilac-blue flowers only partly open; they are bottle-shaped with several in a terminal cluster or in the axils of the upper leaves (Fig. 5-19).

CULTURE: Grow in fertile, sandy loam, pH 4.5–6, in light shade. Space the plants 10–12 in. apart in groups of 3–7. Soapwort Gentian grows in slightly drier soils than other Gentians.

HABITAT AND RANGE: Found along woodland creeks and pond margins from New York and Indiana south to Florida and Louisiana.

FLOWER SEASON: September–November.

PROPAGATION: Division or seeds.

RELATED SPECIES: *Gentiana autumnalis,* the Pine Barren Gentian, is a striking species for an acid soil and light shade; *G. andrewsii* is a beautiful plant for wet, sunny areas; *G. decora* is a southern, mountain plant with acuminate leaves and blue flowers; *G. villosa* has greenish to yellowish white corollas.

COMMENTS: Gentians are lovely plants for the wild garden, with interesting flower shapes and vivid to muted colors. They furnish contrasting color to the yellow typical of so many fall-blooming species. They are more difficult to grow than many natives, so should only be attempted by the experienced gardener.

Geranium maculatum   Wild or Spotted Geranium, Cranesbill
Geraniaceae   Geranium Family

DESCRIPTION: Wild Geranium has an erect stem 1–2 ft. tall arising from a thick rhizome. The basal leaves are hairy and long petioled and are deeply 5–7 lobed. The plant has a single pair of short petioled leaves on the stem below the clusters of pale or deep magenta-pink or quite light purple flowers. The fruits appear after flowering and are pointed, resembling crane's bill (Fig. 5-20).

CULTURE: Best grown in lightly shaded to partly sunny sites in first-class, moist, well-drained soil, pH 4.5–6.

HABITAT AND RANGE: Native in mature woodlands from Maine to Georgia and Mississippi.

FLOWER SEASON: March–May.

PROPAGATION: Seeds or division.

COMMENTS: Use *Geranium maculatum* in drifts in the woodland garden. In the perennial border, the plant adapts to more light. One of the better natives for garden use.

Hydrophyllum canadense — Waterleaf
Hydrophyllaceae — Waterleaf Family

DESCRIPTION: Waterleaf is an erect leafy plant, 1–2 ft. tall, from a creeping rhizome. Its leaves are palmately lobed and coarsely toothed. Half hidden in the leaves, the flowers are in cymose clusters, with a white, bell-shaped corolla about ¼ in. long (Fig. 5-21).

CULTURE: This plant must be grown in a moist, shaded, woodland garden with abundant humus, pH 4.5–6.5. If the soil is allowed to dry out, the foliage turns black.

HABITAT AND RANGE: Grows naturally in moderate to deep shade in rich, moist woods from Vermont to Wisconsin and Missouri south to Georgia and Alabama.

FLOWER SEASON: May–June.

PROPAGATION: Seeds and division.

RELATED SPECIES: Hydrophyllum macrophyllum, H. virginianum, and H. appendiculatum are all excellent for the woodland garden if sufficient moisture is available.

COMMENTS: In early spring the leaves of Waterleaf are mottled with splotches of gray.

Phacelia bipinnatifida — Spotted Phacelia
Hydrophyllaceae — Waterleaf Family

DESCRIPTION: Spotted Phacelia is a biennial species, 8–24 in. tall. The plant forms a cluster of pinnately divided leaves, the basal ones blotched with gray. The flowers are lavender-blue, borne in masses of recurved cymes (Fig. 5-22).

CULTURE: This biennial plant has been grown for several years in the woodland garden at Piccadilly Farm where it has prospered, new flowering plants forming each year from natural, annual regeneration. It requires moist, shaded soil at a pH of 5.5–7.

HABITAT AND RANGE: Found in moist, fertile woods, on calcareous bluffs and ledges, and in ravines from Virginia to Ohio, Illinois and Missouri south to Georgia, Alabama, and Arkansas.

FLOWER SEASON: April–May.

PROPAGATION: Seeds. It self-sows freely to form natural drifts on humus-rich, woodland slopes; however, it is not aggressive nor invasive.

COMMENTS: Although Phacelia bipinnatifida is not perennial as are all others in this chapter, it is included because it is easily naturalized in the wooded garden, it contributes so much to the garden, is a most attractive plant, and regenerates well thereby having the characteristics of a perennial.

Sisyrinchium angustifolium — Blue-eyed Grass, Irisettes
Iridaceae — Iris Family

DESCRIPTION: Forming stiff, erect, grass-like clumps, 6–20 in. tall; flowers on somewhat twisted, flat stalks rising slightly above the leaves. The violet blue flowers consist of 6 divisions; the center of the flower is beautifully marked with a star-like yellow eye. When in bloom, Blue-eyed Grass is a charming sight (Fig. 5-23).

CULTURE: Quickly forms large clumps, thriving in moist, lightly shaded to partially sunny areas. Grow in average garden soil, pH 4.5–6. Plant in drifts where it can be seen in the morning when the flowers are open.
If not divided from time to time, the clumps decline in vigor.

HABITAT AND RANGE: Found naturally in low meadows, fields, and open woods from Newfoundland to Minnesota south to Louisiana.

FLOWER SEASON: May–June.

PROPAGATION: Division.

RELATED SPECIES: The species of *Sisyrinchium* are generally difficult even for botanists to distinguish. Most are of ornamental value and should be tried in the garden.

COMMENTS: Blue-eyed Grass is useful in rock gardens or in drifts at the edge of the wild garden. The fine, grass-like foliage is of great garden value and should be used to contrast with the foliage of other species.

Blephilia ciliata — Wood Mint
Labiatae or Lamiaceae — Mint Family

DESCRIPTION: A woodland species forming a clump about 1–2 ft. tall. The oblong to lance-shaped, opposite leaves are whitish beneath and have shallowly toothed blades. The numerous, pale purple or violet, two-lipped flowers are about ½ in. long and crowded into whorl-like clusters in the axils of the upper leaves.

CULTURE: Grow Wood Mint in well-drained, average soil, pH 4.5–6.5, in thin shade. Space the plants 18 in. apart in groups of 3–5.

HABITAT AND RANGE: Look for it in thin woodlands, often on granitic rocks or limestones from Massachusetts to Wisconsin south to Georgia and Mississippi.

FLOWER SEASON: May–August.

PROPAGATION: Division.

RELATED SPECIES: *Blephilia hirsuta* is similar but taller; its landscape value is often reduced due to insect damage on the leaves.

COMMENTS: Wood Mint contributes much needed summer flowers to the lightly shaded woodland garden.

Allium tricoccum — Ramp, Wild Leek
Liliaceae — Lily Family

DESCRIPTION: Ramp arises from bulbs with scale-like outer coverings. It has large, flat leaves, 8–10 in. long and about 1 in. or more wide, reminding one of Lily-of-the-Valley or Tulip leaves. The greenish white flowers, arranged in an umbel, arrive in June-July after the leaves have withered away. Ramp is strongly onion scented.

CULTURE: Ramp should be grown in fertile damp soil, at a pH of 5.5–6.5, in shady, deciduous woods. The leaves require some early season sunshine to generate food for later flower production. Overplant with Wild Ginger to insure ground cover during the summer. This species is not suited to the lower South.

HABITAT AND RANGE: Found in rich, humus-abundant soils of cool north-facing, wooded slopes or limestone bluffs from New Brunswick to Minnesota south to Georgia.

FLOWER SEASON: June–July.

PROPAGATION: Division.

RELATED SPECIES: *Allium burdickii,* only recently recognized, has a similar range but smaller leaves and fewer flowers.

COMMENTS: Useful for the shaded, humid, rich, wooded garden. The leaves are quite attractive in the early spring. The young leaves may be used as a seasoning in soups or cut up in salads. A Ramp festival is held each year in the mountains of North Carolina where the bulbs are eaten.

Amianthium muscaetoxicum   Fly Poison, Crow Poison
Liliaceae   Lily Family

DESCRIPTION: Fly Poison is 20–60 in. tall from a bulbous base, having numerous narrow, elongated, channeled, flattened, Daylily-like leaves arising from the base. The flowers are in a dense, quite showy raceme, at first white, later turning yellow-green or green (Fig. 5-24).

CULTURE: Grow this plant in damp, acid soil, pH 4.5–5, in light shade for blooms in late spring or early summer.

HABITAT AND RANGE: In nature, Fly Poison occurs on mesic, wooded slopes, seepage areas, and low pinelands from New York to Missouri south to Mississippi and Florida.

FLOWER SEASON: May–July.

PROPAGATION: Seeds.

COMMENTS: The terminal, white raceme contributes some interest at a time when few other woodland species are in flower. The leaves spread outward and arch downward, imparting an unusual effect. The leaves and underground bulb are poisonous to sheep and cattle. The bulb, mixed with sugar, was once used as a fly poison in the southern Appalachians.

Camassia scilloides   Wild Hyacinth, Eastern Camas, Indigo-squill
Liliaceae   Lily Family

DESCRIPTION: The Wild Hyacinth develops from an edible bulb and becomes 18–20 in. tall. The leaves are narrow and elongate, chiefly basal, and the flowers, in loose racemes, are star-like and bluish white.

CULTURE: This plant does well in a semi-shaded, wild garden. Grow in a rich loam, moist, but not wet, containing plenty of humus, pH 6–7.

HABITAT AND RANGE: Found in low, rich woods, thinly wooded glades, or rocky slopes, often on limestone from Pennsylvania to Wisconsin south to Texas and Georgia.

FLOWER SEASON: April–May.

PROPAGATION: Division of clumps.

COMMENTS: Wild Hyacinth is a dependable companion plant for spring bulbs and for accent in the lightly shaded, wild garden. American Indians believed *Camassia* gave their horses strength and endurance.

Chamaelirium luteum   Devil's Bit, Blazing Star, Squirrel Tail
Liliaceae   Lily Family

DESCRIPTION: The stalk of this plant grows 12–30 in. tall from a basal rosette of flat, lanceolate leaves. Male and female flowers are on separate plants, the male bearing a white, feathery, spike-like raceme, 4–8 in. long and the female a shorter and more slender spike. The male flowers have a yellow tint from the color of the stamens, and the raceme, at first erect, becomes curving and wand-like (Fig. 5-25).

CULTURE: Devil's Bit grows best under hardwoods in fertile, loamy soil with adequate soil moisture, pH 5.5–6.5.

HABITAT AND RANGE: Inhabits hardwood slopes and low grounds from Massachusetts to Nebraska south to Florida and Arkansas.

FLOWER SEASON: May–June.

PROPAGATION: Seeds.

COMMENTS: An attractive accent plant for a wooded slope, providing much-needed late spring and early summer flowers for the woodland garden. It is best used in groups of 5–7 plants for maximum impact.

Clintonia umbellulata   Bead Lily; Speckled Wood Lily
Liliaceae   Lily Family

DESCRIPTION: Bead Lily is a stoloniferous, low plant, 6–20 in. tall with broad, glossy, green leaves. The white, green and purple speckled flowers have a sweet odor and are arranged in an umbel borne on a stalk 9–20 in. tall; they are followed by small, globular, black berries (Fig. 5-26).

CULTURE: It must be grown in cool, humid, first-class soil, pH 5–6, in shaded, deciduous woods. It benefits from being mulched and should be watered during droughts.

HABITAT AND RANGE: Found in lush, cool, mountain woods from New York to Ohio south to Georgia.

FLOWER SEASON: May–June.

PROPAGATION: Seeds or division of clumps.

RELATED SPECIES: *Clintonia borealis,* the Bluehead Lily, ranges more to the north in cold, moist woods and has yellow flowers and blue fruits. It is regarded as more difficult to grow than *C. umbellulata.*

COMMENTS: Clintonias are of outstanding value due to the long-lasting leaves that remain green all summer. They are not, however, adapted to the warmer parts of the Southeast. Naturalize them in drifts in a cool, shady spot.

Disporum lanuginosum   Fairybells, Yellow Mandarin
Liliaceae   Lily Family

DESCRIPTION: Another wild flower with nodding, bell-shaped flowers, Fairybells reach 1–3 ft. in height, growing from a knotty rhizome. The stem is forked and the leaves have prominent veins. The greenish yellow flowers are borne at the tips of the stems, followed by red berries. The species resembles *Uvularia* in habit but differs in that the fruit is a smooth red berry in contrast to the 3-angled capsule of *Uvularia.*

CULTURE: The plant favors fertile soil with a pH of 5–6 and moist shaded woods and should never be allowed to become dry. Space the plants in clumps of 3 about 12–15 in. apart.

HABITAT AND RANGE: Found in rich, cool, mountain woods from New York and Ontario south to Georgia and Alabama.

FLOWER SEASON: April–early June.

PROPAGATION: Seeds or by division of the rootstock.

RELATED SPECIES: *Disporum maculatum,* the Nodding Mandarin, is similar but has yellow to whitish petals with black dots. The larger flowers of this species tend to be hidden by the leaves. Both species grow under similar conditions.

COMMENTS: Fairybells, with its late spring flowers, add a touch of interest to the shaded, wild garden. The strongly veined, light green leaves are unusual and help make the planting attractive when dense colonies have become established.

Erythronium umbilicatum (E. americanum)   Trout Lily, Dog-tooth Violet,
                                        Adder's Tongue
Liliaceae   Lily Family

DESCRIPTION: A low, perennial herb, 5–10 in. tall, with pointed, maroon-purple, mottled leaves, 4–8 in. tall, originating from a deeply buried corm. Each corm generally produces two fleshy leaves and a nodding, solitary, lily-like flower bearing sepals that are yellow on the inside and purple on the back, and petals that are also yellow, but with a purple streak on the mid-rib (Fig. 5-27).

CULTURE: Grow Trout Lily in the damp, shaded, wild garden at a pH of 5–6. Add generous amounts of humus to the soil. The plants self-sow and, given sufficient time, form drifts.

HABITAT AND RANGE: Grows naturally in moist, rich woods, often on talus or along streams from Nova Scotia to Minnesota south to Georgia and Alabama.

FLOWER SEASON: Late February–May, one of the earliest spring wild flowers, often commencing to bloom in the last days of February in Georgia.

PROPAGATION: Seeds or division. Occasionally one may be able to collect corms at sites about to be disturbed by construction.

RELATED SPECIES: *Erythronium albidum*, the White Trout Lily, tends to be a better bloomer. Its flowers are white, or dull, pale violet-tinged outside and yellow-tinged at the heart inside; the 6 divisions of the flower are strongly recurved. Add some ground dolomitic limestone to the soil to grow this species.

COMMENTS: The trout lilies are mainly of interest because of their fleshy, mottled leaves and their early appearance in the garden. They should be interplanted with other later species such as the native ferns to give interest later in the season. Although also commonly known as the Dog-tooth Violet, they are not related to the true violets. The tuber is said to resemble the fang of a dog, hence the common name.

Hymenocallis occidentalis   Spider Lily, Basket Flower
Liliaceae (including the Amaryllidaceae)   Lily Family

DESCRIPTION: Spider Lilies are perennial herbs with strap-like leaves growing from a rather large, tunicated bulb. Flowers terminate the scape rising centrally from the bulb, the clusters subtended by 2–4 membranous bracts. The perianth is composed of 6 narrow, white segments; within the perianth is a conspicuous, white, flaring, cup-like corona (Fig. 5-28).

CULTURE: Grow the Spider Lily in soil with abundant humus and high fertility. Although it prefers moist sites, it does well in the woodland garden if given adequate water during droughts. In the senior author's garden at Piccadilly Farm, it blooms each year on a well-drained, wooded slope. In soggy areas, it transplants readily and grows well under Yellow Poplars amid a colony of ferns. Plant it on 18 in. centers in groups of 3 or more.

HABITAT AND RANGE: Low woodlands, swamplands, and shoals of rivers and streams, often in slightly acid soils from Indiana and Missouri south to Texas, Florida and North Carolina.

FLOWER SEASON: June–August.

PROPAGATION: Seeds or division.

RELATED SPECIES: In the Southeast, it is difficult to identify the species of Spider Lilies with any certainty. Godfrey and Wooten (1979) recognized the difficulty, suggested the genus is incompletely understood, and did not distinguish among the species. *Hymenocallis occidentalis* is the most widely distributed of the species and the name is widely recognized, so we use this name.

COMMENTS: A handsome and interesting species well worth a try in the garden.

Lilium superbum — Turk's Cap Lily, Lily Royal
Liliaceae — Lily Family

DESCRIPTION: Turk's Cap Lily reaches 3–9 ft. in height arising from a scaly bulb. The leaves are in whorls. The showy, nodding, red to orange flowers, spotted with purple, are produced in clusters of 3 to many (Fig. 5-29). Remarkable for its completely reflexed sepals and petals which leave the handsome stamens, tipped by brown anthers, fully exposed to view.

CULTURE: This lily requires uniformly moist soil, well laced with organic matter, pH 5–6.5. While it grows well in light to partial shade, optimum conditions include 2 hours of full sun daily.

HABITAT AND RANGE: Found in meadows and coves from New Brunswick to Minnesota south to Florida.

FLOWER SEASON: July–August.

PROPAGATION: Seeds or by planting some of the outer bulb scales in deep, fertile, humic soil.

RELATED SPECIES: *Lilium michauxii,* Michaux's Lily, is similar, but usually bears only 1–3 (rarely 15) blooms (Fig. 5-30). The Wood Lily, *L. philadelphicum,* is a rare plant of higher balds and mountains with 1–2 erect flowers.

COMMENTS: *Lilium superbum* makes a spectacular show against a background of shrubs or dark, low, coniferous trees. It is easier to cultivate than some of the other native lilies and is the best species for gardens.

Medeola virginiana — Indian Cucumber Root
Liliaceae — Lily Family

DESCRIPTION: The slender stem, 8–12 in. tall, has a whorl of 5–9 leaves near the middle with 3 leaves at the stem tip subtending a few-flowered umbel of nodding, inconspicuous, greenish yellow flowers, accented by the reddish color of the 6 stamens. In September, 2 or 3 purple-black berries accent the tips of the plants. It is perennial from a rhizome (Fig. 5-31).

CULTURE: Flourishes in lush, damp soil, pH 4.5–6 in deep shade. Grow it in masses of 12–15 plants spaced 10 in. apart. It is ideal for interplanting among low-growing native ferns.

HABITAT AND RANGE: Indian Cucumber Root is found in moist, shaded woods from Nova Scotia to Quebec and Minnesota south to Alabama and Georgia.

FLOWER SEASON: April–July.

PROPAGATION: By division of rhizome.

COMMENTS: Indian Cucumber Root is not a showy species when in flower, but the small, delicate, greenish yellow flowers followed by purple berries are rather neat. It is actually at its best in the autumn when the leaves become flushed with purple. The succulent, thickened rhizome may be eaten raw, tasting somewhat like a cucumber.

Melanthium virginicum   Bunch Flower
Liliaceae   Lily Family

DESCRIPTION: An impressive, coarse, erect plant, with strong stems 3–5 ft. tall; the narrow elongated leaves mainly clustered at the base of the plant are nearly 1 in. wide, the few upper ones, small, linear or grass-shaped. The tiny yellowish to greenish flowers have 6 separate divisions and are in a large branched cluster held high above the leaves. The fruit is an ovoid, three-lobed capsule.

CULTURE: Bunch Flower requires an acid (pH 4.5–5.5), peaty, moist soil and thin shade to part sun.

HABITAT AND RANGE: Inhabits meadows and pinelands from New York to Indiana south to Florida and Texas.

FLOWER SEASON: June–August.

PROPAGATION: Seeds.

RELATED SPECIES: *Melanthium woodii* and *M. parviflorum* (= *Veratrum parviflorum*) both have wide leaves and are often called Hellebore; *M. latifolium* (= *M. hybridum*) has narrow leaves and is similar to *M. virginicum*. All three of these species are worth growing.

COMMENTS: Bunch Flower is impressive when it blooms and is excellent for providing summer flowers and foliage.

Polygonatum biflorum   Solomon's Seal
(= *P. commutatum* and = *P. canaliculatum*)
Liliaceae   Lily Family

DESCRIPTION: This common and well known plant grows 1–4 ft. tall from a knotted, creeping rhizome. The graceful, erect or arching stem bears alternate leaves arranged on either side of the stem. The flowers are produced in the axils of the leaves and resemble greenish white bells drooping down and hanging on slender stalks, more or less hidden by the foliage. The flowers are followed by blue-black berries resembling small grapes (Fig. 5–32).

CULTURE: Solomon's Seal is almost effortlessly grown in lightly or deeply shaded woodlands. It can serve as a ground cover or be used in clumps tucked here and there.

HABITAT AND RANGE: It grows in woodlands from Massachusetts to Manitoba south to Florida and northern Mexico.

FLOWER SEASON: April–June.

PROPAGATION: Seeds or division.

RELATED SPECIES: *Polygonatum pubescens* is similar but its leaves are hairy on the veins on the lower surface. Most botanical authorities now include *P. commutatum* and *P. canaliculatum* as part of *P. biflorum* rather than as separate species. The complex is rather confusing due to polyploidy (multiplication of the number of chromosomes) as well as environmental variation. The populations of these plants are difficult to classify because of overlapping and intergrading characteristics. The array of ecological deviations and growth forms are bewildering and the populations are best considered as one species, *P. biflorum*.

COMMENTS: The plant is named for the scars on the rhizome from previous years' attachment of stems. A graceful and pretty plant when under cultivation. Although Solomon's Seal is widely known, False Solomon's Seal, *Smilacina racemosa*, is handsomer, with its easily seen, terminal cluster of white flowers followed by red berries.

Fig. 1-1. A small Wisconsin wild flower garden, adjacent to a house, with numerous species of flowering plants and ferns (Morrison).

Fig.1-2. A massive, formal, perennial border with many native perennials at the North Carolina State University Arboretum. Although of interest, its scale is overwhelming for most garden situations.

Fig. 1-3. Drifts of *Phlo* *divaricata* used to hide *Narcissus* foliage in the woodland garden at Piccadilly Farm. Later area will be covered v Hostas.

Fig. 1-4. Thrift, *Phlox subulata,* grows well on poor, tight, clay soils and controls erosion on steep banks.

Fig. 1-5. Green and G *Chrysogonum virginicu* Nancy Arrington's ga in Manassas, VA (Staunton).

Fig. 2-1. Pink Lady Slipper, *Cypripedium acaule.*

Fig. 2-2. This garden will not please everyone, but if the owner is pleased, it is fine. Personal taste is important.

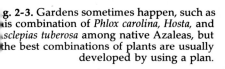

g. 2-3. Gardens sometimes happen, such as ⎫is combination of *Phlox carolina, Hosta,* and *sclepias tuberosa* among native Azaleas, but the best combinations of plants are usually developed by using a plan.

Fig. 2-4. Site analysis is important: a west-facing woodland edge, garden s at Piccadilly Farm, with l afternoon sun; a pine t with a bad "face" that m be removed; several old gullies, the one at the ba eventually left unfilled ▸ provide topography and microhabitats; an east facing slope.

Fig. 2-5. A simple woodland border with Threadleaf Coreopsis, Daylilies, Bee Balm, and Artemisia at Piccadilly Farm.

Fig. 2-6. A drift of *Ligusticum canadense* designed by nature.

Fig. 2-7. A planted drift of *Tiarella cordifolia* at Piccadilly Farm.

Fig. 2-8. *Sagittaria latifolia* effectively used in a small pool to provide height and contrast.

Fig. 2-9. *Phlox carolina* cv. ss Lingard used against variegated *Miscanthus ensis* in an island bed at Piccadilly Farm.

Fig. 5-1. Jack-in-the-Pulpit, *Arisaema triphyllum*.

Fig. 5-2. Green Dragon, *Arisaema dracontium*. Note the long, whip-lik spadix resembling the tongue of a dragon.

Fig. 5-3. Attractive leaves of the Skunk Cabbage, *Symplocarpus foetidus*.

Fig. 5-4. Ginseng, *Panax quinquefolium,* in fruit.

5-5. Blue Cohosh, *Caulophyllum thalictroides*.

Fig. 5-6. Umbrella Leaf, *Diphylleia cymosa*.

Fig. 5-7. The leaves of Twinleaf, *Jeffersonia diphylla* form an interesting ground cover.

Fig. 5-8. May Apple, *Podophyllum peltatum*.

Fig. 5-9. Virginia Bluebells, *Mertensia virginica.*

Fig. 5-10. The notched (pinked) petals of Fire Pink, *S virginica,* are typical of those of the Pink family.

Fig. 5-11. The very rare *Silene polypetala.*

Fig. 5-12. The perennial Giant Chickweed, *Stellaria pubera,* is an excellent choice for the woodland gar

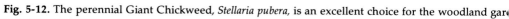

Fig. 5-13. Spiderwort, *Tradescantia virginiana,* easily grown in the garden.

Fig. 5-14. *Coreopsis auriculata,* one of the best natives for the woodland edge.

5-16. Wild Bleeding Heart, *Dicentra eximia,* blooms from March to ▪vember at Piccadilly Farm; a must for a woodland garden.

Fig. 5-15. Golden Ragwort, *Senecio aureus,* very showy in the spring.

Fig. 5-17. The interesting flowers of Dutchman's Britches, *Dicentra cucullaria.*

Fig. 5-18. Squirrel Corn, *Dicentra canadensis.*

Fig. 5-19. Soapwort Gentian, *Gentiana saponaria.*

Fig. 5-20. Wild or Spotted Geranium, *Geranium maculatum.*

5-21. Waterleaf, *Hydrophyllum canadense.*

Fig. 5-22. *Phacelia bipinnatifida.*

Fig. 5-23. Blue-eyed Grass, *Sisyrinchium angusti-folium.*

Fig. 5-24. Fly Poison, *Amian-um muscatoxicum.*

Fig. 5-25. Devil's Bit, *Chamaelirium luteum.*

Fig. 5-26. Clinton's Lily, *Clintonia umbellulata.*

Fig. 5-27. Dog Tooth Violet or Trout Lily, *Erythronium umbilicatum,* delightful in the very early spring.

Fig. 5-28. Spider Lily, *Hymenocallis.*

5-29. The best native lily for the [gard]en, Turk's Cap Lily, *Lilium superbum*.

Fig. 5-30. Michaux's Lily, *Lilium michauxii.*

[5]-31. Cucumber Root, *Medeola virginiana,* in fruit and with fall color.

Fig. 5-32. Solomon's Seal, *Polygonatum biflorum.*

Fig. 5-33. Excellent in the garden, False Solomon's Seal, *Smilacina racemosa.*

Fig. 5-34. *Trillium grandiflorum,* delightful in the garden, but to serve the species, purchase only nursery-propagated plants

Fig. 5-35. *Trillium catesbaei.*

Fig. 5-36. *Trillium erectum.*

5-37. *Trillium decipiens.*

Fig. 5-38. The foliage of Bellwort, *Uvularia perfoliata,* provides interest all season.

Fig. 5-39. The terrific floral display of Rain Lily, *Zephyranthes atamasco.*

Fig. 5-40. A favorite native wild flower, Indian Pink, *Spigelia marilandica.*

Fig. 5-41. A perfect group of Yellow Lady's Slippers, *Cypripedium calceolus* var. *pubescens*.

Fig. 5-42 Bloodroot, *Sanguinaria canadensis*, informing the world that spring has arrive

Fig. 5-43. A nice clump of Bloodroot adds excitement to any garden.

Fig. 5-44. Wood Poppy, *Stylophorum diphyllum*, flowers over the entire growing season.

Fig. 5-45. *Phlox carolina* growing among *Rhododendron canescens* at Piccadilly Farm.

Fig. 5-46. The white *Phlox* cultivar 'Miss Lingard' against a background of *Miscanthus sinensis* 'Variegatus' at Piccadilly Farm. All *Phlox* cultivars have been developed from *Phlox* native to North America.

5-47. Blue Woodland Phlox, *Phlox divaricata,* with stmas Fern (Arrington and Staunton).

Fig. 5-48. *Phlox divaricata* from Chattahoochee, FL, known in the nursery trade as 'Chattahoochee'. Note the dark eye in the center.

Fig. 5-49. *Phlox stolonifera,* note the stolon.

Fig. 5-50. Jacob's Ladder, *Polemonium reptans,* blo
over a long period.

Fig. 5-51. Spring Beauty, *Claytonia caroliniana.*

Fig. 5-52. Shooting Star, *Dodecatheon meadia,* with its unusual-shaped flowers, is bound to command attention in the garden.

Fig. 5-53.
Lysimachia tonsa.

5-54. Baneberry, *Actaea pachypoda,* with its long-
ng foliage and attractive fruit, is very useful in the
dland garden.

Fig. 5-55. Red Baneberry, *Actaea rubra.*

Fig. 5-56. Columbine, *Aquilegia
canadensis,* self-sows and forms
attractive natural drifts of color in
the wild garden.

Fig. 5-58. Wind Flower, *Thalictrum thalictroides*.

Fig. 5-57. The white, candle-like flower clusters of Black Cohosh, *Cimicifuga racemosa*, light up a dark background.

Fig. 5-59. Goat's Beard, *Aruncus dioicus*.

Fig. 5-60. Indian Physic, *Poteranthus trifoliatus.*

Fig. 5-61. *Chelone lyonii,*
Pink Turtlehead.

Fig. 5-62. The flowers of *Chelone glabra* are shaped like the head of a snapping turtle.

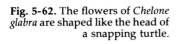

Fig. 6-1. Blue Star or Texas Star, *Amsonia tabernaemontana.*

Fig. 6-2. Butterfly Milkweed, *Asclepias tuberosa.*

Fig. 6-3. The Cardinal Flower, *Lobelia cardinalis.*

Fig. 6-4. The Great Lobelia, *Lobelia siphilitica,* blo◄ over a long period of time.

6-5. New England Aster, *Aster novae-angliae*.

6-6. Heath Aster, *Aster ericoides*.

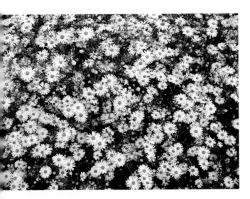

Fig. 6-7. White Woodland Aster, *Aster divaricatus*.

Fig. 6-8. *Boltonia asteroides*, 'Snow Bank', a selection from the species.

Fig. 6-9. Thread Leaved Coreopsis, *Coreopsis verticillata*.

Fig. 6-10. *Coreopsis* 'Moonbeam', a selection from native *C. verticillata* known for its long flowering period.

Fig. 6-11. Purple Cone Flower, *Echinacea purpurea*.

Fig. 6-12. The rare *Echinacea pallida*.

6-13. Joe Pye-weed.

Fig. 6-15. Helen's Flower,
Helenium autumnale.

6-14. *Gaillardia pulchella.*

Fig. 6-16. *Helianthus angustifolius.*

Fig. 6-17. *Heliopsis helianthoides,* 'Summer Sun', a long blooming selection.

Fig. 6-18. *Liatris elegans.*

Fig. 6-19. Prairie Coneflower, *Ratibida pinnata.*

Fig. 6-20. A container grown, *Rudbeckia fulgida,* 'Goldstrum', a superior selection of Perennial Blackeyed Susan.

6-21. *Solidago ulmifolia,*
of the best Goldenrods
gardens.

Fig. 6-22. *Solidago altissima,* use this
Goldenrod in meadow plantings.

Fig. 6-23. *Solidago odora.*

6-24. A widely grown native, Stokes' Aster, *Stokesia laevis.*

Fig. 6-25. *Vernonia gigantea,* Ironweed.

Fig. 6-26. Blue
False Indigo,
Baptisia australis, the
best of the native
Baptisia.

Fig. 6-27. *Thermopsis villosa,* Carolina Bush Pea.

Fig. 6-28. Oswego Tea or Bee Balm, *Monarda didyma.*

6-29. Wild Bergamot, *Monarda fistulosa.*

Fig. 6-30.
The invasive *Physostegia virginiana,*
the Obedient Plant.

6-31. *Pycnanthemum pycnanthemoides.*

Fig. 6-32. *Pycnanthemum tenuifolium.*

Fig. 6-33. *Salvia azurea* var. *azurea*.

Fig. 6-34. Colic Root, *Aletris farinosa*.

Fig. 6-35. *Lilium canadense*.

Fig. 6-36. Sea Shore Mallow, *Kosteletzkya virgin*

Fig. 6-37. Sundops, *Oenothera fruticosa.*

Fig. 6-38. *Oenothera speciosa.*

6-39. *Phlox paniculata,* Summer Phlox.

Fig. 6-40. Three-toothed Cinquefoil, *Potentilla tridentata,* excellent in the rock garden.

Fig. 6-41. Small's Penstemon, *Penstemon smallii.*

Fig. 6-42. *Veronicastrum virginicum.*

Fig. 6-43. *Verbena canadensis.*

Fig. 6-44. *Verbena rigida.*

Fig. 7-1. An August morning at the restored Green Prairie of the University of Wisconsin Arboretum (Morrison).

Fig. 7-2. Prairie vegetation around a dining terrace at a corporate headquarters (Morrison).

Fig. 7-3. Freeway interchange planting of Blackeyed Susans (Michigan DOT and National Wildflower Research Center).

Fig. 7-4. Prairie restoration at a General Electric corporate site 6 years after the initial seeding (Morrison).

Fig. 7-5. A 6-year old prairie restoration shortly after burning (Morrison).

Fig. 7-6. A control burn at Greenwood Plantation, Thomasville, Georgia.

Fig. 7-7. Liatris in a fire-maintained Long Leaf Pine savanna at Greenwood Plantation.

Fig. 7-8. A colorful, fire-maintained savanna in the Apalachicola National Forest in Florida.

Fig. 7-9. Harrell Prairie Hill, a virgin prairie maintained with the aid of fire in Scott County, Mississippi.

Fig. 7-10. Broomsedge, *Andropogon virginicus,* maintained by an annual spring mowing, Saint Catherines Island, Georgia.

Fig. 7-11. Indian grass moving with the wind.

Fig. 7-12. A meadow with drifts of Goldenrod in the mountains of North Carolina.

Fig. 7-13. Direct-seeded flowers are colorful but do not reflect the true prairie dominated by grasses (Texas DOT and the National Wildflower Research Center).

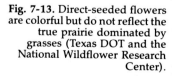

Fig. 7-14. Exotics such as these provide color but are not native wild flowers and rarely establish themselves.

Fig. 7-15. Direct-seeded flowers at the G. D. Hines Development, Sugarland, Texas (Wildseed, Inc. and National Wildflower Research Center).

Fig. 7-16. Jens Jenson's sense of the prairie movement captured by the Missouri Botanical Garden's restored Shaw Prairie near St. Louis.

Fig. 7-17. Native Big Blue Stem, Liatris and Rattlesnake Master in the Shaw Prairie.

Fig. 8-1. The interesting fruiting inflorescence of Bushy Beard Grass, *Andropogon glomeratus,* is attractive either out-of-doors in a meadow or in dried arrangements for inside the home.

Fig. 8-2. *Chasmanthium latifolium,* Upland Sea acquires a marvelous brownish purple color i full sun, yet it is one of the few grasses that gro some shade.

Fig. 8-3. Switch Grass, *Panicum virgatum,* is equally at home in a meadow planting or in the perennial border as here at André Viette's garden in Virginia.

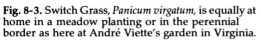

Fig. 8-4. Sea Oats, *Uniola paniculata,* is a picturesque grass used to bind coastal sand dunes.

Fig. 8-5. A lush carpet of *Carex pensylvanica* in an Arkansas forest (Rettig).

Fig. 8-6. The rare Fraser's Sedge, *Cymophyllus fraseri*.

Fig. 8-7. Fraser's Sedge in a natural setting with Trilliums (Manhart).

Fig. 9-2. The fine-textured Northern Maiden Hair Fern, *Adiantum pedatum.*

Fig. 9-3. Lady Fern, *Athyrium filix-femina,* forms a cool green carpet.

Fig. 9-4. The Walking Fern, *Camptosorus rhizophyllus,* produces new plants at the tips of the fronds.

Fig. 9-5. The Hayscented Fern, *Dennstaedtia punctilobula,* forms delicate drifts of foliage and is an excellent ground cover.

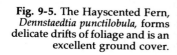

9-6. The Marginal Wood Fern, *Dryopteris*
ginalis, is evergreen, providing interest
ughout the year.

Fig. 9-7. The green stems of
Equisetum hyemale, the Scouring
Rush, are unusually attractive.

Fig. 9-8. The Small Chain Fern,
Lorinseria areolata, sometimes
called *Woodwardia areolata,* is
excellent in wet, shady soil.

Fig. 9-9. A wet meadow in New
England with Ostrich Fern,
Matteuccia struthiopteris.

Fig. 9-10. The Sensitive Fern, *Onoclea sensibilis,* can be invasive in a small garden.

Fig. 9-11. Cinnamon Fern, *Osmunda cinnamomea,* requires moist soil but is one of the most handsome of native ferns.

Fig. 9-13. *Osmunda regalis,* the Royal Fern.

Fig. 9-12. The Interrupted Fern, *Osmunda claytonia.*

Fig. 9-14. Resurrection Fern, *Polypodium polypodioides,* on a tree limb.

Fig. 9-15. The evergreen Christmas Fern, *Polystichum acrostichoides,* is one of the first ferns to produce new fiddleheads in the spring.

Fig. 9-16. The Broad Beech Fern, *Thelypteris hexagonoptera,* is a handsome species for fertile, moist woodlands.

Fig. 9-17. The Widespread Maiden Fern, *Thelypteris kunthii,* is a favorite in southern gardens.

Fig. 10-1. *Asarum shuttleworthii*, 'Callaway', a selection made by Fred Galle.

Fig. 10-2. Wild Ginger, *Asarum canadense*, a fast growing, deciduous species, perhaps the best native ginger for use as a ground cover.

Fig. 10-3. Allegheny Spurge, *Pachysandra procumbens*, a native that merits wide use in shady gardens.

Fig. 10-4. Pussy-toes, *Antennaria plantaginifolia*, thrive poor, dry soil where it covers the ground with flat, si patches.

10-5. Green and Gold, *Chrysogonum virginianum*, 'Piccadilly'.

10-6. The rare Oconee Bells, *Shortia galacifolia*.

Fig. 10-7. Crested Dwarf Iris, *Iris cristata*.

Fig. 10-8. Wood Anemone,
Anemone quinquefolia.

Fig. 10-9. *Hepatica americana,* Liverleaf, one of the earliest spring wild flowers.

Fig. 10-10. Bishop's Cap or Mitrewort, *M diphylla.*

Fig. 10-11. Foam Flower, *Tiarella cordifolia* var. *collina.*

Fig. 10-12. A drift of Foam Flower in the woodland garden at Piccadilly Farm.

Fig. 11-1. Floating Heart, *Nymphoides aquatica.*

Fig. 11-2. *Nymphoides cordata.*

Fig. 11-3. Yellow Lotus, *Nelumbo lutea,* the native water lotus.

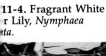

11-4. Fragrant White
r Lily, *Nymphaea*
ta.

Fig. 11-5. Water Lettuce, *Pistia stratiotes,* a free-floating aquatic.

Fig. 11-6. *Sagittaria latifolia,* Arrowhead, a common emergent aquatic.

Fig. 11-8. A large colony of Golden Club in black creek in northern Florida.

Fig. 11-7. The golden-yellow spadix of *Orontium aquaticum,* Golden Club.

Fig. 11-9. Spoon Flower or White Arum, *Peltandra sagittaefolia.*

Fig. 11-10. Wild Rice, *Zizania aquatica;* the lo drooping branches bear staminate flowers a the upper the pistillate flowers.

Fig. 11-12.
Southern Blue Flag,
Iris virginica.

11-11. Red Flag,
ulva.

Fig. 11-13. Yellow
Flag, *Iris pseudacorus,*
widely naturalized in
North America.

1-14. A large colony of *Crinum americanum* in a bayou
ississippi.

Fig. 11-15. A planting
of *Thalia dealbata.*

Fig. 11-16. Water Clover, *Marsilea vestita,* an unusual fern.

Fig. 11-17. Pickerel Weed, *Pontederia cordata.*

Fig. 11-18. Bur Reed, *Sparganium americanum.*

Fig. 11-19. Common Cattail, *Typha latifolia.*

11-20. Bullrush, *Scirpus cyperinus.*

Fig. 11-21. Softrush, *Juncus effusus.*

11-22. Rose Mallow, *Hibiscus moscheutos.*

Fig. 11-23. Swamp Candles, *Lysimachia terrestris.*

Fig. 11-24. *Sarracenia purpurea.*

Fig. 11-25. *Sarracenia minor,* Hooded Pitcher Pl

Fig. 11-26. Lizard's Tail, *Saururus cernuus.*

Fig. 11-27. Grass of Parnassus, *Parnassia asarifolia.*

Smilacina racemosa   False Solomon's Seal, False Spikenard
Liliaceae   Lily Family
DESCRIPTION: An arching, leafy perennial, 1–3 ft. tall, growing from a horizontal rhizome. The stem bears alternate leaves in 2 ranks and a terminal cluster of small, white flowers. The berries, smaller than peas, are at first green, then yellowish white speckled with madder brown and finally a dull ruby-red (Fig. 5-33).

CULTURE: A fine plant for the woodland garden or used in masses as a ground cover. It is neat tucked in here and there among other plants. It is easily grown in almost any good woodland site where the soil is rich and moist, pH 4.5–6. Use mass plantings of this species on 12 in. centers in groups of 5–11 or scatter clumps of 1–3 plants about the shady garden.

HABITAT AND RANGE: Grows in fertile woods from Nova Scotia west to British Columbia south to Georgia and Arizona.

FLOWER SEASON: April–June.

PROPAGATION: Seeds.

RELATED SPECIES: *Smilacina stellata* is similar but has flowers in a raceme rather than a panicle. It spreads rapidly by rhizomes and is useful as a ground cover. *S. trifolia* is a much smaller plant found in cold, wet, sphagnum bogs.

COMMENTS: A really beautiful woodland plant; every woodland garden must have some False Solomon's Seal. The white flowers show up well against a dark setting. Over its long season, it contributes highly visible flowers in the spring and ever changing colored fruit that finally become a notable, showy red.

Streptopus roseus   Rosy Twisted Stalk, Rose Bells, Rose Mandarin
Liliaceae   Lily Family
DESCRIPTION: Rosy Twisted Stalk grows 12–30 in. tall from a rhizome, the larger plants are branched and bear alternate, sessile, coarsely ciliate leaves; the light green leaves are arranged on zigzag stems. The small, curly, whitish to pinkish or purple-pink flowers are about ½ in. long and are borne solitary or paired in the leaf axils; the flowers are dainty, drooping, and bell-like. The flower stalks are twisted, hence the common name. The fruit is a red, round berry, nearly ½ in. in diameter.

CULTURE: Grow Rosy Twisted Stalk in humus rich, neutral to slightly acid (pH 6–6.5) soil, in moist but not wet sites. It does best on cool, north-facing slopes and should not be attempted in the South except at higher elevations in the mountains.

HABITAT AND RANGE: Occurs naturally from Newfoundland to Minnesota south to New Jersey, Pennsylvania and Michigan south along the Appalachians and Blue Ridge into northern Georgia.

FLOWER SEASON: April–July.

PROPAGATION: Seeds or division.

RELATED SPECIES: *Streptopus amplexifolius* is comparable but has cordate, clasping leaves and greenish flowers.

COMMENTS: Use this native species in small groups or in large colonies for ground cover in high, cool shade.

Trillium grandiflorum   Great Trillium, White Wake Robin, Trinity Lily
Liliaceae   Lily Family
DESCRIPTION: This Trillium grows 12–18 in. tall from a short, stout rhizome. It has 3 ovate to lance-ovate leaves whorled around the top of the stem with a single terminal flower. The flower consists of 3 green sepals and 3 white petals, the latter

often fading to pink as they grow older (Fig. 5–34).

CULTURE: Grow the Great Trillium in light to dense shade in moist, but not wet, soil with abundant humus and a pH of 6–7. When used in mass to form natural-appearing drifts, space the plants on 10 in. centers, or put them in clumps of 3–5 and tuck them in here and there in the garden for accent.

HABITAT AND RANGE: Occurs in fertile, moist woodlands from Quebec and Maine south to Arkansas, and along the mountains into northern Georgia.

FLOWER SEASON: April–June.

PROPAGATION: As many as 7 years are required to grow Trilliums from seed. If the rhizomes are wounded, plants can be propagated asexually, as the wounding causes offsets to be produced. Most commercially available Trilliums have been collected in the wild, endangering the natural populations that are often protected by law or the landowner. Purchase only nursery propagated material. Another possibility is a salvage dig on sites about to be destroyed; however, never attempt a salvage dig without the landowner's written permission.

RELATED SPECIES: All of the Trilliums are worthy of cultivation in the woodland garden, but space is too limited to mention all of them. Some of the better include: The pink or whitish *Trillium catesbaei,* an ideal subject for the southern, Piedmont garden (Fig. 5-35); the Red Trillium, *T. erectum,* is easy to grow, with appealing red flowers (Fig. 5-36); the Little Sweet Betsy, *T. cuneatum,* with maroon, sessile flowers, naturalizes easily by self-sowing; *T. decipiens* blooms early and is effective for a long time (Fig. 5-37); *T. luteum* has yellow petals; *T. decumbens* has brownish purple petals and is decumbent in growth form; the flowers of *T. cernuum* are borne on a stalk that curves downward, hence the name Nodding Trillium. The colorful *T. undulatum,* or Painted Trillium, is difficult to grow except in a moist, cool, acid site.

COMMENTS: Every woodland garden should have a few Trilliums.

Uvularia grandiflora　　　　　　　　　　Bellwort, Merry Bells, Straw Flower
Liliaceae　　　　　　　　　　　　　　　　　　　　　　　　　　Lily Family

DESCRIPTION: Bellwort is a perennial, 1–2 ft. tall, growing from a slender rhizome and forming a leafy clump with forked stems. The leaves are perfoliate, reaching full size only after flowering. At the tip of each fork there is one, nodding yellow flower followed by an interesting 3-cornered fruit.

CULTURE: Bellwort grows best in shade in a productive humus soil to which some lime has been added.

HABITAT AND RANGE: It inhabits wooded areas, often in calcareous soil, from Quebec to Minnesota south to Georgia and Mississippi.

FLOWER SEASON: April–May.

PROPAGATION: Seeds or division; once established, it will self-sow.

RELATED SPECIES: A graceful woodland plant, *Uvularia perfoliata,* is similar, but is a clump former (Fig. 5-38), which *U. grandiflora* is not. *U. puberula* (= *U. pudica*), *U. sessilifolia* and *U. floridana* are similar to *U. perfoliata,* but lack perfoliate leaves.

COMMENTS: Bellwort is a superb accent plant for shady gardens. With clumps located here and there, it provides interest and attracts attention. At Piccadilly Farm, we have clumps of *U. perfoliata* scattered about in our woodland garden which regularly elicit comments from vistors.

Zephyranthes atamasco   Atamasco Lily, Rain Lily, Zephyr Lily
Liliaceae (including the Amaryllidaceae)   Lily Family
DESCRIPTION: Small, white lilies, 8–15 in. tall, rising from a bulb, with thick, linear, channelled, sharp-edged leaves rising from sheaths near the base. The white, rarely pink, flower is solitary, the perianth of 6 distinct lobes, united and funnel-shaped (Fig. 5-39).

CULTURE: Atamasco lilies are easy to grow in an open, low woodland where the plants receive approximately 2 hours of direct sunlight each day. They grow in moist, acid soil (pH 5–6).

HABITAT AND RANGE: This lily is sporadic in roadside ditches, wet woods, meadows, and bottomlands from Virginia to Mississippi.

FLOWER SEASON: March–early June.

PROPAGATION: Seeds or division of mature clumps.

RELATED SPECIES: *Zephyranthes treatiae* of Florida is similar but smaller and has narrower, half-rounded leaves with rounded margins.

COMMENTS: This southern lily produces flowers in great quanities and is easily adapted for garden use, but it is not hardy where the ground freezes deeply. It is most effective when used in masses to form drifts.

Spigelia marilandica   Indian Pink, Pinkroot, Worm Grass
Loganiaceae   Logania Family
DESCRIPTION: A clump-forming perennial, 12–18 in. tall, with 4–7 pairs of leaves; the terminal flowers have a deep red to scarlet, tubular corolla, ending in 5 yellow lobes (Fig. 5-40).

CULTURE: Grow Indian Pink in part shade to part sun in a fertile, moist soil, pH 5.5–7. It thrives under a tall, open hardwood overstory or along edges of small wood openings.

HABITAT AND RANGE: Indigenous to mesic open woods and wood edges from North Carolina to Indiana and Missouri, south to Florida and Texas.

FLOWER SEASON: May–July.

PROPAGATION: Seeds or division.

COMMENTS: Use this stunning plant near a path where it can be viewed as a focal point. It is one of the senior author's favorite native wild flowers.

Cypripedium calceolus var. *pubescens*   Yellow Lady's Slipper
Orchidaceae   Orchid Family
DESCRIPTION: This perennial orchid forms large clumps of erect, leafy-stemmed plants 18–24 in. tall. Its leaves are broadly ovate. The lip of the flower is pale yellow and the sepals and two lateral petals are greenish yellow to brownish purple and are usually twisted (Fig. 5-41).

CULTURE: The most satisfactory of the Lady's Slippers in the garden; plant it in neutral to slightly acid (pH 6–7) soil, with a generous supply of humus, in a shady spot.

HABITAT AND RANGE: Prefers bogs or moist woods, mostly north facing slopes, sometimes on disturbed soil; the species is circumboreal and south along the mountains to Georgia and Arizona.

FLOWER SEASON: April–July.

PROPAGATION: Division of large clumps in the spring.

RELATED SPECIES: The Showy Lady's slipper, *Cypripedium reginae*, is difficult to cultivate but can be grown on hummocks over a calcareous bog. The Pink Lady's Slipper, *C. acaule*, bears a single flower and 2 basal leaves; its flower stalk is leafless. It needs strongly acid soil (pH 4.5–5) in deep pine needle litter, and is often difficult to establish in the garden. Lady's Slippers require an association with a fungus in the soil; if this relationship is not established, the plants dwindle away.

COMMENTS: Yellow Lady's Slipper, with its golden yellow moccasin, as well as the other two species, are desired by all who see them. Since they are difficult to establish, they are not recommended for the average gardener. At the present time, Lady's Slippers purchased from nurseries represent collected material as commmercial propagation is not yet feasible. Commercial digging of the plants from the wild is a deplorable practice.

Sanguinaria canadensis   Bloodroot
Papaveraceae   Poppy Family
DESCRIPTION: Bloodroot is a perennial herb, 3–9 in. tall, from a thickened, elongated rhizome which, when broken, exudes a red sap. The leaves are basal, palmately lobed, orbicular to reniform. The solitary, white flowers are star-like and fragile with 8–12 white petals and numerous yellow stamens. When the plant first appears in early spring, the budding flower is enclosed in the curled leaf (Figs 5–42 & 5–43).

CULTURE: Bloodroot grows well in soils rich in humus and nutrients, acid to neutral (pH 4.5–7), and well drained. If leaf litter is removed from around the plants exposing bare mineral soil, Bloodroot can be encouraged to self-sow.

HABITAT AND RANGE: Found in rich woods from Nova Scotia to Manitoba south to Florida and Oklahoma.

FLOWER SEASON: March–April.

PROPAGATION: Seeds.

COMMENTS: Although Bloodroot flowers are relatively short-lived, they herald the welcome arrival of spring and are a welcome sight. Their leaves, however, remain throughout most of the summer providing much garden value. Bloodroot can be grown in large drifts or tucked in here and there in the woodland garden. Double-flowered selections such as 'Flore Pleno' are available in the nursery trade, but it is hard to imagine who would want a double Bloodroot when one has observed the simplicity, satiny beauty, and glow of the single form.

Stylophorum diphyllum   Wood Poppy, Celandine Poppy, Yellow Poppy
Papaveraceae   Poppy Family
DESCRIPTION: A pleasant plant producing large, yellow, poppy-like flowers on grayish green, leafy stalks. It is 1–2 ft. tall with orange yellow roots and pinnately lobed leaf blades. Showy, clear yellow flowers with 4 petals are produced in few-flowered clusters over a long season, followed by light green spiny fruits (Fig. 5-44).

CULTURE: The Wood Poppy should be grown in moist, fertile soil, pH 6–7, abounding with organic matter. They are at their best in a woodland garden with high, filtered shade. Plant in groups of 3 or more, 2 ft. apart.

HABITAT AND RANGE: Found in lush, damp woods, often in calcareous soil, sometimes in talus from carbonate outcrops, from Pennsylvania to Wisconsin south to Georgia and Arkansas.

FLOWER SEASON: March–April, with scattered flowers to October.

PROPAGATION: Seeds; it self-sows freely and forms natural drifts but is not aggressive.

COMMENTS: This marvelous woodland species is little known and infrequently grown. Given a favorable location and supplied with moisture, the Wood Poppy will reward the gardener with gorgeous flowers throughout the growing season.

Phlox carolina   Carolina Phlox, Thick-leaved Phlox
Polemoniaceae   Phlox Family

DESCRIPTION: This Phlox is erect, 24–30 in. tall, with slender, solitary or clustered flowering stems that are green or sometimes streaked with red. The leaves are bright green, the blades narrow on those at the base of the stem, widening on those up the stem to lanceolate or ovate-oblong. The flowers, with lavendar to pink, rarely white, petals, are in a loose, broadly cylindrical cluster (Fig. 5-45).

CULTURE: Grow *Phlox carolina* in ordinary, well drained soil, pH 5–6, in thin, high shade, or ideally in woodland openings or along woodland edges where it receives some direct sunlight each day. It is resistant to powdery mildew and is one of the best, tall, native Phloxes for garden use.

HABITAT AND RANGE: It is commonly found in thin, well-drained, open woods from North Carolina west to Missouri south to Florida and Texas.

FLOWER SEASON: June, with intermittent blooming until frost.

PROPAGATION: Cuttings and divisions. Carolina Phlox self-sows but is not at all aggressive.

RELATED SPECIES: *Phlox glaberrima,* with a cylindrical calyx rather than the campanulate calyx of *P. carolina,* is similar. The former requires moist soils so does not succeed if transplanted to dry places. *P. carolina* is a variable species because it intergrades with both *P. maculata* and *P. glaberrima;* thus the plants are hard to name. The white cultivar 'Miss Lingard' is a sterile triploid and thought to be a hybrid between *P. carolina* and *P. maculata* (Fig. 5-46). The pink cultivar 'Rosalinda' appears to have been derived from *P. carolina.* Both cultivars share the species' resistance to mildew.

COMMENTS: Carolina Phlox is grown at the edge of the senior author's woodland garden at one of the entrances, prompting much favorable comment.

Phlox divaricata   Blue Phlox, Blue Woodland Phlox
Polemoniaceae   Phlox Family

DESCRIPTION: Blue Phlox is a low perennial with decumbent, persistent, sub-evergreen, sterile shoots, sending up flowering stems 8–18 in. high in early spring. The leaf blades on the sterile shoots are broadly elliptic while those on the flowering shoots are ovate to lanceolate.The lovely violet to lavender or pinkish petals with notched petal lobes are in loosely branched, flat, terminal clusters. The flowers have a delicate honeysuckle odor (Fig. 5-47).

CULTURE: Blue Phlox is easily grown in the moist, fertile woodland garden where it forms natural drifts on hillsides because it self-sows so readily.

HABITAT AND RANGE: Found in rich, mesic woods from New England and Quebec to Michigan, south to North Carolina, Florida, and Texas.

FLOWER SEASON: March–April.

PROPAGATION: Division or harvesting of self-sown plants.

RELATED SPECIES: The more westerly *Phlox divaricata* spp. *laphamii* is of deeper hues, ranging to violet or purple with an intense eye in the center of the corolla sometimes forming a purple ring. *Phlox* 'Chattahoochee' is a cultivar of spp. *laphamii* from calcareous river bluffs along the Apalachicola River near the town of Chattahoochee, Florida and is available in the nursery trade (Fig. 5-48). Masses of 'Chattahoochee' are breathtaking especially when seen in the wild. *Phlox divaricata* is also available at perennial nuseries in white cultivars including 'Alba', 'Fuller's White', and 'Dirgo Ice'. *Phlox stolonifera,* Creeping Phlox, with spreading runners and roundish leaves, is an excellent ground cover plant which thrives in light shade (Fig. 5-49). Its flowers are borne about 6–8 in. off the ground and vary in color from violet to lavender, purple, and lilac. Those in the plant trade tend to be pink. A white cultivar of Creeping Phlox is also available.

COMMENTS: Plant *Phlox divaricata* on a rich bluff or hillside and enjoy the sight of the plants drifting down the hillside over the years. The senior author plants Narcissus and Hostas with Blue Phlox. The Narcissus blooms first, after which its foliage is hidden by the Blue Phlox; then the Hostas appear, hiding the partially dormant phlox.

Polemonium reptans   Jacob's Ladder, Blue Bell Valerian, Greek Valerian
Polemoniaceae   Phlox Family

DESCRIPTION: Jacob's Ladder is a low, branching perennial, 1–2 ft. tall, with well developed rootstocks. The leaves are alternate and pinnately divided. The small blue flowers are in terminal clusters held slightly above the leaves (Fig. 5-50).

CULTURE: In the upper South, Jacob's Ladder requires thin shade for best results but in the North it may be grown in almost full sun. It requires a fertile, damp soil, pH 6–7, so the addition of dolomitic limestone to most soils is helpful. Unfortunately, this lovely species is marginal in the middle to lower South where it tends to rot during hot, humid weather.

HABITAT AND RANGE: Found in neutral soil of moist woodlands from New York to Minnesota south to northern Georgia and Arkansas.

FLOWER SEASON: March–June.

PROPAGATION: Division or seeds; it self-sows readily.

RELATED SPECIES: The rarer *Polemonium van-bruntiae* occurs from Vermont along the mountains into West Virginia; it is taller and has a narrow panicle of larger flowers with exserted stamens.

COMMENTS: Use Jacob's Ladder to create a splash of delicate blue color for accent. Try interplanting it with *Mertensia virginica* to provide interest in the area after the Virginia Bluebells have gone dormant.

Claytonia virginica   Spring Beauty
Portulacaceae   Purslane Family

DESCRIPTION: A dainty little plant, appearing very early in the spring, 3–6 in. tall, arising from small, tuber-like corms, each slender stem bearing a pair of opposite, narrow leaves and a loose cluster of 5-petaled, star-like pink flowers with deeper colored veins (Fig 5–51).

CULTURE: This species should be grown in light shade, in good, damp soil, pH 5–6, with an abundance of humus. The plants disappear rapidly following flowering so they should be interplanted with native ferns to carpet the ground.

HABITAT AND RANGE: Spring Beauty occurs in moist woods and along streams, often covering the ground in favorable habitats, from Nova Scotia to Minnesota south to Georgia and Texas.

FLOWER SEASON: March–April.

PROPAGATION: Division or seeds; this species self-sows in the garden.

RELATED SPECIES: *Claytonia caroliniana* is similar but has relatively short, broad leaf blades.

COMMENTS: Use Spring Beauty to carpet low, moist, shady areas with a display of charmingly delicate early spring flowers distinguished by their flush of pale crimson pink and veins of deeper pink.

Dodecatheon meadia   Shooting Star, American Cowslips
Primulaceae   Primrose Family

DESCRIPTION: Shooting Star is 10–16 in. tall, perennial from a short fragile root-stock. The white to pink flowers are borne on a tall flower stalk in an umbel; the petals are so reflexed they resemble the tails of a shooting star. The leaves form a basal rosette and disappear after flowering (Fig. 5–52).

CULTURE: Readily grown in light shade in damp, well-drained soil at a pH of 6–7. Plant Shooting Star in clumps of at least 3–5, among limestone rocks along paths where they may be easily seen and enjoyed. The flowers never cease to thrill.

HABITAT AND RANGE: Native to fertile, moist woods, usually on a calcareous sub-strate, from Maryland to Wisconsin south to Georgia and Texas.

FLOWER SEASON: April–June.

PROPAGATION: Seeds, division or root cuttings.

RELATED SPECIES: *Dodecatheon pulchellum* (= *D. amethystinum, D. radicatum*) is similar to *D. meadia* but blooms later and is a rather rare, smaller plant, with white to reddish purple flowers.

COMMENTS: A most interesting and exciting plant when in flower, sure to attract notice and conversation.

Lysimachia ciliata   Fringed Loosestrife
Primulaceae   Primrose Family

DESCRIPTION: This attractive, sprawling perennial forms large masses of foliage on wet soil along streams and has pretty, yellow flowers. It can reach 2–3 ft. in height and has numerous opposite leaves; the hairy petioles are the basis of the name, Fringed Loosestrife. The yellow-petaled flowers are arranged in whorls, and borne on slender stalks arising from the leaf axils.

CULTURE: Readily grown in wet, garden soil in light shade to partial sun. It can become invasive in favorable conditions.

HABITAT AND RANGE: Fringed Loosestrife occurs naturally along streams, usually in moist, shaded places, but sometimes in full sun in the northern part of its range; Nova Scotia to British Columbia south to New Mexico and Florida.

FLOWER SEASON: June–September.

PROPAGATION: Cuttings or division.

RELATED SPECIES: *Lysimachia tonsa* is an upright plant of well-drained upland woods (Fig. 5-53); *L. terrestris*, the Swamp Candle, grows in boggy soils; *L. quadrifolia*, the Whorled Loosestrife, has leaves in whorls and grows in moist to dry places. All are worth a try in the wild flower garden if placed in suitable sites.

COMMENTS: The Fringed Loosestrife has attractive flowers and is an excellent choice for naturalizing in a moist, low, woodland garden, but it is aggressive and can overcrowd nearby plants.

71

Actaea pachypoda   Doll's Eyes, White Baneberry
(= A. alba)
Ranunculaceae   Crowfoot Family
   DESCRIPTION: Doll's Eyes is a bushy perennial, 1–3 ft. tall from a hard rootstock.
The large, compound leaves are 3–4 parted, the leaflets sharply toothed. The
flowers, which are small and grouped in a terminal raceme, are followed by a
cluster of china-white fruits, each with a conspicuous black eye, hence the name
Doll's Eyes (Fig. 5-54).
   CULTURE: This species prospers in moist, fertile soil, laced with humus, pH 5–6,
in light to heavy shade.
   HABITAT AND RANGE: Look for Doll's Eyes in damp soil, often at a talus edge, in
deciduous woods from Quebec to Minnesota south to Florida.
   FLOWER SEASON: April–June.
   PROPAGATION: Seeds or division. The seeds of Doll's Eyes, like many members
of the Ranunculaceae, should be planted immediately after maturation and not
stored. Sow in an outdoor bed in a shaded area; germination usually occurs the
following spring but sometimes two years are required.
   RELATED SPECIES: *Actaea rubra,* the Coral Berry or Red Baneberry, has red fruit and
attractive, white flowers (Fig. 5-55). It is also a great plant for the woodland garden.
   COMMENTS: Baneberries are attractive at all seasons and are very useful in the
woodland garden. They are especially attractive when in fruit.

Aquilegia canadensis   Columbine
Ranunculaceae   Crowfoot Family
   DESCRIPTION: Columbine is a graceful, erect plant growing to 30 in. tall from a
short, thick rootstock. The long-petioled compound leaves are borne both basally
and on the stem; they are divided into small, lobed leaflets, light olive green in
color. The flowers are large and nodding with 5 yellow petals, red spurs and 5 red
sepals; the stamens are yellow (Fig. 5-56).
   CULTURE: Columbine flourishes in average, well-drained soil, pH 5.5–6.5, in
light shade. The plants require 18–24 in. of space between clumps. It is one of the
easiest native wild flowers to grow but the old rootstocks do not transplant well. It
is best to buy nursery propagated, pot-grown plants.
   HABITAT AND RANGE: Columbine is native to dry, rocky woods, often in
calcareous soil, from Nova Scotia to Saskatchewan south to Florida and Texas.
   FLOWER SEASON: March–June.
   PROPAGATION: Readily grown from seed scattered on top of the seed bed and
not covered. It self-sows.
   RELATED SPECIES: A pure yellow form is available in the perennial trade.
   COMMENTS: Columbine is ideally used in the lightly shaded woodland garden
either in small clumps scattered here and there or in large naturalized drifts. It is a
good companion species for Hostas. It is highly suited for naturalizing in the wild,
very informal garden.

Cimicifuga racemosa   Black Cohosh, Black Snake Root, Fairy Candles
Ranunculaceae   Crowfoot Family
   DESCRIPTION: This large, bushy perennial is equally at home in the formal shady
perennial border or in a wild garden. Its flower stalk can reach 4–8 ft. in height; the
plant arises from a knotty rhizome. The erect plant bears large, compound, sharply

72

toothed, light green leaves on a stem terminated by a long wand-like raceme of feathery, white flowers (Fig. 5-57).

CULTURE: Easily grown in almost any fertile, moist, humus-filled soil at a pH of 5–6.5. The clumps become large with age so the plants should be spaced at least 2 ft. apart toward the rear of the planting. *Cimicifuga racemosa* is hardy north of its natural range and is preferred in southern gardens over *C. americana*.

HABITAT AND RANGE: Found in rich woods from Massachusetts to Indiana south to Georgia.

FLOWER SEASON: May–July.

PROPAGATION: Division and seeds.

RELATED SPECIES: *Cimicifuga americana* is vegetatively similar to *C. racemosa* but grows to only 3 ft. tall, is a later bloomer, and is useful in the garden because it is not as tall as *C. racemosa*.

COMMENTS: Black Cohosh combines well with ferns, Spiderwort, deciduous Wild Ginger, and Umbrella Leaf in the woodland, native flora garden. It is a showy, long-lived perennial that can stay in one place for years. Place it in the shady perennial border against a dark background where the white candles stand out.

Delphinium tricorne   Dwarf Larkspur, Rock Larkspur
Ranunculaceae   Crowfoot Family

DESCRIPTION: Dwarf Larkspur is a much smaller version of the typical garden larkspur. It is a perennial, 6–18 in. tall with palmately lobed, finely cut, linear leaf segments. The flowers resemble those of a larkspur and have a long, stubby spur, and vary in color from white to blue.

CULTURE: A species readily grown in the lightly shaded woodland garden or in part sun in the perennial border. It requires fertile, moist soil and a pH of 6–7.

HABITAT AND RANGE: Dwarf Larkspur inhabits lush, humid woods, often on a calcareous substrate, from Pennsylvania to Minnesota south to Georgia, Alabama and Mississippi.

FLOWER SEASON: March–May.

PROPAGATION: Seeds or division.

RELATED SPECIES: *Delphinium exaltatum*, the Tall Larkspur, is a large, coarse, woodland plant reaching 6 ft. tall; ideal where a tall native larkspur is needed. Its deep green leaves have generally 5 divergent, lance-shaped or wedge-shaped lobes, and the light purple or blue-violet flowers are borne in a thin raceme. Tall Larkspur usually inhabits calcareous soil. *D. carolinianum* and *D. virescens* are smaller and are often found on thin, rocky soil, the latter on limestone. These two species require 5–6 hours of sunshine each day. Since exotic Delphiniums typically do poorly in the South, the native species should be tried by southern gardeners desiring examples of this genus.

COMMENTS: *Delphinium tricorne* is superb in the early spring woodland garden. Clumps of 3–4 plants should be tucked in here and there for interest and accent.

Hydrastis canadensis   Golden Seal, Orange Root, Eye Root
Ranunculaceae   Crowfoot Family

DESCRIPTION: Golden Seal becomes 6–16 in. tall from a thick, knotty, yellow rhizome. The leaves are maple-like in appearance, palmately veined and lobed; there is usually 1 basal leaf and 2 cauline leaves. The stem is terminated by a single, white flower with yellow stamens followed by a tight cluster of red fruit. The fruits are rather attractive against the dark green leaves.

CULTURE: Golden Seal grows best in deep, humus soil, pH 6–7.

HABITAT AND RANGE: Found in fertile, moist woods, often on calcareous soil from Vermont to Minnesota south to Georgia and Alabama.

FLOWER SEASON: April–May.

PROPAGATION: Seeds, division, or root cuttings.

COMMENTS: Plant Golden Seal in groups of in groups of 1–3 in the woodland garden for a conversation plant and to test your friends' abilities to identify native plants. The roots and sometimes the leaves have long been collected for the drug hydastine, so the plants have become scarce in the wild. This is an endangered species in most states and protected on most public lands; using nursery propagated specimens assists in perpetuating the species.

Thalictrum dioicum Early Meadow Rue, Spring Meadow Rue
Ranunculaceae Crowfoot Family

DESCRIPTION: Grown mostly for its fine textured foliage, Early Meadow Rue is a beautiful, but not showy, perennial, 1–2 ft. tall. The much divided, thinly spreading, compound leaves are bluish olive-green and lustreless. The staminate and pistillate flowers are produced in loose panicles on separate plants; the pistillate flowers are inconspicuously pale green; the staminate flowers have green sepals and long, madder purple stamens.

CULTURE: Easily grown in fertile, moist soil, pH 5–6, in very light shade.

HABITAT AND RANGE: Found in moist woods from Quebec to Manitoba south to Georgia and Alabama.

SEASON: March–April.

PROPAGATION: Seeds.

RELATED SPECIES: Several small and dainty Thalictrums include *T. debile* and *T. clavatum;* species that are tall and coarse are *T. dasycarpum* and *T. revolutum.* For one with showy flowers try *T. pubescens* (= *T. polygamum*). Thalictrums are interesting wild flowers always attracting attention in the garden. They substitute for ferns and are grown primarily for their foliage.

COMMENTS: In the informal woodland garden at Piccadilly Farm, the various species of Thalictrums are used to blend with and soften the foliage of other plants, such as *Helleborus orientalis,* whose mass of leafage is coarser and rougher in texture.

Thalictrum thalictroides Wind Flower, Rue Anemone
(= Anemonella thalictroides)
Ranunculaceae Crowfoot Family

DESCRIPTION: This is a beautiful, little, slender-stemmed plant, perennial from a small, tuberous-appearing rootstock. Typically no more than 3–10 in. high, it has several clusters of divided, attractive leaves, below a gay cluster of white flowers borne on very fragile stalks (Fig. 5-58).

CULTURE: Wind Flower must be grown in humus soil in shaded, protected woodlands at a pH of around 6.

HABITAT AND RANGE: Found naturally in fertile woods from New Hampshire to Minnesota south to Kansas and Florida.

FLOWER SEASON: March–May.

PROPAGATION: Seeds.

COMMENTS: A favorite native species at Piccadilly Farm where the fragile, white flowers held on reddish brown stems above lacy foliage are a pleasant reminder that spring is here. Use the plants along the edge of paths or among rocks in the woodland garden, placing them where they can be seen.

Aruncus dioicus   Goat's Beard, Bride's Feathers
Rosaceae   Rose Family

DESCRIPTION: Goat's Beard is an imposing perennial, 3–5 ft. tall, from a woody rootstock. The stems bear several twice or thrice pinnately compound leaves, the segments prominently toothed; the terminal leaflet is unlobed. Male and female flowers are borne on separate plants, the staminate being more attractive (Fig. 5-59).

CULTURE: Goat's Beard is readily raised from seed and easily transplanted. It establishes readily in shaded borders and wild gardens in ordinary garden soil, pH 5–6, if kept moist during droughts. It is marginal in the deep south.

HABITAT AND RANGE: Look for Goat's Beard in fertile, damp woods from Pennsylvania to Iowa south to North Carolina, Alabama and Arkansas.

FLOWER SEASON: May–June.

PROPAGATION: Division or seeds.

RELATED SPECIES: *Aruncus dioicus* resembles *Astilbe biternata*, the False Goat's Beard of the Saxifragaceae family, and they are often confused. The terminal leaflet of *Astilbe* is usually 3-lobed but is unlobed in *Aruncus*.

COMMENTS: When well grown, *Aruncus dioicus* is striking when in flower. Use it in the wild garden or combine it with exotic perennials such as Hostas.

Poteranthus trifoliatus   Bowman's Root, Indian Physic, False Ipecac
(= *Gillenia trifoliata*)
Rosaceae   Rose Family

DESCRIPTION: A relaxed slender plant, Bowman's Root grows to 2–3 ft. tall from a woody rootstock. One or more stems arise from each crown. The blades of the leaves are divided into three, narrow, toothed lobes; a pair of narrow, small stipules is present where the leaf joins the stem. The whitish flowers have 5 narrow petals and are borne in loose panicles (Fig. 5-60).

CULTURE: Bowman's Root grows best in well-drained soil, pH 5–6, in light shade or along woodland borders. Place it on rocky, shady banks where it receives about 2 hours of sunlight each day.

HABITAT AND RANGE: Occurs naturally along rural roadside banks, in dry to moist, upland woods from Ontario, New York and Michigan south to Missouri and Georgia.

FLOWER SEASON: April–June.

PROPAGATION: Seeds or division; it has been observed to self-sow.

RELATED SPECIES: *Poteranthus stipulatus* (= *Gillenia stipulata*) has smaller petals and blooms later than *P. trifoliatus*. The stipules of *P. stipulatus* are leaf-like, deeply dissected and much larger than those of *P. trifoliatus*.

COMMENTS: An unusual and attractive native for the wild garden, Bowman's Root has showy flowers and a loose, informal growth habit. It adds diversity to the native flora garden and is happy when planted on a bank, in a lightly shady spot, with *Campanula divaricata*.

Astilbe biternata
False Goat's Beard

Saxifragaceae
Saxifrage Family

DESCRIPTION: False Goat's Beard is a tall, 3–6 ft. plant arising from a stout rhizome. The blades of the large leaves are divided 2–3 times, the terminal leaflet three-lobed. The flowers are small, perfect or unisexual, the petals almost white or yellowish, and borne in a large, pyramid shaped panicle. The perfect flowers lack petals.

CULTURE: Grow *Astilbe biternata* in moist, shady soil, pH 5–6.5; space the plants 24 in. apart in groups of 3–5 or as single focal points.

HABITAT AND RANGE: On moist soils of shaded woodlands from Virginia and Kentucky south to Georgia.

FLOWER SEASON: May–June.

PROPAGATION: Division or seeds.

RELATED SPECIES: Resembles *Aruncus* but the terminal leaf of *Astilbe* is lobed, while that of *Aruncus* is unlobed.

COMMENTS: False Goat's Beard is a tall, perennial wild flower with a showy cluster of small, white flowers. It is unusual, and should be placed at the back of the planting because of its height.

Saxifraga virginiensis
Eastern Saxifrage, Early Saxifrage, St. Peter's Cabbage

Saxifragaceae
Saxifrage Family

DESCRIPTION: Eastern Saxifrage forms a basal rosette of oval to ovate leaves borne close to the ground and produces a branching downy stem bearing a cluster of tiny, white, star-like flowers with 5 petals and 10 stamens; the flowers are followed by tiny 2-beaked purplish fruits.

CULTURE: Eastern Saxifrage can be grown successfully in rock gardens if given sufficient shade, drainage, and moisture. Sandstone, gravel, and coarse sand can be used to meet its soil requirements.

HABITAT AND RANGE: On rocky ledges and outcrops from New Brunswick to Manitoba south to Georgia and Mississippi.

FLOWER SEASON: April–May.

PROPAGATION: Seeds and division.

RELATED SPECIES: Others that might be attempted include *Saxifraga micranthidifolia*, a large coarse plant and the smaller species *S. michauxii* and *S. careyana*.

COMMENTS: *Saxifraga virginiensis* is probably the easiest native Saxifrage to grow in North American rock gardens and can be used on moist dripping rocks.

Chelone lyonii
Pink Turtlehead

Scrophulariaceae
Figwort Family

DESCRIPTION: Pink Turtlehead is an erect perennial, 1–3 ft. tall, with dark green, opposite leaves of toothed blades. The flamboyant, snapdragon-like, pinkish flowers are held in spike-like racemes. The flowers resemble the head of a turtle, hence the common name (Fig. 5-61).

CULTURE: Although native to the southeastern Appalachian Mountains, this southerner is quite hardy in the North. Grow the plants in moderately acid soil, pH 5–6, in a fertile loam, with adequate moisture, in light shade or, ideally, with 2 hours of direct sunlight each day.

HABITAT AND RANGE: Pink Turtlehead occupies rich coves and stream banks in Tennessee, North Carolina, and South Carolina.

SEASON: August–September.

PROPAGATION: Seeds, it self-sows readily; also by cuttings and division.

RELATED SPECIES: *Chelone obliqua* reaches 3–4 ft.; *C. glabra* (Fig. 5-62) is but 2–3 ft. tall. All have proved to be worthy additions to the garden and hardy north of their natural ranges.

COMMENTS: The Turtleheads impart a bit of color in the wild garden in late summer and early fall.

| *Zizia aptera* | Heart Leaved Alexander, Golden Parsnip |
| Umbelliferae or Apiaceae | Parsley Family |

DESCRIPTION: *Zizia aptera* is an erect perennial reaching 24 in. high; having simple (rarely three-parted), dark green, heart-shaped, basal leaves, with the margin of the terminal leaflet of the upper stem leaves entire near its base. This species bears an attractive umbel of small yellow flowers.

CULTURE: Grow Heart Leaved Alexander in the wild garden in light shade, or, in the North, in partial to full sunlight. It excels in moist, well drained soil.

HABITAT AND RANGE: Found naturally in moist meadows and open woods from New York to British Columbia south to Arkansas and Florida.

FLOWER SEASON: April–June.

PROPAGATION: Seeds or division; it self-sows but is not aggressive.

RELATED SPECIES: *Zizia aurea*, the Golden Alexander, and *Z. trifoliata* are similar, but taller, and have basal leaves that are once or twice compound. The leaves of *Z. trifoliata* are coriaceous. All three species are worth a try in the native flora garden.

COMMENTS: *Zizia aptera* is a late spring bloomer providing some yellow color at time when few other yellow flowers are in bloom.

| *Viola canadensis* | Canada Violet, Tall White Violet, Summer Violet |
| Violaceae | Violet Family |

DESCRIPTION: A sweet-scented, erect, leafy, stemmed violet, 12–16 in. tall, with long-petioled, heart-shaped, deep green leaves; the margins of the leaf blades are slightly toothed. The flowers, springing from the leaf axils, are largely white but have a spur petal which is yellow at the base and striped with fine, dark lines; the 3 lower petals are purple veined.

CULTURE: Canada Violet grows best in moist, shady, cool woodlands, in fertile, neutral to slightly acid soil, pH 6–7.

HABITAT AND RANGE: Found in cool, shady woods, ranging from Newfoundland to Alberta south to Georgia and South Carolina.

FLOWER SEASON: April–July.

PROPAGATION: Seeds or by division of plants with off-shoots.

RELATED SPECIES: There are numerous species of leafy stemmed violets which can be used in the woodland garden. Their identification can be difficult but here are a few worth considering.

Viola rostrata, Beaked Violet	*V. pubescens*, Downy Violet
V. hastata, Triangle Leaf Violet	*V. tripartita*, Three Leaflet Violet
V. conspersa, American Dog violet	*V. striata*, Cream Violet
V. walteri, Walter's Violet	

COMMENTS: Grow violets in colonies to achieve the maximum visual impact of the gorgeous, tiny blooms.

CHAPTER 6

Native Wild Flower Perennials for the Sun

The plants described and recommended in this chapter require nearly a full day of sun; in the absence of 8 or more hours of sunshine they become unsightly and often fail to bloom. All of the species are perennials native to eastern and midwestern North America. Their native habitats are prairies, open fields, and roadsides. While most grow on well-drained soils, a few inhabit moist soil along streams and around ponds. Unless otherwise noted, they require sun and well-drained, fertile soil typical of that of a vegetable garden.

Amsonia tabernaemontana   Blue Star, Texas Star
Apocynaceae   Dogbane Family
   DESCRIPTION: In full sun this plant forms large, multi-stemmed clumps about 3 ft. tall, with alternate, willow-like leaves which are dull above. It produces clusters of small, pale, clear blue flowers with 5 narrow corolla lobes (Fig. 6-1).
   CULTURE: Easily grown almost anywhere in good garden soil, pH 5–6, in full sun or thin shade. Following flowering, the clumps should be cut back to within 6–8 in. of the ground, which produces a dense foliage that turns pale yellow in August.
   HABITAT AND RANGE: Plants of thin woodlands, rocky slopes and roadsides from New Jersey west to Kansas, southward to Louisiana.
   FLOWER SEASON: March–May.
   PROPAGATION: Seeds, cuttings or divisions.
   RELATED SPECIES: *Amsonia ciliata*, with narrow leaves, is similar, as is *A. illustris*, with leaves shiny on the upper surface. The latter is especially desirable for the garden, but it is not readily available in the nursery trade.
   COMMENTS: These plants are quite handsome with their pleasant foliage and striking, pale blue flowers. Blue Star should be planted in groups of 3–5 in the front or middle of the perennial bed. Their foliage can be especially attractive in an island bed against a group of nice, yellow Day Lilies.

Asclepias incarnata   Swamp Milkweed
Asclepiadaceae   Milkweed Family
   DESCRIPTION: This milkweed grows about 3 ft. tall, has opposite, grayish or deep green leaves. Swamp Milkweed bears mauve, pink, or white flowers which are gathered in many compound umbels to form a large, flat, or slightly convex cluster at the apex of the plant.
   CULTURE: Swamp Milkweed is easily grown in the sunny perennial garden, pH 4–6. It presents no difficulties in transplanting or growing in ordinary garden soil, in spite of the fact that it is a wet soil plant in the wild. Unlike *Asclepias tuberosa* which has a long tap root, *A. incarnata* has shallow cord-like roots and is easily moved from place to place in the garden.
   HABITAT AND RANGE: Grows abundantly in vast colonies in moist meadows and along river bottoms from southeastern Canada to Florida and Utah.
   FLOWER SEASON: June–August.
   PROPAGATION: Easily propagated from seed or by division of the crowns in spring.

78

RELATED SPECIES: A taller species, *Asclepias syriaca*, is very easy to grow and produces attractive clusters of flowers. *A. quadrifolia*, about 1 ft. in height, has two whorls of leaves and pale pink flowers.

COMMENTS: Despite the common name of Swamp Milkweed, *A. incarnata* grows nicely in well-drained soil. It is extraordinarily attractive to butterflies.

Asclepias tuberosa — Butterfly Milkweed, Chiggerweed
Asclepiadaceae — Milkweed Family

DESCRIPTION: Look for a hairy plant, about 2 ft. tall with bright orange, orange-red or yellow flowers. The brilliantly colored flowers are held in upright clusters of umbels. Unlike many milkweeds, its sap is not milky (Fig. 6-2). It has a long, fleshy tap root often producing several stems from the crown. The leaves are alternate and elliptic to obovate.

CULTURE: Butterfly Milkweed responds to cultivation in a well-drained, dry, exposed sunny location, pH 5–7. Transplanting of mature clumps can be aided by cutting back to the ground and allowing the rootstock to resprout. Butterfly Milkweed thrives in hot, dry places where other wildflowers fail. It is attractive when planted in groups and makes a fine border along roadsides or fills rustic fence corners in an impressive way.

HABITAT AND RANGE: Prairies and roadsides from New Hampshire to Minnesota, south to Florida, Arizona, and New Mexico.

FLOWER SEASON: June–August.

PROPAGATION: Grow Butterfly Milkweed from seeds sown immediately after the pod ripens or from terminal cuttings. Young seedlings quickly make long taproots and require a deep pot. It can also be propagated from root cuttings.

RELATED SPECIES: There are many other species of native milkweeds, several with scarlet to orange flowers. One with red to purple, or perhaps magenta flowers, is *Asclepias purpurascens*, whose leaves have downy lower surfaces.

COMMENTS: Butterfly Milkweed is one of the showiest of our native wild flowers. It is especially attractive to the adult Diana, Aphrodite, and Fritillary butterflies. Milkweeds are an important food source for larvae of Monarch and Queen butterflies.

Lobelia cardinalis — Cardinal Flower
Campanulaceae — Bellflower Family

DESCRIPTION: A most beautiful species, remarkable for its deep, rich red flowers which complements the coloring of the foliage and stems. The leafy, unbranched stems are 2–4 ft. tall and bear a terminal cluster of vivid, scarlet flowers; the triple-lobed lips of the corolla are a velvety, cardinal red (Fig. 6-3). The leaves are dark to light green, oblong to lance-shaped and remotely toothed.

CULTURE: Cardinal Flower grows best in the wild in slightly moist, acid soil (pH 4–6), in wet seepage areas, or at the edge of ponds, sometimes in the shade; but in the garden Cardinal Flower can be grown at the moisture level common to most gardens. It transplants easily and should be planted in groups of 5–7 in full sun or in the semi-shade of moist woodlands. It is a short-lived perennial, so new seedlings and offshoots are needed to maintain it in the garden. In the South, leaf litter must be removed from the overwintering rosettes to prevent rot, whereas, in the North some winter mulch is essential to prevent winter kill.

HABITAT AND RANGE: *Lobelia cardinalis* inhabits moist to wet soil of roadside ditches, swamps, and swales, and grows along streams from southeastern Canada west to Minnesota and south to the Gulf Coast.

FLOWER SEASON: July–September.

PROPAGATION: Easily raised from seed.

RELATED SPECIES: Hybrids are known between this species and *Lobelia siphilitica*. A red-leaved cultivar of *L. cardinalis* is called 'Royal Robe'; however, it is a bit over-powering. White forms are also available in the trade.

COMMENTS: Use Cardinal Flower against a dark background of ferns to properly display the brilliant color.

Lobelia siphilitica   Great Lobelia
Campanulaceae   Bellflower Family

DESCRIPTION: Great Lobelia has 2-lipped, bluish violet flowers nearly 1 in. long, borne in terminal racemes, on 2–3-ft. tall bushy plants. The light green leaves are pointed on both ends and are irregularly toothed (Fig. 6-4).

CULTURE: Easily grown in full sun in the perennial border, with moist soils, pH 4–6. It can tolerate a few hours of shade each day. Group the plants in clumps of 3–5 for maximum visual impact. Cabbage Loopers can be a problem late in the growing season.

HABITAT AND RANGE: Moist soil of meadows and along brooks from Maine to Manitoba, south to the Gulf Coast.

FLOWER SEASON: June–September.

PROPAGATION: Seeds, cuttings and divisions; it self-sows so seedlings can be collected from near the parent clumps.

COMMENTS: Because it blooms over a longer period of time and is easily maintained in garden culture, the Great Lobelia is actually a better plant for the garden than the more popular Cardinal Flower.

Aster novae-angliae   New England Aster
Compositae or Asteraceae   Sunflower Family

DESCRIPTION: A familar and common species, New England Aster reaches 3–5 ft. in height and has numerous, narrow, clasping leaves borne on rough stems; the handsome flower heads, which are 1 in. broad, are loosely arranged with lavender, blue, pink or white ray flowers, and with yellow disk flowers in the center (Fig. 6-5).

CULTURE: The plants can reach a height of 5 ft., to avoid overly robust specimens, grow in ordinary garden soil, low in nitrogen. In the landscape, give them plenty of room, and use these toward the rear of the perennial bed or naturalized in moist soil along streams and ditches, but always in full sun.

HABITAT AND RANGE: This Aster occurs naturally in moist, open places from New England west to Wyoming south to Alabama.

FLOWER SEASON: September–October.

PROPAGATION: Seeds, cuttings and divisions. Asexual propagation is the only way to insure the desired flower color. Select and mark forms as field clumps in the fall and divide the following spring. Asters must be divided every few years to maintain their vigor.

RELATED SPECIES: Several cultivars are available in the nursery trade: 'Harrington's Pink' is a light pink selection, 'Fellowship' is a selected deep pink cultivar, and 'Helen Lacy' is purple. More than 60 species of Aster are native to North

America. Among the better species for the garden are: *Aster laevis* (Smooth Aster), with light blue flowers on 2 ft. plants; *A. linariifolius* (Bristly Aster), a dwarf, blue Aster with a nice yellow center, for sunny, moderately dry places; *Aster ptarmicoides* (Frost Flower Aster), a low plant, 12–18 in. tall with white flowers having yellow centers, and attractive dark green leaves; and *Aster umbellatus* (Flat-topped Aster), 3–5 ft. tall, with white flowers with yellow disks, growing best in sunny, moist situations.

COMMENTS: Asters (Fig. 6-6 & 6-7) are delightful in the early autumn provided sufficient space was allowed them in planning the garden.

Boltonia asteroides   Boltonia
Compositae or Asteraceae   Sunflower Family
DESCRIPTION: Boltonia bears small heads of daisy-like, white flowers on a 3–4-ft., rather erect plant. Its leaves are gray-green, narrow, and somewhat grass-like in appearance.

CULTURE: Boltonia is best grown in full sun, in well-drained beds prepared with an abundance of organic matter, and moderately acid soil, pH 4.5–6.

HABITAT AND RANGE: This native wild flower occurs in slightly moist soil from New Jersey to North Dakota south to Florida and Texas.

FLOWER SEASON: July–September.

PROPAGATION: Seeds, divisions and cuttings. Divisions are most successful in the spring.

RELATED SPECIES: The cultivar 'Snowbank' is a prolific bloomer and is more compact than the wild species (Fig. 6-8). It is excellent in the sunny perennial border.

COMMENTS: *Boltonia asteroides* is a useful plant in providing white flowers during a season often dominated by yellows. The shining, light green foliage supplies a contrasting texture to a season dominated by Asters, Goldenrods, and grasses.

Coreopsis verticillata   Thread-leaved Coreopsis
Compositae or Asteraceae   Sunflower Family
DESCRIPTION: This attractive Coreopsis is a rhizomatous perennial with delicate, much divided, dark green leaves and heads of flowers with light yellow rays. It grows 20–30 in. in height (Fig. 6-9).

CULTURE: Try Thread-leaved Coreopsis in full sun, in sandy, well-drained garden soil, pH 5–6. Arrange in groups of 3 or more plants. Although it spreads by means of rhizomes, it can easily be controlled in the garden by lifting and dividing every 3–4 years, which increases the vigor of the plants.

HABITAT AND RANGE: Scattered on well-drained soils at woodland edges and along roadsides from Maryland to North Carolina.

FLOWER SEASON: June–July.

PROPAGATION: Propagate by dividing either in the fall or early spring.

RELATED SPECIES: A selection or possible hybrid named 'Moonbeam' has pale yellow ray flowers, is extremely compact and blooms without deadheading from June–September (Fig. 6-10). Another selection, 'Zagreb', is more compact and with deep yellow ray flowers. *Coreopsis lanceolata* and *C. grandiflora* and their cultivars are commonly sold in the trade, but are inferior garden plants, definitely not for the well-cared for perennial border; they are not reliably perennial and self-sow readily, becoming weedy. These latter two are better used in meadow plantings.

COMMENTS: The fine texture of the leaves and the attractive flowers make Thread-leaved Coreopsis an ideal foil when used with Day Lilies or Iris.

Echinacea purpurea — Purple Cone Flower
Compositae or Asteraceae — Sunflower Family

DESCRIPTION: An erect, leafy perennial, 3–4 ft. tall, bearing stunning, rather stiff, terminal, flower heads with drooping, pinkish ray flowers and a cone of dark purple disk flowers. The alternate, dark green leaves are coarsely toothed (Fig. 6-11).

CULTURE: Grow the Purple Cone Flower in well-drained, moderately fertile soil, pH 6–7. The sturdy plants should be spaced about 18 in. apart in groups of 3–7 or more. If necessary, add lime to the soil to maintain a near neutral pH.

HABITAT AND RANGE: This Coneflower inhabits prairies and occasionally roadsides from Ohio to Iowa south to Georgia and Mississippi in neutral or alkaline soil.

FLOWER SEASON: June–July.

PROPAGATION: Purple Cone Flower is best propagated by seeds.

RELATED SPECIES: Less common but just as attractive are *Echinacea laevigata* and *E. pallida* (Fig. 6-12). An especially beautiful Coneflower is the rare *E. tennesseensis*, endemic to the cedar glades of central Tennessee. It is on the Federal List of Endangered Species, but is being propagated under permit, and can be purchased from several nurseries featuring native wild flowers. All three species merit inclusion in gardens. Several cultivars of *E. purpurea* are sold in the trade, including 'Bright Star' and 'White Lustre', but the wild species is not to be overlooked as an attractive, sturdy addition to the garden.

COMMENTS: A group of Purple Cone Flowers makes a striking focal point when placed near the front of a perennial border where they become the centerpiece during the heat and drought of midsummer.

Eupatorium fistulosum — Joe Pye-weed
Compositae or Asteraceae — Sunflower Family

DESCRIPTION: Joe Pye-weed and related Eupatoriums have whorls of 3–7, roughish, pointed, ovate, toothed, light green leaves borne on tall, stout stems, and bear long, terminal clusters of purple to pink flowers grouped into numerous, small heads. *Eupatorium fistulosum* has hollow stems and each flower head contains 5–7 disk flowers.

CULTURE: Joe Pye-weed is grown in moist, moderately acid soil, pH 4.5–6, in full sun or very light shade. Because plants may become 6–10 ft. tall, they are best used at the back of a perennial border to form a background for other species, or in the wild garden along a stream flowing through a meadow.

HABITAT AND RANGE: Common in bottomlands from Maine south to Florida and Texas.

FLOWER SEASON: July–September.

PROPAGATIONI: Seeds.

RELATED SPECIES: *Eupatorium maculatum* (3–8 ft.), *E. dubium* (3 ft.), and *E. purpureum* (3–6 ft.) are all similar in appearance and culture to *E. fistulosum*.

COMMENTS: Joe Pye-weed is an excellent addition to the garden when a tall, coarse plant is needed (Fig. 6-13). Joe Pye-weeds are important sources of honey and pollen and attract pollinators by the score.

Gaillardia pulchella   Firewheels, Blanket Flower
Compositae or Asteraceae   Sunflower Family
DESCRIPTION: *Gaillardia pulchella* is perennial along the sandy Gulf Coast but annual further north; a loose, sprawling plant 1–2 ft. tall, freely branching from the base. The flowers are in showy heads, the ray flowers purple to brownish red to yellow or purplish, often tipped with yellow (Fig. 6-14).

CULTURE: Grow in sandy, dry garden soil, pH 5–6. Since it does not overwinter, treat as an annual and replace it annually.

HABITAT AND RANGE: *Gaillardia* lives in dry, often sandy soils of the Great Plains and near the shore from Texas to Virginia.

FLOWER SEASON: June–October.

PROPAGATION: Seeds.

RELATED SPECIES: *Gaillardia aristata* is similar but has yellow ray flowers. It is more often perennial. A widely available yellow to red cultivar is named 'Goblin'.

COMMENTS: Treated as an annual, *Gaillardia* can be counted on to provide color during the hot, dry midseason. It reseeds, so seedlings often appear where they are not wanted. Due to its straggling habit, it can crowd out other better species. Its striking flowers are the sole reason for including it in the wild flower garden; probably best used in cottage gardens on sandy soil along the southern coast. It can withstand salt spray.

Helenium autumnale   Helen's Flower
Compositae or Asteraceae   Sunflower Family
DESCRIPTION: Helen's Flower is a 2–4-ft. plant with numerous, oblong, nearly smooth, toothed leaves, their bases decurrent as wings along the stem. Ray and disk flowers are both golden yellow; the decorative heads are daisy-like in appearance and 1–2 in. broad (Fig. 6-15).

CULTURE: Helen's Flower needs a dampish spot in the garden, perhaps a slight depression that can be given a good soaking during droughts. It responds to a good, fertile garden soil. Arrange the plants in groups of 3–7, 18 in. apart.

HABITAT AND RANGE: A plant of bottomlands and swales ranging from Canada south to Florida and Arizona.

FLOWER SEASON: July–September.

PROPAGATION: Seeds.

RELATED SPECIES: *Helenium flexuosum* and *H. brevifolium* are similar. Several cultivars are available: 'Crimson Beauty', a bronze-red; 'Moerheim Beauty', also bronze-red; and 'Magnificum', a yellow.

COMMENTS: Helen's Flower needs a wetter soil than is often available in gardens but in a suitable site provides color during late summer.

Helianthus angustifolius   Sunflower
Compositae or Asteraceae   Sunflower Family
DESCRIPTION: A tall, coarse, perennial Sunflower, 4–8 ft. in height, bearing numerous, small, sunflower-type heads, about 2–3 in. broad, with yellow ray flowers and purplish red disk flowers. The rough, narrow, lance-shaped leaves are opposite on the lower part of the stem and alternate below the flower cluster (Fig. 6-16).

CULTURE: Grow this sunflower in full sun in ordinary garden soil, pH 4.5–6. Too rich a soil leads to weak, succulent growth. An established clump requires 6 to 9 sq. ft. of space so it is definitely a plant for the back of the bed. Typically, only a single plant is needed.

HABITAT AND RANGE: Found in open woods and meadows along the coast from New York south to Texas and inland to Kentucky and Missouri.

FLOWER SEASON: September–October.

PROPAGATION: By cuttings or division.

RELATED SPECIES: Other perennial sunflowers used in the garden include: *Helianthus atrorubens* (4–6 ft.), the Dark-eyed Sunflower; *H. decapetalus* (4–5 ft.), the Thin-leaved Sunflower; *H. grosseserratus* (6–7 ft.), the Saw-toothed Sunflower; *H. mollis* (4 ft.), the Ashy Sunflower; and *H. salicifolius* (5–7 ft.), the Willow Leaved Sunflower. A double yellow sunflower often found in old gardens is sold as 'Flore Plenus'.

COMMENTS: A well-grown plant of *Helianthus angustifolius* yields a marvelous display of golden yellow sunflowers in September–October. Prune in midsummer to reduce the height of the plants and to eliminate the need for staking.

Heliopsis helianthoides (including *H. scabra*) — Ox-eye
Compositae or Asteraceae — Sunflower Family

DESCRIPTION: An erect perennial, 4–5 ft. tall, with opposite, lance-ovate, irregularly toothed, light green leaves. The stem bears many attractive, solitary, sunflower-like heads, 2–3 in. broad, composed of yellow ray and disk flowers.

CULTURE: This is an undemanding plant and better for the garden than many of the true sunflowers. Plant in groups of 3–5, allowing about 30 in. between plants.

HABITAT AND RANGE: The Ox-eye is native to woodland edges from Canada south to Georgia and New Mexico.

FLOWER SEASON: June–September.

PROPAGATION: Easily grown form seed.

RELATED SPECIES: The selection 'Summer Sun' is outstanding in the garden, much more attractive than wild material (Fig. 6-17). 'Gold Greenheart' is golden and 'Gold Feather' is a double yellow.

COMMENTS: Excellent for providing midsummer color. During dry weather the plants need extra water as they wilt easily. Plants often flower the first year following sowing indoors in late winter.

Liatris spicata — Blazing Star, Spiked Gay-feather
Compositae or Asteraceae — Sunflower Family

DESCRIPTION: An erect, slender plant from a corm-like base, reaching a height of 3–4 ft. The leaves are linear and grass-like, and clumped toward the base of the plant, but extend up the stem to the flower cluster. The flower heads are arranged in a long dense, spike-like array composed of purple disk flowers only.

CULTURE: This species grows without difficulty in moist, ordinary garden soil, pH 5–6, providing it is in full sun. If shaded, the overall effect of the plants is unsatisfactory. Do not over-fertilize which encourages rank growth. Space the plants 18 in. apart in groups of 3–7.

HABITAT AND RANGE: Blazing Star favors the moist soil of meadows and openings from New York to Michigan south to Florida and Louisiana.

FLOWER SEASON: August–September.

PROPAGATION: By seeds or division in the early spring.

RELATED SPECIES: Most species belonging to the beautiful genus *Liatris* have garden value and can be used for naturalizing. Among the better choices are: *Liatris aspera, L. elegans* (Fig. 6-18), *L. pycnostachya, L. scariosa* and *L. squarrosa;* all reach a height of around 2–3 ft.

COMMENTS: The purple flowers of *Liatris spicata* make a superb contrast with the yellows of many of the other fall blooming members of the Compositae family.

Ratibida pinnata   Prairie Coneflower
Compositae or Asteraceae   Sunflower Family

DESCRIPTION: A rather coarse, stout growth habit distinguishes this 3–5 ft.-tall plant with alternate, pinnately divided, rough-feeling leaves. The leaves are rather stiff and coarse in texture. The flower heads are large, with long, drooping, pale yellow ray flowers and an elevated, globose, cone-like center, with purple disk flowers (Fig.6-19).

CULTURE: Prairie Coneflower prefers well-drained ground with good soil, pH 6–7. The addition of ground dolomitic limestone benefits the species in acid soils.

HABITAT AND RANGE: This Coneflower is a native of dry prairies, typically on calcareous soil, from Minnesota and South Dakota south to Georgia and Mississippi.

FLOWER SEASON: June–August.

PROPAGATION: Seeds.

RELATED SPECIES: A smaller species, *Ratibida columnifera,* has a much longer cone of purplish brown disk flowers, surrounded by a ring of yellow or purple ray flowers.

COMMENTS: The drooping, light yellow ray flowers and the interesting, elongated heads make this species a conversation piece in the wild border garden.

Rudbeckia fulgida   Perennial Blackeyed Susan
Compositae or Asteraceae   Sunflower Family

DESCRIPTION: A vigorous grower, 2–3 ft. tall, with rough, stiff, toothed leaves. The flowers, borne in heads 3 in. broad, resemble those of Blackeyed Susans with yellow ray flowers and a center of dark disk flowers. The species is highly variable with numerous botanical varieties.

CULTURE: This perennial member of the Blackeyed Susan genus is easily grown in full sun in fertile garden soil, pH 5.5–6. It produces numerous off-sets and self-sows. Scatter the plants about 2 ft. apart in groups of 3–5 or use them in masses.

HABITAT AND RANGE: This species is found growing naturally in moist soil of thin woods from Pennsylvania to Michigan south to Florida and Texas.

SEASON: July–October.

PROPAGATION: By seeds or division. It is known to produce asexual seed and for this reason comes true to type.

RELATED SPECIES: The selection *Rudbeckia fulgida* 'Goldstrum' rewards the gardener with bushy, compact plants, dark green, attractive foliage and award-winning flowers over a long season (Fig. 6-20). *Rudbeckia fulgida* is superior to the more familar *R. hirta,* the Blackeyed Susan, which is not reliably perennial nor as attractive. *R. hirta* is best used in a meadow planting. *Rudbeckia laciniata,* the Cutleaf Coneflower, is a large plant ranging from 4–9 ft. tall; the coarsely toothed leaves are large, pinnately divided,or sometimes merely 3-lobed. Its flower heads are composed of greenish disk flowers in a conical mass, and long, drooping, yellow ray flowers. The Cutleaf Coneflower is an excellent plant for the summer wild garden if grown in part shade and in moist soil.

COMMENTS: Use Perennial Blackeyed Susan in the front to center of the perennial border for midsummer flowers. It can add color after the Daylilies and Phlox have flowered. Combine it with native or exotic grasses.

Solidago odora — Sweet Goldenrod
Compositae or Asteraceae — Sunflower Family

DESCRIPTION: Perennial, 2–4 ft. tall, with short rhizomes. The smooth, bright green leaves have an anise odor when bruised, and, when held to the light, minute dots can be seen; the lateral veins are indistinct. The small, yellow flower heads, with 3–4 golden rays, are in a much branched flower cluster with recurved branches.

CULTURE: Grow Sweet Goldenrod in ordinary, well-drained garden soil, pH 4.5–5.5, in direct sun. Unlike some Goldenrods, *S. odora* is easily kept in bounds.

HABITAT AND RANGE: This species grows in thin hardwoods and pine woods, and along roadsides from New England to Ohio south to Florida and Texas.

FLOWER SEASON: July–October.

PROPAGATION: Plant after digging field grown clumps, selected and marked the previous season, in late winter or early spring.

RELATED SPECIES: North America is home to numerous species of Goldenrods, most are difficult for even experienced botanists to identify. *Solidago odora* was chosen to feature here because it is easily identified and does not normally become weedy in the garden. Goldenrods are sometimes avoided, thanks to the false notion that they produce hay fever. The real cause of the allergy is usually Ragweed (*Ambrosia* spp.), which blooms at the same time. Europeans have long recognized the merits of our native Goldenrods and numerous cultivars are available in the trade. Some of the better species for cultivation include: *Solidago bicolor,* the White Goldenrod, with creamy flowers; *S. caesia,* the Blue-stemmed Goldenrod, with purplish colored stems; *S. rugosa,* the Rough-leaved Goldenrod; *S. juncea,* the Early Goldenrod; and *S. ulmifolia,* the Elm-leaved Goldenrod (Fig. 6-21). The latter is the pick of the group with deep yellow flowers against dark green, elm-like foliage. The Seaside Goldenrod, *S. sempervirens,* native to the Atlantic and Gulf Coasts, is handsome, with deep yellow flowers. It does not spread by rhizomes nor become invasive as do some of the other Goldenrods. It should be used in naturalistic plantings along the coast and in seaside cottage gardens as it is resistant to salt spray. For meadow plantings, try *S. altissima* (Fig. 6-22), *S. gigantea,* and *S. fistulosa.* These three species spread rapidly by rhizomes and form attractive drifts of golden yellow flowers. The last three do not have a place in the perennial border as they are too aggressive.

COMMENTS: The fragrant leaves of *Solidago odora* (Fig. 6-23) can be used for making tea. Use it either as an individual focal plant or in clumps of 3–5 in the sunny perennial garden. Combine Goldenrods with Asters, ornamental grasses, Boltonia and Sunflowers for a delightful late season effect.

Stokesia laevis — Stokes' Aster
Compositae or Asteraceae — Sunflower Family

DESCRIPTION: A low perennial, 12–18 in. tall, with a basal cluster of dark green, lance-shaped leaves. The flowers are borne in large, 2–3-in., showy heads, and bear attractive, sky-blue ray flowers (Fig. 6-24).

CULTURE: An old favorite among natives, easily grown in well prepared soil, pH 4–6, in full sunlight. Space the plants about 18 in. apart. It performs well in the heat and humidity of the deep South.

HABITAT AND RANGE: Stokes' Aster grows in moist, acid soil of pine savannas, and Pitcher Plant bogs of the the southeastern Coastal Plain from South Carolina west into Louisiana and Mississippi.

FLOWER SEASON: May–October.

PROPAGATION: Seeds or divisions; it readily self-sows.

RELATED SPECIES: Several cultivars, including a white form, 'Silver Moon', and the blue 'Blue Danube' are listed in perennial catalogs. The white cultivar is not a pure white and 'Blue Danube' seems little different from plants found in wild populations.

COMMENTS: An excellent source of blue color in the early summer garden. Use it in masses toward the front of the perennial border together with Daylilies.

Verbesina helianthoides
Compositae or Asteraceae

Crown-beard
Sunflower Family

DESCRIPTION: An erect, coarse plant about 3 ft. tall, with winged stems; the leaves alternate, lanceolate to narrowly ovate. The flowers are grouped into sunflower-like heads with drooping yellow rays.

CULTURE: Crown-beard is easily grown in ordinary garden soil, pH 5–6.5.

HABITAT AND RANGE: Found in thin woodlands from Ohio and Oklahoma south to Texas and Georgia.

FLOWER SEASON: May–September.

PROPAGATION: Seeds.

RELATED SPECIES: *Verbesina alternifolia* is similar, but the flower heads are globose and the plant prefers moist situations.

COMMENTS: The sunflower-like heads are attractive and produced over a relatively long season. Crown-beard is a nice addition to the wild garden.

Vernonia noveboracensis
Compositae or Asteraceae

New York Ironweed
Sunflower Family

DESCRIPTION: A tall, clump-forming perennial, becoming 5–8 ft. tall. The usually slightly rough stem bears lance-shaped, deep green leaves. The flowers are borne in ½ in. heads in a large, loosely branched, terminal cluster; they are all of the disk type and are reddish purple, a unique color which has been described as Vernonia purple.

CULTURE: New York Ironweed is easily grown in full sun in ordinary garden soil, pH 5–6. Space the plants on 3-ft. centers.

HABITAT AND RANGE: Occurs in moist soil of meadows and pastures, and along roadsides from Massachusetts and Ohio south to Florida.

FLOWER SEASON: August–September.

PROPAGATION: Seeds or by division of field grown clumps.

RELATED SPECIES: The senior author grew all 17 species of *Vernonia* native to eastern North America in an experimental garden for a number of years. They are all easily grown and make excellent garden plants. *Vernonia arkansana* (= *V. crinita*) from the Ozarks of Arkansas and Missouri has the largest heads, about 1. in. across and very attractive. It has a stiff upright habit and grows about 2–5 ft. tall. *V. lettermanii* of Arkansas and Oklahoma is a smaller plant, 12–18 in., with dark green foliage. *V. gigantea* (= *V. altissima*), a common, wide-ranging species over much of the eastern United States, is similar in habit to *V. noveboracensis,* but has much smaller flower heads (Fig. 6-25). *V. angustifolia* ranges widely over the southeastern Coastal Plain, is about 2–3 ft. in height, and has narrow, linear leaves. Natural hybrids are common in *Vernonia* and all of the 17 eastern North American species form fertile hybrids when intercrossed.

COMMENTS: Ironweeds have been grown in England since the 1700s and are now beginning to attract the attention of gardeners in their native North America. Try any of the species and be rewarded with a unique reddish purple color borne on erect clumps of plants. Use with Perennial Blackeyed Susans and Goldenrods.

Baptisia australis   Blue False Indigo
Fabaceae   Legume Family
DESCRIPTION: The racemes, often 6–10 in. long, of the blue, pea-like flowers are striking, but the chief garden worth of *Baptisia australis* is its striking foliage. The dense, shrub-like plants, 3–4 ft. in height, and unique bluish green foliage persist throughout the summer. Seeds are produced in inflated, pea-like pods which rattle when the blackened pods are ripe (Fig. 6-26).

CULTURE: Full sun is required for the Blue False Indigo, as well as good garden soil, pH 5–6.5. The plant forms a large clump so allow plenty of space between plants, perhaps 30–36 in. Plan carefully when planting since this species is long-lived and difficult to move about.

HABITAT AND RANGE: Found along woodland borders, often on limestone soils, from Pennsylvania and Indiana south to North Carolina and Georgia.

FLOWER SEASON: April–June.

PROPAGATION: Seeds or division. The seeds have a hard seed coat and germination is sporadic; try soaking the seeds in water for 48 hours or placing them in a mechanical rock polisher to wear away some of the seed coat prior to planting.

RELATED SPECIES: Most of the species of *Baptisia* are of garden value. Among the better are: the Wild White Indigo, *Baptisia pendula,* with white flowers; Yellow False Indigo, *B. cinerea,* with yellow flowers; White False Indigo, *B. alba,* with white flowers; Prairie False Indigo, *B. leucantha,* also with white flowers; and the Plains False Indigo, *B. leucophaea,* with creamy white flowers. Each of these species reaches 2–3 ft. in height with the exception of *B. leucantha* which can reach 6 ft. under ideal conditions. The yellow flowers of the Yellow Wild Indigo, *B. tinctoria,* are too small for the species to be of exceptional garden value. The southern *B. perfoliata* has unusual, perfoliate foliage which is interesting in dried flower arrangements.

COMMENTS: The unique, long lasting stem and leaf patterns of *Baptisia australis* makes it the most showy of the Baptisias. Use it in the middle or the back of the perennial bed and surround it with contrasting foliage plants such as Thread-leaf Coreopsis, Upland Seaoats, or Phlox.

Lupinus perennis   Eastern Wild Lupine
Fabaceae   Legume Family
DESCRIPTION: A deep-rooted, finely textured perennial, 1–2 ft. tall. The leaves are palmately divided into 7–11 narrow leaflets. The flowers are pea-like, borne on erect racemes, blue with a touch of purple.

CULTURE: The Eastern Wild Lupine grows best in full sun, in well-drained, sandy-loam soil, pH 4–6. Use young seedlings since older plants are difficult to establish. Space the seedlings 8–12 in. apart in groups of 5–7 or more.

HABITAT AND RANGE: Native to dry, sandy soils from Maine and Minnesota south to Florida and Louisiana.

FLOWER SEASON: May–June.

PROPAGATION: Seeds. Use some of the soil from around the mother plants in the seed bed to insure the presence of the specific nitrogen-fixing bacteria which are associated with roots of *Lupinus perennis*. If possible, plant newly ripened seed.

COMMENTS: Used in a mass, more or less as a ground cover, this species is one of the more beautiful wild flowers, but it requires a full day's sun and well-drained sandy-loam to be satisfactory. Because of its low habit of growth, it is ideal for massing at an entranceway.

Thermopsis villosa   Carolina Bush Pea
(= T. caroliniana)
Fabaceae   Legume Family

DESCRIPTION: A stout, very erect, clump-forming perennial, 4–5 ft. tall. The leaves are palmately 3-foliate, the light green leaflets hairy beneath. The flowers are yellow and pea-like, standing erect in racemes; the legume fruits are densely hairy and closely appressed to the axis of the raceme (Fig. 6-27).

CULTURE: Fertile garden soil, pH 5–6, and full sun are required for this native legume. Two or more seasons are needed in the garden for this old favorite to become fully established and productive, after which it persists for many years. Space the plants 30 in. apart in groups of 3.

HABITAT AND RANGE: Found along woodland edges in North Carolina, Tennessee, Georgia, and Alabama, but hardy in New England and the Midwest.

SEASON: May–June.

PROPAGATION: Seeds and division.

RELATED SPECIES: *Thermopsis mollis* is similar but shorter; it is less desirable than *T. villosa*.

COMMENTS: Attractive flowers, interesting seed pods, and handsome foliage early in the season make Carolina Bush Pea ideal for sunny situations in the perennial border. Place it towards the center or the back of the bed and use it in combination with Blue Star, Daylilies, and ornamental grasses.

Monarda didyma   Bee Balm, Oswego Tea
Labiatae or Lamiaceae   Mint Family

DESCRIPTION: An erect, aromatic perennial, 3 ft. tall, spreading by rhizomes. The stems are square and the leaves opposite, both typical of members of the mint family; the dark green leaves are broadly lance-shaped and sharply toothed, the stem hairy-rough. The flowers, borne in tight clusters at the tops of the plants, have 2-lipped, scarlet-red corollas (Fig. 6-28).

CULTURE: The brilliant and showy Bee Balm is easily grown in full sun in moist garden soil, pH 5–6. Under ideal growing conditions, the plants spread aggressively by rhizomes so divide them every 3–4 years. Additional water is required during droughts. Powdery mildew can be a problem with Monardas.

HABITAT AND RANGE: Found along wooded streams and on mountain slopes from Maine to Michigan south along the mountains into Georgia.

SEASON: June–July.

PROPAGATION: Divisions in the early spring.

RELATED SPECIES: White, rose and purplish cultivars, selected from among hybrids of the native species, are available through perennial nurseries, including: 'Cambridge Scarlet', 'Croftway Pink', 'Snow Maiden', the dark purple 'Prairie Knight', and others. In some instances, these cultivars have more to offer than the native species. Among the better native Monardas are: *Monarda fistulosa*, the Wild Bergamot (Fig. 6-29), grows to 3–4 ft. in drier soil than *M. didyma* and has pinkish to purple flowers; *M. punctata,* the Spotted Monarda, grows 2–3 ft. tall in dry, sandy soil and has pale yellow corollas spotted with purple; *M. clinopodia* grows 2–3 ft. tall, has whitish to pinkish corollas, and is more delicate than *M. fistulosa.*

COMMENTS: *Monarda didyma* is unexcelled in providing vivid scarlet color to a summer perennial border and is particularly attractive to butterflies. Use it among yellow Daylilies or Perennial Blackeyed Susans and against a dark shrub background. Bee Balm has been used as a folk remedy for bee stings.

Physostegia virginiana   Obedient Plant, False Dragonhead
(= *Dracocephalum*)
Labiatae or Lamiaceae   Mint Family

DESCRIPTION: This commonly grown native is a rhizomatous, sprawling perennial, 2–3 ft. tall. The stems are smooth and square; the leaves opposite, narrowly lance-shaped, and coarsely toothed. The snapdragon-like flowers are arranged in 2 rows, crowded in terminal, leafless spikes, and have pinkish purple corollas (Fig. 6-30).

CULTURE: Obedient Plant grows well in full sun, in ordinary, moist garden soil, pH 5–6. Space plants about 1 ft. apart, giving each plenty of room since it is an aggressive spreader. Confine the plants in buried 3-gal. nursery containers, lifting and dividing every couple of years. It has been a real pest in the perennial border at Piccadilly Farm.

HABITAT AND RANGE: Found in moist meadows from Maine to Alberta south to Georgia and Texas.

FLOWER SEASON: July–September.

PROPAGATION: Seeds or divisions.

RELATED SPECIES: The white cultivar, 'Alba', of *Physostegia virginiana* is sold by most perennial nurseries. Other native species are *P. purpurea, P. angustifolia,* and *P. intermedia;* all similar in size, habit and flower color to *P. virginiana,* differing only in technical features.

COMMENTS: Forming dense stands by virtue of its underground rhizomes, Obedient Plant is best used in the wild garden or in a meadow planting and kept out of the more formal areas of the perennial garden. Obedient Plant owes its name to the ease with which a corolla, calyx, or stem can be turned and directed to a new position.

Pycnanthemum incanum   Mountain Mint
Labiatae or Lamiaceae   Mint Family

DESCRIPTION: This stiff, erect clump-forming mint has whitened leaves subtending the flower clusters. The aromatic plants, with a mint-like odor, are 3–6 ft. tall and have flowers borne in terminal clusters about 1 in. across and composed of numerous, small, two-lipped corollas varying from whitish to lavender, with purple spots.

CULTURE: When supplied with adequate moisture, Mountain Mint can be grown in ordinary garden soil, pH 4.5–6. Since it can become invasive, the clumps should be lifted and divided every 3–5 years. *Pycnanthemum incanum* is best used in the informal wild garden.

HABITAT AND RANGE: Thin woodlands and roadsides, from Vermont to Illinois south to Georgia.

FLOWER SEASON: June–July.

PROPAGATION: Best propagated by cuttings or divisions.

RELATED SPECIES: Species suitable for gardens and similar in size and appearance to *Pycnanthemum incanum* are: *P. pycnanthemoides* (Fig. 6-31), *P. muticum, P. montanum, P. virginianum,* and *P. verticillatum.* Less tall (2 ft.), rather stiff, erect, and compact species with narrow leaves are *P. tenuifolium* (Fig. 6-32) and *P. flexuosum.* The latter two have a place in the more formal perennial garden.

COMMENTS: Mountain Mint is ideal for the wild garden used along the woodland edge. Once established, it is easily grown and will reappear year after year. It is not at all aggressive.

Salvia azurea var. *grandiflora*   Blue Sage
(= *S. pitcheri*)
Labiatae or Lamiaceae   Mint Family

DESCRIPTION: This attractive Salvia is a semi-erect, sprawling perennial about 3 ft. tall, with narrow, toothed, green leaves. The large (0.75–1 in.), sky-blue, 2-lipped flowers are borne in clusters of 6–12 toward the end of the stems.

CULTURE: Blue Sage is an excellent plant for the late summer and fall garden. It grows well in dry, well-drained, sunny situations at a soil pH of about 6. If grown with too much moisture, fertilizer, and/or shade, it tends to become floppy. Variety *grandiflora* is best for garden use.

HABITAT AND RANGE: On limestone glades, in prairies, and occasionally on roadsides from Minnesota to Nebraska south to Kentucky, Texas and Arkansas.

FLOWER SEASON: August–October.

PROPAGATION: Seeds and cuttings.

RELATED SPECIES: *Salvia azurea* var. *azurea* from the southeastern Coastal Plain has smaller flowers and is more compact (Fig. 6-33).

COMMENTS: The sky-blue corollas are a welcome addition to the garden late in the season when yellows are so common. In spite of its floppy habit, it is enjoyed each fall in the perennial border at Piccadilly Farm.

Teucrium canadense   Germander, Wood Sage
Labiatae or Lamiaceae   Mint Family

DESCRIPTION: A downy, clump-forming perennial 1.5–3 ft. tall, with stiff erect stems, the plants brownish pubescent; the thick, unevenly toothed leaves are whitish beneath, the blades lance-shaped. The flowers are borne in a rather long terminal cluster and are pink to purple or dull white in color; the lower lobe of the flower is broad and prominent, forming a convenient landing site for visiting insects.

CULTURE: Germander is grown in moist garden soil, pH 4.5–6. It is often found near the coast and the coastal ecotypes are resistant to salt spray. Use in naturalistic landscapes in moist soils or in cottage gardens near the sea coast.

HABITAT AND RANGE: Moist soil of meadows and swales from Canada southward throughout much of the United States.

FLOWER SEASON: July–September.

PROPAGATION: Cuttings and divisions.

COMMENTS: This handsome, rugged species should be used in the landscape due to its ability to withstand salt spray and to grow in moist places where many other species are unsatisfactory.

Aletris farinosa
Liliaceae

Colic Root
Lily Family

DESCRIPTION: Forms a basal cluster of grass-like leaves and sends up a leafless scape 1–2 ft. tall. The flowers are round, white, about ⅜ in. long, and covered with rough projections (Fig. 6-34).

CULTURE: Colic Root grows best in acid soil with a pH of 4.5–5.5, on moist to dry sites, and in full sun. It is easily transplanted at almost any time.

HABITAT AND RANGE: Meadows and upland woods from Maine to Minnesota south to Florida and Texas.

FLOWER SEASON: June–July.

PROPAGATION: Seeds.

RELATED SPECIES: *Aletris obovata* has white, obovate flowers; *A. aurea* and *A. lutea* have yellow to golden flowers.

COMMENTS: Of interest for the wild garden because of its unique appearance and small size.

Allium cernuum
Liliaceae

Nodding Onion, Summer Wild Onion, Lady's Leek
Lily Family

DESCRIPTION: Perennial, 8–24 in. tall from a reddish purple bulb with a membranous outer coat. The leaves are onion-like in appearance and the flowers are borne on a leafless scape terminated by nodding, white to purple flowers.

CULTURE: Easily grown in relatively dry, poor, well-drained garden soil, pH 5.5–6, in full sun to very light shade.

HABITAT AND RANGE: Inhabits dry woods, rocky banks, and prairies from New York south to Georgia and Mississippi.

FLOWER SEASON: July–September.

PROPAGATION: Seeds or division of existing clumps.

RELATED SPECIES: *Allium stellatum*, the Wild Onion, has showy rose to pink flowers and does well in cultivation when grown on a sunny exposure in a limey, rocky soil. *Allium cuthbertii*, the Striped Garlic, is an attractive, spring-flowering onion.

COMMENTS: *Allium cernuum* provides interest in the rock garden in late summer when few other species are blooming.

Lilium canadense
Liliaceae

Wild Yellow Lily, Canada or Yellow Bell Lily
Lily Family

DESCRIPTION: A tall, native lily, 3–8 ft. in height, rising from a scaly bulb, bearing flat, mostly whorled, lance-shaped leaves and crowned with beautiful, pendulous, lily-type flowers; the perianth segments slightly recurved, yellow on the outside, reddish orange with dark spots on the inside (Fig. 6-35).

CULTURE: Successful cultivation of the Canada Lily requires a cool, moist location where it receives at least 8 hours of full sun each day. The soil should be dug to a depth of about 18 in. and plenty of organic matter added.

HABITAT AND RANGE: Meadows from Quebec to Minnesota south to Alabama.

FLOWER SEASON: June–July.

PROPAGATION: Start *Lilium canadense* from bulb scales or from seed. Remove the outer, small scales from a bulb and plant them in a humus-rich bed. Patience is necessary as 4–6 years are required to obtain flowering-size plants from either seeds or bulb scales.

COMMENTS: Canada Lily is truly a beautiful native species. Single clumps placed against a background of shrubs or dark, dwarf conifers, are a sight to behold in any garden. The graceful curves of its pendulous flowers are unsurpassed in any wild flower.

Kosteletskya virginica   Seashore Mallow
Malvaceae   Mallow Family

DESCRIPTION: A coarse perennial, 3–5 ft. tall, covered with rough, star-shaped hairs, the leaf blades triangular-ovate, with a triangular lobe on either side of the leaf base. The flowers are like *Hibiscus,* the petals a lovely, light pink, about 1–2 in. long (Fig. 6-36).

CULTURE: Although normally found along the edges of salt marshes, Seashore Mallow is easily grown in full sun, in typical garden soil, pH 5.5–6, to which some sand has been added. Under garden conditions, the plants become quite large so adequate space must be provided; allow about 1.2 sq. ft. per plant.

HABITAT AND RANGE: Seashore Mallow inhabits the edges of salt or brackish marshes from Long Island southward along the coast to Texas.

FLOWER SEASON: June–October.

PROPAGATION: Seeds or cuttings.

COMMENTS: Useful in the wild garden along the edge of a salt or brackish marsh, this species adds beauty to such natural landscapes and makes a fitting transition to a wild seascape. Use it also as a background plant in the perennial border.

Oenothera fruticosa   Sundrops
(= O. tetragona)
Onagraceae   Evening Primrose Family

DESCRIPTION: A perennial, 18–24 in. tall, with erect, diffusely clustered, or unbranched stems. The leaves are simple, lanceolate to lance-elliptic, 2–3 in. long, and very slightly toothed. The showy, golden-yellow flowers average 2 in. in diameter and have 4 petals (Fig. 6-37).

CULTURE: Sundrops is a another native wild flower that loves the sun, growing well in ordinary garden soil, pH 5–6. While it spreads rapidly under favorable conditions, it is not invasive. Although flea beetles can be a problem in early spring, they can be controlled following the recommendations of an extension agent. Space the plants 18 in. apart in groups of 3 or more. In the South, the overwintering basal leaf cluster is evergreen and reddish purple in appearance, presenting a nice effect.

HABITAT AND RANGE: Woodland edges and roadsides from Nova Scotia to Michigan south to Mississippi and South Carolina.

FLOWER SEASON: April–May.

PROPAGATION: Seeds and by divisions.

RELATED SPECIES: Some other yellow-flowered Evening Primroses are *O.*

missouriensis, which is semi-prostrate, aggressively spreading, and with large flowers. Another is *O. perennis,* also called Sundrops, a small, hairy plant with delicate, small flowers.

COMMENTS: Sundrops perform ably in the front of the perennial border or along a sunny woodland edge where the bright, golden yellow blooms stand out sharply against the dark, forest background. They are wonderful along roadsides or in meadow plantings.

Oenothera speciosa   White Evening Primrose
Onagraceae   Evening Primrose Family

DESCRIPTION: *Oenothera speciosa* is 6–18 in. tall, sprawling to erect, with lanceolate to oblanceolate leaves 1.5–2 in. long. The flower buds appear to nod and the numerous, white to pink flowers are borne in the upper leaf axils. There are 4 white to pink petals, with the pink typically borne along the petal edges (Fig. 6-38).

CULTURE: *Oenothera speciosa* grows naturally in poor, gravely soils along roadsides. When placed in the better growing conditions of the prepared soil of a typical perennial bed, it explodes into growth covering nearby plants. For best results in the garden grow it in poor, well-drained soil, pH 5–6.5.

HABITAT AND RANGE: Roadsides and prairies, from Missouri southward into Mexico and across the southeastern states.

FLOWER SEASON: May–July.

PROPAGATION: Division.

COMMENTS: An excellent native perennial for roadsides and meadow plantings. It is too aggressive for most perennial borders, although it produces masses of flowers over a long period. *Oenothera speciosa* is best used in meadow plantings, or, if planted in fertile soil, use it alone or along roads and entrances.

Phlox paniculata   Summer Phlox
Polemoniaceae   Phlox Family

DESCRIPTION: An erect, clump-forming perennial reaching a height of 3–4 ft. The leaves are elliptic-lanceolate, 4–7 in. long and 1–1.5 in. wide. The flowers are borne in a terminal cluster 4–8 in. broad, with bright pink, lavender, or, rarely, white corollas (Fig. 6-39).

CULTURE: The mainstay of many perennial borders, this species grows superbly in fertile, moist soil, pH 5–6. The plants need at least 6 hours of direct sunlight daily. Space them about 18 in. apart in arrays of 3–7. Powdery mildew is a frequent problem.

HABITAT AND RANGE: Found in fertile, moist soil along roadsides and in meadows from New York to Missouri south to northern Georgia.

FLOWER SEASON: June–August.

PROPAGATION: Stem or root cuttings, division or seeds.

RELATED SPECIES: *Phlox glaberrima,* the Smooth Phlox, and *P. maculata,* the Meadow Phlox, are similar in habit and appearance. The species of *Phlox* are highly variable, sometimes hybridizing in nature, thereby making identification difficult. Numerous cultivars of the tall Phlox are available in the perennial trade.

COMMENTS: Useful at the edge of woodlands in the wild garden or as a formal part of a perennial border at the back or middle of the bed.

Phlox pulchra   Alabama Phlox
Polemoniaceae   Phlox Family
   DESCRIPTION: A low, sprawling perennial, becoming 12 in. tall, originating from
a branching rhizome. The leaves are elliptic, 1–2 in. long and 0.5–0.75 in. wide. The
striking cluster of flowers bears 12–36 individual, lilac, pink, or, rarely, white
flowers of great beauty, with a faint fragrance.
   CULTURE: Alabama Phlox is readily grown in good garden soil, pH 5–6, in full
sun. The plants spread rapidly so should be planted alone or in groups of 3
allowing 24–30 in. of space between them. It is not invasive and remains under
control.
   HABITAT AND RANGE: Woodland margins in central Alabama.
   FLOWER SEASON: April with occasional rebloom.
   PROPAGATION: Divison or cuttings.
   RELATED SPECIES: *Phlox ovata* is similar, but the gorgeous hues of *P. pulchra* are
much superior. This species deserves wider recognition and use than it has yet
received. Some perennial nurseries are beginning to list the Alabama Phlox. The
Chalice Phlox, *Phlox amoena* is another low (8–20-in.) Phlox at home in full sun and
useful in rock gardens. It has two distinct stem forms, one sterile and persistent, the
other erect and flowering. Chalice Phlox has purple to pink flowers in compact
clusters.
   COMMENTS: The little-known Alabama Phlox has been described as one of the
best low-growing Phlox for garden use. Place this colorful species at the front of
the perennial border or use it in rock gardens. It is delightful when scattered along
the sunny edge of the woodland garden.

Phlox subulata   Thrift, Moss Pink, Rock Pink, Ground Pink
   DESCRIPTION: Thrift is a perennial, forming evergreen mats of needle-like
foliage, covered by masses of flowers in various shades of pink, purple or white.
   CULTURE: This plant grows best in full sun and well-drained soil, pH 5–6. Even
in the poorest of soils it swiftly covers a bare slope, stops erosion, and stabilizes
freshly disturbed clay banks.
   HABITAT AND RANGE: Found on dry, sandy, or rocky soil from New York to
Michigan and to the mountains of Tennessee and North Carolina. It has escaped
from cultivation elsewhere or remains about old house sites.
   FLOWER SEASON: March–June.
   PROPAGATION: Division or cuttings.
   RELATED SPECIES: *Phlox bifida* and *P. nivalis* are similar but not as colorful as *P. sub-
ulata*. Numerous cultivars of *P. subulata* have been selected and named: 'Apple
Blossom', pale, pink-eyed; 'Coral eye', blush and red; 'Crimson Beauty', red;
'Millstream Jupiter', blue; 'Red Wings', light red; 'White Delight', white. Thrift is so
common in cultivation that few recognize it as a native species.
   COMMENTS: Often over-used, invaded by grasses and weeds, or poorly sited,
Phlox subulata can be a colorful addition to the landscape, especially in rock gardens
if properly cultivated.

Potentilla tridentata   Three-toothed or Wineleaved Cinquefoil
Rosaceae   Rose Family
   DESCRIPTION: A low growing plant, 3–10 in. high, with shining, evergreen
leaves. The leaves are palmately compound with three leaflets, each leaflet having

95

3 teeth at its apex, the leaflets becoming scarlet in the fall. The flowers are white and numerous in crowded arrays (Fig. 6-40).

CULTURE: Grow *Potentilla tridentata* in cool, acid, gravely soil, pH 4–5. Do not attempt it in the mid-to-deep South.

HABITAT AND RANGE: Found on rocky and sandy shores from Greenland to Canada and on hilltops and exposed mountain summits southward along the Applachians into northern Georgia and westward into Michigan, Minnesota, and North Dakota.

FLOWER SEASON: June–August.

PROPAGATION: Divisions, cuttings or seeds.

RELATED SPECIES: The Five Finger, *Potentilla canadensis,* has been used in gardens but is best considered a weed.

COMMENTS: *Potentilla tridentata* makes a splendid rock garden plant when grown in freely draining, fine gravel. It is an endangered species in Georgia and rare to uncommon as far north as Virginia where it is confined largely to the most wind-swept eminences; it is more common in the gravels of Labrador and Greenland. Southern Appalachian colonies are disjunct relicts from the Ice Age and should be preserved to maintain their genetic diversity.

Filipendula rubra
Queen-of-the-meadow
Rosaceae
Rose Family

DESCRIPTION: Queen-of-the-meadow is a single-stemmed, rhizomatous, perennial herb, 3–6 ft. tall. Its leaves are deeply pinnately divided into 5–9 lobes, the terminal leaflet kidney-shaped. The terminal cluster of small pinkish flowers is arranged into a large, flat topped panicle.

CULTURE: Grow this native species in full sun and very moist soil, pH 6–7.

HABITAT AND RANGE: Wet meadows and bogs are the natural habitat for this species, and it can be found from Pennsylvania to Michigan and Iowa south to Missouri and North Carolina.

FLOWER SEASON: June–July.

PROPAGATION: Division and seeds.

RELATED SPECIES: 'Venus Magnifica' is a selected cultivar and is superior to the wild material.

COMMENTS: Although best adapted to streamsides and pond margins, it can be used in perennial borders if given adequate moisture.

Penstemon smallii
Small's Beard Tongue
Scrophulariaceae
Figwort Family

DESCRIPTION: Small's Beard Tongue is an erect, perennial herb arising from a rosette of petioled, basal leaves. The stem leaves are opposite, broadly lanceolate and cordate-clasping at their bases. The flower cluster is leafy and the corolla purplish to pink. Each flower has 4 fertile stamens and one bushy, yellow, modified stamen called a staminode (Fig. 6-41).

CULTURE: Penstemons require an acid soil, pH 4.5–5.5; add some sand and fine gravel to insure drainage and to provide a nutrient poor substrate. Use in a rock garden or plant in well drained soil in the wild garden near woodland edges.

HABITAT AND RANGE: Woodland edges and roadsides of the mountains of North Carolina, South Carolina, and Georgia.

FLOWER SEASON: May–June.

PROPAGATION: Cuttings, division, or seeds.

RELATED SPECIES: Over 250 species of *Penstemon* are native to North America, mostly in the western portions. Some eastern and midwestern species should be considered for use in the garden as short-lived perennials. These include: *Penstemon australis, P. calycosus, P. digitalis, P. hirsutus, P. laevigatus, P. multiflorus,* and *P. tenuiflorus.* All are nearly identical in appearance so difficult to identify to species.

COMMENTS: Collect seeds of the local Penstemons and try them in the garden. Local species are most likely to perform well because they evolved under the same climatic and edaphic conditions.

Veronicastrum virginicum   Culver's Root
Scrophulariaceae   Figwort Family

DESCRIPTION: One of the taller native perennials, reaching 4–7 ft. in height and having narrow, whorled leaves. The pink and white flowers are borne in terminal clusters like a large garden Veronica (Fig. 6-42).

CULTURE: Although found in nature in wet meadows, Culver's Root grows well in ordinary garden soil, pH 5–6.5, which has been enriched with an ample amount of organic matter. During dry spells, treat the plants to extra water. It performs well in the perennial bed at Piccadilly Farm.

HABITAT AND RANGE: Meadows, prairies, and edges of woodlands from Vermont to Ontario south to Georgia and Louisiana.

FLOWER SEASON: July–August.

PROPAGATION: Division, seeds or cuttings.

COMMENTS: Use Culver's Root in the native garden or at the middle or back of the perennial border. Its long flower spikes provide a textural contrast to many other perennials. Use it as fresh cut flowers or dry it for dried arrangements.

Verbena canadensis   Rose Verbena
Verbenaceae   Verbena Family

DESCRIPTION: A low, spreading plant resembling garden Verbena, reaching only 8–12 in. in height. The leaves are much divided and the blade is decurrent on the petiole. The flowers are in dense, almost flat-topped appearing spikes which continue to elongate; the corollas are pink to blue, purple, or white (Fig. 6-43).

CULTURE: Rose Verbena requires full sun and well-drained garden soil, pH 5–6. Sand should be added to clay soils for better drainage. Do not overfertilize.

HABITAT AND RANGE: Grows on the thin soil of roadsides, sandy outcrops, woodland edges, and rocky areas from Pennsylvania west to Illinois and south to Florida.

FLOWER SEASON: March–August.

PROPAGATION: Cuttings or divisions.

RELATED SPECIES: The low, creeping *Verbena tenuisecta,* from the sandy southeastern Coastal Plain is a useful ground cover on well-drained soils. It can be found in a variety of colors from lilac to pink or white. *V. rigida* is an erect plant 12 in. high and purple in color (Fig. 6-44). Cultivated in the prepared, enriched soil of perennial beds, it can become very invasive. Two upright, white to pale purple species are *V. hastata* and *V. stricta;* both have garden potential. A coarse prairie species is *V. bipinnatifida;* it is 12–18 in. tall with purple flowers.

COMMENTS: Rose Verbena is useful as a low plant at the front of the perennial border or as a rock garden plant. In a mass planting, it forms a solid cover over the soil. In nature *Verbena canadensis* is highly variable in flower color and habit of growth. It is a good example of a wide-ranging species from which desirable forms can be selected. Recently some species of the genus *Verbena* have been shifted to *Glandularia.*

CHAPTER 7
Meadows

During the past 10 years, attractive containers of seeds of wild flower mixtures have appeared in garden centers. Numerous magazine articles with photographs of colorful displays of massed blossoms have trumpeted the virtues and the ecological soundness of meadows filled with brilliant wild flowers. Seed companies and other opportunistic promoters have jumped on the band wagon urging gardeners, landscape designers, and managers to convert lawns to meadows and for that purpose to use their seed mixes. It is suggested these meadows will put us in touch with our historical roots, summon nostalgic remembrances of pleasant episodes in our past—fields of Blackeyed Susans, Goldenrods, and Asters—and bring us closer to nature. Before running out to plant the lawn with a wild flower mix purchased on impulse because the gorgeous pictures on the can were appealing—or it seemed a possible way to discard the old lawn mower—it is best to examine just what is meant by the meadow gardening concept. It is essential to acquire a thorough understanding of what is actually involved in a true meadow gardening approach. This is the intent of this chapter.

DEFINITIONS

The word "meadow" is derived from the old English, meaning "to mow," and refers to land predominantly in grass or to a tract of low-lying, moist grassland. The grasslands of the Midwest are often called prairies. The word "prairie" is usually attributed to the French word for meadow and is defined as a more or less treeless tract of grassland. Prairies historically extended from North and South Dakota, Nebraska, and Kansas into the Midwest as far east as Ohio. Prairie-type vegetation also occurred in the Blackbelt of Alabama and Mississippi, the Cedar Glades of Tennessee, the Pine Savannas of the southeastern Coastal Plain, and in the Barrens of Kentucky. These areas originally were predominantly covered in grasses and deep-rooted, perennial wild flowers, with scattered woody vegetation.

A modern popular book on gardening defines a meadow as a sunny grassland found in forested regions with open patches of grasses and wild flowers. The very definitions of meadows and prairies indicate they are areas dominated by grasses. In fact, when botanists carefully measure and study the makeup of prairies, they find the dominant plants are various species of grasses. Such natural areas are, in fact, quite different from what the color photographs of 20th century marketing techniques suggest are meadows. Thus the picture on the can of wild flower seed mix is not a true meadow or prairie.

MEADOW CONCEPT

The concept of meadows as a form of planting design has its roots in the prairie restoration movement of the Midwest beginning some 100 years ago (Fig. 7-1). Although the ideas of the pioneer proponents of meadows or restored prairies as a landscape form were not widely accepted at once, they have recently become very popular. The original idea was to restore the beauty of these former grasslands by bringing changing form and color to the landscape. The techniques of prairie restoration have largely been developed since the 1930s, beginning with the early efforts of botanists J. T. Curtis and H. C. Greene at the University of Wisconsin's prairie at Madison. Their early attempts at establishing plants in a prairie landscape have been followed by many other successful projects at arboreta, state parks, and other public properties. With the development of practical procedures, meadows or prairies can now be found surrounding industrial plants and corporate headquarters, and along some highway right-of-ways. The use of prairie vegetation as a form of landscape is now recognized as a practical approach by trade publications such as the *American Nurseryman.* Such plantings are based upon native American grasses ranging from one to several feet in height, these grasses forming the mainstay of the prairie or meadow landscape design (Figs. 7-2, 7-3, 7-4, & 7-5).

The meadow movement has gained favor in direct proportion to the dissatisfaction with prevailing contemporary designed landscapes. Such landscapes of ordered, smooth lawns broken up by dark green, trimmed shrubs used in mass or as hedges, acccompanied by symmetrically shaped trees planted in rows, or groups of individuals of a similar size and species, are seen everywhere. Such designs are found throughout the country and it becomes impossible to determine if one is in Georgia, Indiana, or New York. Such standard planting designs result in landscapes with little or no resemblance to the natural landscape of the region in which they occur. On the other hand, naturalistic meadow plantings make use of plants native to the area to provide a unique yet intrinsically compatible visual experience. Species selected for meadows are those that occur locally to reflect regional identity and cohesion.

The goals and objectives of a meadow or prairie planting vary with the function to be served by each project and with the interests of the property owner. Some meadows are educationally oriented with the idea of introducing a large number of native American species to students or to the public, and in the process provide the visual experience of a grassland. Other plantings are more functional, designed to slow run-off and to control erosion on a newly developed site. Others are aesthetically oriented, recreating the visual essence of the prairie landscape of tall grasses intermingled with native, perennial, North American wild flowers.

Still other plantings are directed toward providing a scene in which colorful blossoms predominate, the majority of which are not native to the area and are largely annuals with only a few native, perennial, wild flowers. For the purpose of this chapter, the latter approach is termed direct seeded flowers. A short section on *direct seeded flowers* is presented at the conclusion of this chapter; it is not recognized as the true, naturalistic meadow approach.

A *prairie meadow* or simply a *meadow,* as used here means a planting of native, North American grasses and perennial wild flowers consistent with the sense of the prairie restoration movement. The term "wild flower meadow" is not used here since it hints at a dominance of showy, flowering species rather than one of a grass dominated meadow. In a book such as this, oriented to gardening with native plants, this purist or traditional approach to meadows seems advisable. What is meant is a mixture of native, sun-loving, perennial wild flowers interplanted in a grassland dominated by tall, native, perennial grasses. By native, we mean the species growing naturally in the general area prior to the arrival of European settlers. Examples are the two grasses, Little Bluestem and Big Bluestem, or wild

100

flowers such as Butterfly Milkweed or Purple Cone Flowers. *Naturalized species* such as Queen Anne's Lace or Corn Flower (introduced and established) are excluded together with *exotic* species such as California Poppy not native to the general area of eastern North America.

PRACTICAL CONSIDERATIONS

With the terms defined, the practical problems inherent in meadow plantings must be considered. First of all, while meadows look simply marvelous to some, others see them as utter chaos. To dissenters, meadows appear untidy, pose fire hazards, and serve as havens for rats or snakes. Legal covenants or ordinances in some cities limiting the height of grasses have led to home owners in several places having been hauled into court and forced to mow their meadows. So before any serious planning begins, be sure to understand the covenants and regulations that might affect planting a meadow. Communicate with neighbors, explaining what is being attempted. Make it clear that the meadow is part of the total landscape plan and not simply an area where mowing is to be forgotten. Keep in mind that it is difficult for some to accept the idea of something other than the standard mowed lawn and neatly trimmed shrubs. Be sure to learn clearly how a meadow planting might be greeted by neighbors.

It is essential to know what objectives are desired in a meadow planting and how particular goals can be realized. Although plantings of native grasses and wild flowers are ecologically sound, they never produce the gawdy display pictured on packages of seed mixes. True meadows rely heavily on the use of native species and natural processes, the outcomes of which cannot be speeded up. While planting a meadow is highly commendable, understand that it requires hard work and 4–6 years before the meadow is securely established. Keep in mind that the native plants used in the meadow will face severe competition from naturalized weedy grasses, broad-leaved weeds, and invasive trees or shrubs. These must be removed by hand. All of this adds up to hard work.

In most cases, several years of monthly weedings are needed in most sites to establish a meadow. After a meadow is successfully established, however, an annual controlled burn or mowing may be the only maintenance required. Regardless, the likelihood of success is enhanced by a basic understanding of natural prairies and their structure and composition.

Nearly all meadow plants require a bright, sunny exposure and do not grow well in the shade. Every species used in a meadow has fairly specific and narrow moisture or soil preference—each one growing best on sand or clay, in dry upland sites, in moist, or even in wet soils of low places, etc. Success with meadows depends upon a clear understanding that natural meadows are temporary stages in an ecological succession. For example, an old corn field is soon invaded by a series of annual grasses and broad-leaved weeds, followed by herbaceous perennials, then by shrubs and trees. In much of eastern and midwestern North America, a climax forest vegetation will eventually be reached in 150–200 years. If a meadow is to remain a meadow, woody plants must be removed or else held in check by either mowing or burning. Natural meadows were found originally in much of North America only in situations where inadequate rainfall, fire, soil, bed rock, water table, or other conditions combined to allow succession to proceed only to the perennial grass/wild flower stage. Otherwise the area supported tree growth. Management of a meadow is essential to prevent the reversion of the site to trees and shrubs.

LANDSCAPE DESIGN CONSIDERATIONS

If properly done, meadows provide landscapes that are both ecologically sound and aesthetically satisfying. A mix of native meadow or prairie perennials might be used to replace the typical landscape sequence of spring bulbs, summer annuals, and fall chrysanthemums. Big Blue Stem and Little Blue Stem provide most of the cover so a prairie-like effect can be achieved without using a large number of species of perennial native wild flowers. During the growing season, meadows are in constant transition, with changes occurring in the predominant flower colors, plant heights, and landscape character of the setting. Naturalistic meadow landscapes are always changing due both to long-term successional and short term seasonal events. These changes add interest to the landscape so are highly desirable in the eyes of many gardeners.

Colors and textures of meadows are typically subtle and diverse. The diversity of the texture in a meadow is due largely to the fine textures of the grasses. Grasses provide a linear form and unify the meadow visually. Flowers in a meadow do not occur as a solid mass of color as is typical of standard bedding plants such as Begonias, Marigolds, and Geraniums, used in the more formal designed landscape. What really happens is that several species usually occur together in a meadow where the bold colors of the wild flowers are filtered and made more subtle by the linear leaves of the native tall grasses. Meadows produce a flowing, open sense of space bending out of sight and yielding a degree of mystery. The grasses move with the wind creating the prairie image in the landscape. Wild flowers provide the diversity and should be used to form drifts of colors and textures.

Meadows offer a wide range of landscape possibilities incorporating plant species native to the region in the appropriate microhabitat. So their use can result in reduced inputs of water, fertilizer, and specialized management and maintenance procedures. Expensive, labor-intensive plantings can be reduced or eliminated. Meadow plantings can be of any size, so they may cover several acres or only a corner of a small back yard. The site should be chosen to blend comfortably with the topography and with the features of the immediate vicinity. Fences or woodland borders may serve as appropriate backgrounds. Paths are provided to beckon people into the meadow to enjoy the plants at close range, as well as to give easy access for weeding.

Before beginning a meadow design, local grasslands should be observed to determine which species are found in nature and how they are distributed. Much can be learned from getting out into the field and observing natural plant communities. The distribution pattern of a particular species as it occurs naturally provides a logical basis for the placement of the same species in a meadow landscape setting. Many species show some degree of aggregation which becomes important in creating the visual patterns of a meadow. This aggregation results from the vegetative spreading of such species to form drifts that are dense near the center but thin out along the edges. A design intended to duplicate nature features drifts of species with transitional zones where textures and colors blend.

Basically, it is possible to plant any sunny, well-drained site with native grasses and wild flowers to form a meadow. Meadows, like perennial borders, however, look best against a wall, fence, shrub border, or woodland edge. Use native shrubs at the edge of a woodland, blending them into native Asters and Goldenrods. A large open area, such as a field or sunny slope, may be utilized for a meadow planting. Island beds of native perennial grasses and wild flowers can be established in what was once lawn, forming a part of the overall landscape setting. Advantage should be taken of the "lay" of the land, of topography. Use slopes and swales in the design and emphasize the topography by deepening the swales and adding the excavated soil to the tops of the slopes.

When planting, do not succumb to the temptation of omitting the grasses, favoring only wild flowers. Consider using a ratio by weight of 60–80% grass seed of 2–3 species to 20–40% wild flowers of 8–12 species. Match the species to the microhabitats of the site, especially in relation to the moisture available. For example, Purple Cone Flowers can be utilized in drier, elevated spots while some of the native, wetland irises are suitable for wet, lower spots. Design plantings in sweeps and drifts of single species. In neighboring areas plant two species to be dominant but gradually blend into the dominant sweep of wild flowers of other areas. Another possibility is to apply a seed mixture of all the species uniformly and at random over the entire area, allowing nature to select the ones best suited for each microhabitat. Choose wild flowers to provide for a succession of bloom in the meadow. Additionally, the height of the species selected should be considered, placing lower-growing species along the front and at the edges of paths.

PLANTING THE MEADOW

One cannot simply throw seeds out and expect a meadow to apppear. Because weeds are one of the major obstacles to establishing a meadow planting, careful preparation of the soil is required. Several months prior to planting (usually in July), spray the persistent weeds and tough grasses such as Tall Fescue, Bluegrass, Bermuda Grass, and Johnson Grass with a non-persistent, recommended herbicide. About one week later till the area to a depth of 1–2 in. to expose the weed seeds hidden in the top layer of the soil. Allow a couple of weeks and again spray the entire area with herbicide. Cultivate shallowly again and spray yet a third time. Do not cultivate too deeply or additional weed seeds will be brought up to surface where they can germinate.

In most regions, it is best to plant the grass and wild flower seed in the cool, moist months of autumn. Some species germinate in the fall and overwinter as rosettes establishing a root system; others require a cool, moist period such as winter to break dormancy, and so germinate the following spring. Some wild species do not germinate until the second year after planting, so patience is required.

Immediately prior to planting, till the area to a depth of about 1 in. again, being careful not to bring weed seeds to the surface. Break up any clods and smooth the surface before sowing. A hand carried, mechanical seeder such as a Cyclone Seeder works well for many species, especially grasses. Small wild flower seed should be mixed with damp sand and scattered by hand on a windless day. Spreading a commercial mix evenly is difficult because of the differing size and weight of the seeds in the mix. For that reason, it is best to purchase each species separately, seeding one species at the time. A meadow should be seeded at the rate of about 1 lb of total seed (grass and wild flower), consisting of about 60–80% grass seed, per 1,000 sq. ft. Use Big Blue Stem, Little Blue Stem, Switch Grass, and Indian Grass. The annual grasses, Oats and Canadian Wild Rye, can be added to prevent erosion and to provide some cover for the planting during the first year.

It is most important in the planting process to insure good seed/soil contact so the optimum amount of moisture can enter the seed and also to protect the seed from bird and rodent predation. Once seeded, the area should first be raked lightly to cover the seed with 0.25 in. of soil, then rolled with a lawn roller or tamped to firm the soil. Fertilizer should not be applied in a meadow planting, although liming may be advisable if the soil is extremely acid. Fertilizer serves to encourage weeds and causes excessive, undesirable growth of the native grasses and wild flowers. If at all possible, water throughly once a week if fall rains do not appear. If spring rains are non-existent, periodic watering is again required.

Introducing plants by seed is generally the cheapest method of establishing a meadow. It is possible, however, to use nursery grown plugs of both wild flowers and perennial grasses as an economically feasible alternative in establishing a meadow. Transplants are best planted in the fall in the deep South or in the spring in the North, thereby avoiding the problem of frost heaving in northern climates. An alternate method is to direct seed the grasses, followed by transplanting plugs of wild flowers. Use only nursery grown plants; never dig plants from the wild.

Another approach is the collection of seed from local populations, to be germinated in flats and later transplanted to the meadow, and hand weeded for the first several growing seasons. Keep in mind that the appearance of first year meadows is at best discouraging. Perennial grasses and wild flowers require time to develop root systems capable of growing out to fill the spaces between plants.

Commercially prepared seed mixes, while seemingly easier to purchase and use, often contain filler in the form of grass seeds such as Annual Rye Grass, Orchard Grass, Timothy, Blue Grass, and Tall Fescue that are not desirable in a meadow. Before buying mixed seed, know exactly what the seed company is selling. In our opinion, it is best to buy seed of individual species from quality sources. This approach gives better control over what is planted so only desirable species are included. Native seeds can be obtained in quantity from commercial sources in areas where those species are planted in rangeland for grazing. The Soil Conservation Society of America [7615 Northeast Ankeny Road, Ankeny, IA 50021] has a list of sources ($3.00). A list of seed sources is also included near the end of this book.

Where individual species of wild flowers are seeded or transplanted into drifts on the site, it is wise to insert labels or else prepare a carefully drawn map to aid in weeding later. Regardless of the method, be aware that it will take 5–10 years for a meadow planting to approach the final appearance of a prairie. Do not expect too much too soon.

MAINTENANCE

As has been repeatedly stressed, meadows take several years to become established. During this time some of the species planted will die while others will thrive and multiply. Initially, the principle maintenance task is weeding, mostly hand pulling, although some weeds can be eliminated by carefully applying an approved herbicide with a wick applicator. Keep in mind that seedlings of weeds and woody plants are easiest to remove if pulled when small. Care must be taken not to remove desirable seedlings, so learn to recognize the weeds.

Mow the meadow planting to a height of 4–8 in. in late winter, or in very early spring prior to the resumption of growth following the first complete growing season, to improve the visual aspects of the site. Use a mower with a rotary blade rather than a sickle bar; the former disperses and grinds the litter so that it does not inhibit plant growth. Mow every spring thereafter until the meadow is established. Once established, usually 4–6 years following planting, the meadow will benefit from an annual, early spring, controlled burn. If it is not possible to burn the site, early spring mowing should be continued.

Before burning, obtain the necessary burning permits and the cooperation of your neighbors and local fire department. Establish fire breaks, that is, a swath cut around the edges to stop the fire while still in the meadow, burn only on a calm day and have plenty of help, water, and firefighting equipment. Controlled burning accomplishes several things: it reduces surface debris to the basic chemical elements, reintroducing them to the soil; it reduces the risk of wild fires by eliminating fuel buildup; it slightly elevates the pH; it controls unwanted woody plants; it causes the soil to warm earlier due to the black ashes; it promotes the growth of the desirable plants; and it creates a favorable situation for the germination of grass and wild flower seeds (Figs. 7-6, 7-7, 7-8, 7-9, & 7-10). There is evidence to suggest that an annual late winter or spring burn produces less pollution than the spring to autumn mowing of the same area in turf grass. This is due to the exhaust gases produced during mowing. As to costs: maintenance of a high-quality, turf grass lawn costs over $1,500/acre per year. On the other hand, using controlled burns, a managed meadow costs around $100/acre per year to maintain.

SELECTION OF SPECIES

The species used should be those found native in the region (Fig. 7-11 & 7-12). Standard floristic references should be consulted, such as state or provinical floras or Gleason and Cronquist's *Manual of Vascular Plants* to determine if the range of the species selected is to be found in the general area in which the meadow is located. A list of species native to the Midwest and Eastern Seaboard and suitable for sunny meadows is given below. In many instances additional species in the genus may also be suitable and may be found in the local region. Again, consult one of the standard floristic manuals before making a final selection.

Some suggested species of grasses for meadow plantings (See Chapter 8 for a more complete discussion of some of these grasses):

Andropogon gerardii, Big Blue Stem, Turkey Foot Grass
Andropogon virginicus, Broomsedge
Avena sativa, Oats, an annual non-native used to control erosion
Bouteloua curtipendula, Side-oats Grama Grass
Elymus canadensis, Canada Wild Rye, use for initial erosion control
Elymus virginicus, Virginia Wild Rye, use for initial erosion control
Eragrostis spectabilis, Purple Love Grass
Panicum virgatum, Switch Grass
Schizachyrium scoparium, Little Blue Stem (= *Andropogon scoparius*)
Sorghastrum nutans, Indian Grass
Spartina pectinata, Prairie Grass, Slough Grass (good in wet areas)

Sporobolus heterolepis, Prairie Dropseed (good in dry soil)
Sporobolus junceus, Pineywoods Dropseed
Stipa spartea, Needle Grass
Tridens flavus, Purple Top

Some suggested species of native wild flowers suitable for meadow plantings. Moisture requirements are indicated as follows: dry = well drained upland or sandy soils; wet = more or less permanently wet soil along drainage-ways or ponds; mesic = soil that is typically neither wet nor dry; and moist = soil that has a tendency to remain damp most of the season.

Apocynum cannabinum, Indian Hemp, flowers white, soil dry-mesic
Asclepias amplexicaulis, Sand Milkweed, flowers greenish purple, soil dry
Asclepias syriaca, Common Milkweed, flowers purple to green, soil dry-mesic
Asclepias tuberosa, Butterfly Weed, Butterfly Milkweed, flowers orange to reddish orange or yellowish, soil dry
Aster azureus, Sky Blue Aster, Azure Aster, flowers blue, soil dry-mesic
Aster ericoides, White Heath Aster, flowers white, soil dry-mesic
Aster laevis, Smooth Aster, flowers blue to purple, soil dry-moist
Aster novae-angliae, New England Aster, flowers reddish purple, rosy or blue, soil moist-mesic
Aster pilosus, Hairy Aster, flowers white, pink or purple, soil dry
Aster sagittifolius, Arrowleaved Aster, flowers pale blue or lilac, soil dry
Aster umbellatus, Flat Topped Aster, flowers white, soil wet
Baptisia australis, Blue Wild Indigo, flowers blue, soil dry-mesic
Baptisia leucantha, White Wild Indigo, flowers white, soil moist-dry
Baptisia leucophaea, Cream Wild Indigo flowers cream, soil mesic-dry
Blephilia ciliata, Downy Wood Mint, flowers pale purple, soil dry-mesic
Cacalia atriplicifolia, Indian Plantain, flowers white, soil dry-mesic
Coreopsis lanceolata, Lanceleaved Coreopsis, flowers yellow, soil dry
Coreopsis tripteris, Tall Coreopsis, flowers yellow, soil mesic
Desmodium canadense, Showy Tick Trefoil, flowers pale purple, soil wet-mesic
Dodecatheon meadia, Shooting Star, flowers white, soil dry-moist
Echinacea pallida, Pale Cone Flower, flowers purple, soil dry-mesic
Echinacea purpurea, Purple Cone Flower, flowers reddish purple, soil dry-mesic
Eryngium yuccifolium, Rattlesnake Master, Black Snakeroot, flowers white, soil moist-dry
Eupatorium perfoliatum, Boneset, flowers white, soil moist-wet
Euphorbia corollata, Flowering Spurge, flowers white, soil dry-mesic
Gaura biennis, Biennial Gaura, flowers white turning pink with age, soil dry-mesic
Gentiana andrewsii, Bottle Gentian, Closed Gentian, flowers blue, soil wet-mesic
Geum trifolium, Prairie Smoke, flowers purplish, soil dry-moist
Helenium autumnale, Helen's Flower, Sneezeweed, flowers yellow, soil wet-mesic
Helianthus grosseserratus, Saw Tooth Sunflower, flowers yellow, soil mesic
Helianthus mollis, Hairy Sunflower, Downy Sunflower, flowers yellow, soil dry
Helianthus strumosus, Rough Sunflower, flowers yellow, soil dry-mesic
Heliopsis helianthoides False Sunflower, flowers yellow, soil moist-mesic
Iris virginica, Wild Blue Flag, flowers blue, soil wet
Kuhnia eupatorioides, False Boneset, flowers creamy white, soil dry
Lathyrus palustris, Wild Pea, flowers reddish purple, soil wet

106

Lespedeza capitata, Roundheaded Bush Clover, flowers light purple, soil dry-mesic
Lespedeza hirta, Hairy Bush Clover, flowers light purple, soil dry-mesic
Liatris aspera, Rough Blazing Star, flowers pink purple, soil dry-mesic
Liatris cylindracea, Cylindric Blazing Star, flowers pink purple, soil dry
Liatris pycnostachya, Prairie Blazing Star, Kansas Gay Feather, flowers pink purple, soil wet-dry
Liatris spicata, Gay Feather, flowers pink purple, soil wet-mesic
Lobelia cardinalis, Cardinal Flower, flowers scarlet, soil wet
Lobelia spicata, Pale Lobelia, flowers blue to white, soil wet-dry
Lupinus perennis, Perennial Lupine, flowers blue to pink or white, soil dry
Lysimachia lanceolata, Lanceleaved Loosestrife, flowers yellow, soil moist-wet
Monarda fistulosa, Wild Bergamot, flowers pale lavender, soil moist-dry
Monarda punctata, Spotted Horse Mint, flowers pale yellow, soil dry
Oenothera biennis, Common Evening Primrose, flowers yellow, soil dry-mesic
Oenothera fruticosa, Sundrops, flowers yellow, soil dry
Oenothera speciosa, White Evening Primrose, flowers white or pink, soil dry
Parthenium integrifolium, Wild Quinine, flowers white, soil dry
Penstemon digitalis, Smooth Penstemon, flowers white to violet tinged, soil mesic
Penstemon grandiflorus, Largeleaved Beard Tongue, flowers pale purple, soil dry
Penstemon hirsutus, Hairy Penstemon, flowers pale violet, soil dry
Petalostemum candidum, White Prairie Clover, flowers white, soil dry-mesic
Petalostemum purpureum, Purple Prairie Clover, flowers rose purple, soil dry-mesic
Phlox glaberrima, Smooth Phlox, flowers reddish purple, soil moist-mesic
Phlox pilosa, Prairie Phlox, flowers pale reddish purple, soil dry-mesic
Physotegia virginiana, False Dragonhead, Obedient Plant, flowers pink to purple, soil wet-mesic
Potentilla arguta, Tall Silvery Cinquefoil, flowers white, soil dry
Psoralea esculenta, Prairie Turnip, flowers blue, soil dry
Pycnanthemum tenuifolium, Slender Leaved Mountain Mint, flowers light purple, soil dry-mesic
Pycnanthemum virginianum, Virginia Mountain Mint, flowers light purple, soil mesic
Ratibida columnifera, Longheaded Cone Flower, flowers yellow, soil dry-mesic
Ratibida pinnata, Yellow Cone Flower, flowers yellow, soil dry-mesic
Rudbeckia hirta, Blackeyed Susan, flowers yellow, soil dry-mesic
Silphium integrifolium, Rosinweed, flowers yellow, soil dry
Silphium laciniatum, Compassplant, flowers yellow, soil dry
Silphium perfoliatum, Cupplant, Rosinweed, flowers yellow, soil dry
Silphium terebinthinaceum, Prairiedock, Rosinweed, flowers yellow, soil dry
Solidago altissima, Tall Goldenrod, flowers yellow, soil moist-dry
Solidago canadensis, Canada Goldenrod, flowers yellow, soil moist-dry
Solidago juncea, Early Goldenrod, flowers yellow, soil dry
Solidago nemoralis, Oldfield Goldenrod, flowers yellow, soil dry
Tephrosia virginiana, Goat's Rue, flowers pink or pale purple, soil dry
Teucrium canadense, American Germander, flowers pinkish purple, soil wet
Thalictrum dasycarpum, Tall Meadowrue, flowers greenish, soil wet-mesic
Tradescantia ohiensis, Spiderwort, flowers blue, soil mesic
Verbena hastata, Blue Verbena, Erect Verbena, flowers blue, soil dry
Verbena rigida, Rigid Verbena, flowers blue, soil dry

Verbena stricta, Hoary Verbena, flowers deep blue or purple, soil dry
Vernonia fasciculata, Prairie Ironweed, flowers reddish purple, soil wet-mesic
Vernonia gigantea, Ironweed, flowers reddish purple, soil mesic
Veronicastrum virginicum, Culversroot, flowers pink or white, soil wet-mesic
Viola lanceolata, Lanceleaved Violet, flowers white, soil wet
Viola sororia, Hairy Blue Violet, flowers violet to lavender or blue, soil mesic
Zizea aurea, Golden Alexander, flowers yellow, soil moist-mesic

DIRECT-SEEDED FLOWERS

Many agencies, publications, and commercial seed companies have promoted the direct-seeding of various flowering plants including annuals, biennials and perennials (Figs 7-13, 7-14, & 7-15). These are touted as "wild flowers," "wild flower meadows," "wild flower plantings," or "wild flower seed mixes." The species recommended or included in the seed mixes are wild flowers somewhere, but many are not native to the Eastern Seaboard or the Midwest. The list of species included in any mix should be noted before considering purchase. Frequently, mixes include mostly European natives or non-regional natives and contain a great quanity of undesirable grasses as fillers. Such promotions stressing the beauty of our roadsides and meadows may be well-intended, but it should be clearly understood that wild flowers native to eastern North America may or may not be involved.

Certainly there is nothing wrong with direct-seeding of non-native flowers as long as species are not being introduced that may later become weeds. Further, it must be clear to all concerned just what is meant by the term wild flower. Basically, the purist insists that species characteristic of the region be used in such plantings. The authors hope this book encourages its readers to use and enjoy representatives of native, regional floras. Otherwise, every meadow planting will come to resemble every other meadow planting, much as is the case with the standard landscape designs of shrubs and trees used over much of North America. The Texas Department of Transportation has had great success in using many of their native plants along highway right-of-ways. But an attempt to duplicate a Texas roadside in Georgia, Maryland, New York, or Ohio is not only foolish but ecologically and aesthetically misguided.

The techniques for preparing the soil, planting the seed, and maintaining the site of direct-seeded flowers are basically the same as for true meadow planting. The differences turn on the emphasis on the bright, warm colors of annuals used in the seed mixes, and the reduced maintenance, both claimed for the stylized design of the direct-seeded flowers approach. But this approach bears little relationship to the prairie meadow landscape concept with its emphasis on native perennial grasses and the muted colors of wild flowers native to the region. A list of species often recommended for the direct-seeded flower approach is included below so the reader may realize how few of them are native to the eastern half of North America.

Species of annual and perennials frequently recommended for direct-seeded flowers:

Achillea millefolium, Yarrow, introduced, non-native
Centaurea cyanus, Cornflower, Ragged Robins, introduced, non-native
Chrysanthemum leucanthemum, Daisy, Oxeye Daisy, introduced, non-native

Cichorium intybus, Chicory, Blue Sailors, introduced, non-native
Coreopsis lanceolata, Lanceleaved Coreopsis, native
Coreopsis tinctoria, Plains Coreopsis, introduced, non-native
Cosmos bipinnatus, Cosmos, non-native
Cosmos sulphureus, Yellow Cosmos, non-native
Daucus carota, Wild Carrot, Queen Anne's Lace, introduced, non-native
Eschscholtzia californica, California Poppy, non-native
Gaillardia aristata, Blanket Flower, marginally native
Oenothera biennis, Common Evening Primrose, native
Oenothera missouriensis, Missouri Evening Primrose, native
Oenothera speciosa, White Evening Primrose, native
Papaver rhoeas, Corn Poppy, non-native
Phlox drummondii, Drummond Phlox, non-native
Rudbeckia hirta, Blackeyed Susan, native

If a commercial "wild flower" seed mix is being considered, the list of grasses included in the mix should also be reviewed before purchase. Non-native turf and forage grasses that are relatively inexpensive are often included. Such grasses may be fine in a lawn or pasture but not in a meadow. Among those commonly included, all non-native, are:

Dactylis glomerata, Orchard Grass
Festuca arundinacea, Tall Fescue
Lolium multiflorum, Rye Grass
Phleum pratense, Timothy
Poa pratensis, Blue Grass

If an area of direct-seeded flowers is needed for color, the best thing to do is to find a reliable seed company and order the desired species individually. By doing this, one has total control over what is being planted. The typical mixes are planned with the knowledge that not all the species will flourish, but that only a few will establish themselves and provide color. Additionally, the gardener will find that several species contained in most mixes will grow and bloom the first year, but relatively few will reappear the second. The point is: purchase only desirable species known to perform well in the local area. There is simply no reason to purchase seeds of plants that do not perform in the local region.

MEADOWS OR PRAIRIES

Are meadows or prairies the answer to every gardener's dreams? It would certainly seem so if one can believe the numerous, appealing advertisements and the colorful containers of seed mixtures which line the shelves of garden centers and beckon gardeners to pursue the latest fad. In most cases the results have been disappointing. Promoted by a combination of gross commercialism and well-intended naiveté, these so-called "wild flower" seed mixtures have done little to encourage what has been touted as a new form of gardening. If one is genuinely interested in native species, the prevalance of exotic flowers and non-native grasses in such commercial seed mixtures is not just disturbing, but down right discouraging, for such plants have nothing to do with wild flora gardening.

The true concept of meadows or prairies as a practical form of landscape design is rooted in the prairie restoration movement that began about 100 years ago under the influence and leadership of Jens Jenson. A landscape designer who practiced in the Midwest, Jenson attempted in this work to recreate the tapestry of living colors seen by the early pioneers in the region, and stressed the importance of the beauty of native plants and the natural landscape (Fig. 7-16). In such a natural prairie or meadow, clumpforming, warm season, native grasses cover about 80% of the ground area, though the native, deep-rooted wild flowers are more obvious. A meadow of muted colors, softened by grasses, simulates nature (Fig. 7-17). This ideal comes closest in appearance to the natural plant communities which once flourished across wide expanses of North America. Fortunately, the establishment of such prairies has now become a routine procedure, thanks to the availability of the required seed and plants of desirable, native grass and wild flower species. Effort is required to establish a meadow, but the goals of Jens Jenson are now within reach of anyone willing to understand the planning and attention required.

CHAPTER 8

Grasses, Sedges and Rushes

Grasses and grass-like plants, such as sedges and rushes, offer an amazing variety of landscape possibilities with their remarkable diversity and range of form. Native grasses meet many landscaping needs, ranging from focal points or background settings in the formal perennial garden to forming the backbone of the naturalistic meadow planting. Although grasses are usually thought of only as turf grasses suitable for lawns and forming an opening to mow, gardeners have come in the past 10 years to recognize that a number of native grass species can make a significant contribution to a native garden or perennial border.

Although widely used in Europe, especially in Germany, grasses have been virtually unknown to all but a handful of North Americans. The innovative use of grasses in plantings around public buildings in Washington, D.C., in numerous horticultural gardens, and in the landscaping of corporate buildings by several landscape designers have brought grasses to the attention of both gardeners and professional horticulturists on this continent. With the increasing awareness of the value of green plants and a reduced emphasis on brightly colored bedding plants, grasses have come into their own and are being freely used by the better landscape designers. The facts that grasses blend well with other plants and flower in late summer or early autumn have brought a new dimension to the perennial border. Grasses are especially striking in island beds since they provide useful contrast to the form of other landscape plants. Additionally, the recent popularity of meadows has attracted the attention of many who realize that grasses form the major component of prairies and meadows.

Grasses add lightness and texture to any planting. They provide a constantly shifting, curving line as their blades stir in the breeze. Grasses reward the gardener with flower clusters of varying sizes and contrasting textures. Their long linear leaves are especially attractive and useful around water, providing a perfect contrast to a sheet of water and making a lovely combination. Grasses are adapted to a wide range of soil, moisture and climatic conditions, so a dependable assortment can be selected to suit almost any site. Some are at home on dry coastal sand dunes where they help to bind the beach sand and are tolerant of salt spray. Others can withstand conditions of waterlogged soil or heavy clay. A few grasses even tolerate light shade, although most are at their best in full sun. The species mentioned in this chapter are all perennials that will return year after year with relatively little maintenance.

In meadow planting, grasses are usually established by means of seeding (see the chapter on meadows for further discussion). While grass seeds germinate readily if properly planted and maintained in the perennial garden, grasses for this use are usually either propagated by division and transplanted directly to their growing site, or purchased from nurseries as container grown stock. The soil should be carefully prepared as for any perennial—add plenty of organic matter and 10-10-10 fertilizer at the rate of 3–4 lbs. per 100 sq. ft. of bed. A similar amount of fertilizer should be provided early each spring.

While perennial grasses die back to the ground after frost, their dry stems, leaves, and plumes add interest to the garden throughout the winter. The only real chore in gardening with perennial native grasses is the annual pruning of the plants in late winter. The dead stems must be cut back to 6 in. above the ground before new growth begins. The plants are not at all fragile and are difficult to damage. In the nursery at Piccadilly Farm, we run the tractor and bush hog over the clumps to remove the dead shoots, which is surely rougher treatment than the typical gardener can possibly give them.

The Grass family is one of several families, such as the Compositae or Asteraceae and the Labiatae or Lamiaceae, that have two absolutely correct botanical names—Gramineae or Poaceae. This family of plants is of greater economic importance than any other family of flowering plants since it provides food for humans and animals (grasses such as Rice, Wheat, Oats, Barley and Corn), forage for livestock (Fescue, Coastal Bermuda, Orchard Grass and Timothy), shelter (Bamboo), lawn grasses (Blue Grass, Tift Bermuda, Fescue and Zoysia), plants for soil conservation (Fescue and Coastal Bermuda), wildlife food and cover (Pearl Millet and Broom Sedge), and ornamental species (Maiden Grass). Human culture itself has evolved around the cultivation and utilization of a wide variety of grass species and would be impossible save in terms of the continued cultural utilization of the grass family.

Grasses may be confused with two other families of grass-like plants: the Sedge family (Cyperaceae) and the Rush family (Juncaceae). Grasses typically have round hollow stems and grains as fruits; the stems of sedges are triangular in cross section and their fruits are lens-shaped or triangular nutlets; the rushes produce round solid stems and fruits of many seeded capsules. In contrast with the grasses, the sedges and rushes are of practically no economic importance; however, several of our native Cyperaceae and Juncaceae do have garden value and are discussed in this chapter. For detailed information on the morphology of the grasses, sedges and rushes, see: Jones and Luchsinger, 1986, *Plant Systematics,* 2nd ed. McGraw-Hill Book Co., New York.

RECOMMENDED NATIVE SPECIES OF GRASSES, SEDGES AND RUSHES

For the purposes of organization the grasses are listed first followed by the rushes and sedges.

Andropogon gerardii   Big Blue Stem, Turkeyfoot
Gramineae or Poaceae   Grass Family
DESCRIPTION: Big Blue Stem is a perennial, clump-forming grass with bluegreen stems 4–8 ft. tall, topped by finger-like racemes of fruiting clusters. The entire flowering cluster resembles an upside down turkey foot, hence one of its common names.

CULTURE: Grow the Big Blue Stem in moist, fertile, well-drained soil in full sunlight. In meadows, maintain it by an annual, early spring, controlled burn or by mowing in late winter.

HABITAT AND RANGE: Once the major component of the tall grass prairie, a grassland with native grasses 5–8 ft. high that once covered the present day Corn Belt, extending northward into Manitoba and southward into Texas; this prairie species is found in moist soil and in woodland openings and ranges from Quebec to Saskatchewan south to Florida and Arizona.

112

FLOWER SEASON: Late summer and early fall.

PROPAGATION: Seeds or division of superior clones.

COMMENTS: A valuable grass for naturalistic planting in meadows and restored prairies. It is used in clumps in a perennial border to provide points of interest in the late summer and fall. Big Blue Stem is one of North America's great prairie grasses, a robust species and a favorite of livestock. The plants turn a splendid shade of light reddish brown in autumn.

Andropogon virginicus　　　　　　　　　　　　　　　　　Broom Sedge
Gramineae or Poaceae　　　　　　　　　　　　　　　　　Grass Family

DESCRIPTION: Broom Sedge is a tufted, clump-forming perennial grass, turning brownish with the onset of autumn, with inconspicuous flowers. The flower cluster is elongate, the 2–4 racemes 1.25 in. long and partially enclosed in the inflated tawny bracts.

CULTURE: Readily grows in poor, dry soil of abandoned fields and in areas with scattered trees. Plantings can be maintained by burning or mowing in the very early spring. It should not be fertilized.

HABITAT AND RANGE: Commonly found in dry to moist soil of old fields and thin woods from Massachusetts to Kansas south to Central America.

FLOWER SEASON: Early fall; its stems are attractive all winter.

PROPAGATION: Seeds or division.

RELATED SPECIES: *Andropogon glomeratus,* the Bushy Beardgrass, is similar but has a denser and more feathery flower cluster (Fig. 8-1). It occurs in wet soils of swales and ditches and makes a handsome, dried flower arrangement.

COMMENTS: Use Broom Sedge in meadow plantings or in pure stands for a low maintenannce cover on old fields or along roadsides. The reddish brown color of the stems and leaves holds well through the winter months. Broom Sedge, largely unappreciated yet so common on old fields, is attractive, especially when a slight breeze waves the stems. It provides excellent wildlife cover and is used by many ground nesting birds such as the Bob White Quail.

Bouteloua curtipendula　　　　　　　　　　　　　　　　Side-oats Grama
Gramineae or Poaceae　　　　　　　　　　　　　　　　　Grass Family

DESCRIPTION: A low, stoloniferous, sod-forming, perennial grass with interesting, purplish spikelets that point downward along the main axis of the flower cluster.

CULTURE: Grow Side-oats Grama in full sunlight in ordinary, well-drained garden soil. Mow or burn it in the spring.

HABITAT AND RANGE: Found in prairies and open woodlands from Maine to Montana south to the Gulf of Mexico. It once was a major component of the mixed grass prairies of the plains of the central part of North America, a region characterized by moderately restricted rainfall.

FLOWER SEASON: Summer.

PROPAGATION: Seeds.

RELATED SPECIES: *Bouteloua gracilis,* the Sand Love Grass, or Blue Grama, native to the limited rainfall, high plains area of the short grass prairie region, is ideally suited to both garden and meadow situations.

COMMENTS: Use Side-oats Grama in meadow plantings or to form a tough low-maintenance sod to replace the typical lawn grasses having high water and maintenance requirements. As water use becomes increasingly restricted in many areas of North America, serious consideration must be given to alternatives to high water use plantings. Side-oats Grama is the answer for a sod-former for many landscape applications in drier regions. It is attractive in sunny, well-drained rock gardens.

Chasmanthium latifolium   Upland Sea Oats
(= Uniola latifolia)
Gramineae or Poaceae   Grass Family

DESCRIPTION: A perennial grass 30–50 in. tall, from a short, stout rhizome, bearing large, open, drooping panicles of flowers. The leaf blades are flat, narrowly lanceolate and the branches of the inflorescence bear a few, large, very flat spikelets (Fig. 8-2).

CULTURE: Readily grown in moist, well drained soil in full sun to partial shade.

HABITAT AND RANGE: Found in moist, wooded, sandy levees along streams from New Jersey to southern Illinois and Kansas south to Florida and Texas.

FLOWER SEASON: Summer and fall.

PROPAGATION: Seeds or division.

COMMENTS: Upland Sea Oats is a valuable grass for the garden and one of the few grasses that grows in some shade. The plant has a pleasing form and turns a rich brownish color in the fall, especially if grown in full sun. The flower clusters are outstanding for dried arrangements. This plant is greatly under-used, yet exceedingly attractive.

Eragrostis spectabilis   Purple Love Grass
Gramineae or Poaceae   Grass Family

DESCRIPTION: An erect or ascending perennial, clump-forming grass, 12–24 in. tall, with open and diffusely branched panicles. The flowering and fruiting spikelets are reddish purple. The entire panicle breaks away with the winter wind, spreading the seed.

CULTURE: Grow in full sunlight in well-drained soil.

HABITAT AND RANGE: Inhabits well-drained soil of open fields from Maine to Minnesota south to Florida and Texas.

FLOWER SEASON: Late summer and fall.

PROPAGATION: Seeds or division.

COMMENTS: Purple Love Grass has a pleasing, open form with a fruiting cluster of an attractive reddish purple. Viewed from a distance, natural drifts of Purple Love Grass provide visual enhancement to a meadow.

Erianthus contortus   Plume Grass, Beard Grass
Gramineae or Poaceae   Grass Family

DESCRIPTION: Plume Grass is a tall, coarse perennial grass with long leaves and a large terminal panicle appearing late in the summer. The panicles are conspicuously silky as a result of the hairs extending from the spikelets.

CULTURE: Grow Plume Grass in full sunlight in ordinary moist soil.

HABITAT AND RANGE: Found in moist, open areas and along roadsides of the Coastal Plain from New Jersey south to Florida, Texas, Arkansas, and Oklahoma.

FLOWER SEASON: Late summer or fall.

PROPAGATION: Seeds or division.

RELATED SPECIES: Several species of *Erianthus* are of value for the garden including: *E. alopecuroides,* the Silver Plume Grass; *E. brevibarbis;* and the extra large *E. giganteus,* the Sugarcane Plume Grass.

COMMENTS: Plume Grass is a coarse, erect grass providing charming contrast and interest in the wild garden. It is best used in large, natural areas.

Panicum amarum   Beach Panic Grass
Gramineae or Poaceae   Grass Family

DESCRIPTION: The Beach Panic Grass is stout-stemmed and bluish waxy in appearance. The flowers and fruit are arranged in an elongate panicle. The somewhat decumbent plant ranges in height from 10–28 in. and is perennial from creeping rhizomes.

CULTURE: Grow Beach Panic Grass in the full sunlight in the beach sand of coastal dunes and beach fronts.

HABITAT AND RANGE: Found on sandy shores and dunes along the coast from Connecticut to Louisiana.

FLOWER SEASON: Summer and fall.

PROPAGATION: Easily propagated from cuttings made from its decumbent stems, which typically have adventitious roots. Cuttings with intact roots can be inserted directly into beach front sands.

COMMENTS: One of the best species for binding the sand of coastal dunes. It is tolerant of salt spray. The glaucous forms can be quite attractive when used in landscape settings of beach front property.

Panicum virgatum   Switch Grass
Gramineae or Poaceae   Grass Family

DESCRIPTION: Switch Grass is a tall, erect, rhizomatous plant bearing diffuse panicles of flowers and fruit. The plants usually occur in clumps with numerous, scaly, creeping rhizomes, and may reach a height of 75 in. (Fig 8-3).

CULTURE: Grow Switch Grass in ordinary garden soil in full sun, allowing generous amounts of space because the clumps become large. It will grow under the poorest of conditions, including lack of drainage and some flooding.

HABITAT AND RANGE: Found in prairies, along roadsides, and in fields throughout much of eastern North America. It was one of the grasses found in the original tall grass prairies.

FLOWER SEASON: Late summer and fall.

PROPAGATION: Division of superior clones is easiest, but it can be grown from seed.

COMMENTS: Switch Grass is used in the perennial border, for screening or privacy, or for the natural, wild look of wildlife habitat. It is ideal for meadow plantings and mixed with various fall-blooming wild flowers such as Asters and Goldenrods. Switch Grass is one of the better native grasses for garden use due to its unusual appearance. The open panicles are extremely pleasing when viewed against a dark background.

Schizachyrium scoparium   Little Blue Stem
(= Andropogon scoparium)
Gramineae or Poaceae   Grass Family

DESCRIPTION: Little Blue Stem is a highly variable species of clump-forming grass. The slender stems are 20–40 in. tall, often freely branching above; the stems and leaves become golden brownish in the fall.

CULTURE: Grow Little Blue Stem in full sun on well drained soil. Burn or mow the clumps in late winter to eliminate woody plant competition in meadow plantings. Little Blue Stem requires less moisture than Big Blue Stem, thus can be used on drier sites.

HABITAT AND RANGE: Common on well-drained soil in old fields, prairies and thin woodlands from New Brunswick to Alberta south to Florida, Texas and Arizona. Little Blue Stem was a major component on drier sites of the original vegetation of the tall grass prairies and the mixed grass prairies. The mixed grass prairie was an area intermediate in rainfall between the tall grass prairie region and the short grass prairies of the high plains.

FLOWER SEASON: Late summer and fall.

PROPAGATION: Seeds.

COMMENTS: Little Blue Stem is valuable for meadow plantings and naturalistic landscapes. Plant it in large drifts, along roadsides or in fields. It can be maintained by one mowing a year.

Sorghastrum nutans — Indian Grass, Indian Reeds
Gramineae or Poaceae — Grass Family

DESCRIPTION: A rather tall grass from short, scaly rhizomes, reaching 3–6 ft. tall, with flat, narrow leaf blades and narrow terminal, yellowish panicles. The gracefully drooping flowering and fruiting structures bear hairs and a long bent and twisted awn.

CULTURE: Grow Indian Grass in full sun in slightly moist to well drained soil. When used in a meadow planting manage the species by an annual, late winter controlled burn or by a mowing during the same season.

HABITAT AND RANGE: Found along roadsides in moist to dry prairies, old fields, open woodlands, and savannas from southern Canada to the Gulf of Mexico; a component of the original tall grass prairie.

SEASON: Late summer and fall.

PROPAGATION: Seeds or by division.

RELATED SPECIES: *Sorghastrum elliottii* and *S. secundum* are similar in appearance and garden value.

COMMENTS: This attractive, fine textured, prairie native is ideally suited for use in perennial borders, island beds, and meadow plantings. Its graceful appearance and fine texture always excite the landscape students in the senior author's classes at the University of Georgia.

Spartina pectinata — Slough Grass, Prairie Cordgrass
Gramineae or Poaceae — Grass Family

DESCRIPTION: A stout, erect, firm, wiry grass from extensively creeping, scaly rhizomes. The leaf blades are long and tough, flat when fresh, rolled in drying, with rough margins. The flower clusters are closely appressed to the central axis.

CULTURE: Grow in moist, fertile soil; the plant is invasive due to an extensive system of rhizomes.

HABITAT AND RANGE: Occurs in wet prairies, in fresh water marshes, on stream banks, and extending into brackish coastal marshes; it ranges from Newfoundland west to Washington south to North Carolina, Texas and New Mexico; found in low wet places in the original tall grass prairies of the present-day Corn Belt.

FLOWER SEASON: Late summer and fall.

PROPAGATION: Seeds or division.

RELATED SPECIES: The cultivar *Spartina pectinata* 'Aureo-marginata' has long, graceful, ribbon-like foliage striped with yellow. *S. alterniflora* is the major component of salt marshes along the coast of the southeast; *S. patens* grows on coastal sands and tolerates salt spray, so it can be used to provide stabilization for beach front property; *S. bakeri* and *S. cynosuroides* can be used in natural landscapes along the coast.

COMMENTS: Spartinas are interesting and unusual grasses meriting garden trials and use in naturalistic landscapes.

Uniola paniculata — Sea Oats
Gramineae or Poaceae — Grass Family

DESCRIPTION: Sea Oats is a grass 3–6 ft. tall from extensively creeping rhizomes. The infloresences of flattened flowering and fruiting structures are dense and branched, arching and drooping (Fig. 8-4).

CULTURE: Sea Oats can be transplanted to coastal sands and dunes. The plants accumulate around themselves deposits of wind blown sand that would seem to pose the inherent danger of self-burial. However, *Uniola paniculata* has a unique ability to grow upwards through accumulating sand as dunes increase in size or the sand in them shifts. The extensive rhizomes of Sea Oats aid in binding sand in place, stabilizing coastal sands. It is resistant to salt spray.

HABITAT AND RANGE: Found on sand dunes from southeastern Virginia to Texas.

FLOWER SEASON: Summer and fall.

PROPAGATION: Seeds and division.

COMMENTS: One of the more picturesque species of native grasses; protected in many states due to overcollecting for dried arrangements.

Juncus coriaceus — Rush
Juncaceae — Rush Family

DESCRIPTION: This Rush has densely clustered, green, upright stems, 16–24 in. tall. The leaves are persistent for 2 years or more and all are basal save for a bracteal leaf extending beyond the flower cluster. The fruits are globose, shining, chestnut-brown capsules.

CULTURE: Grow this Rush in moist soil in full sun.

HABITAT AND RANGE: *Juncus coriaceus* grows in wet soil along swamps, pond and stream margins from New Jersey south to Florida and Texas and in the interior from Kentucky to Oklahoma.

FLOWER SEASON: Summer and fall.

PROPAGATION: Seeds or division.

RELATED SPECIES: Several species of *Juncus* have value in the garden. A few of the better are: *J. canadensis, J. dichotomus,* and *J. scirpoides.* Identification of species is difficult; therefore, when interesting forms can be located in nature, transplant them into the garden where they contribute an unusual form to the plantings.

COMMENTS: The erect, wiry, green stems provide an exciting textural contrast. Many rushes are useful in bog gardens.

Luzula echinata   Wood Rush
Juncaceae   Rush Family
   DESCRIPTION: A clump-forming perennial with light green, grass-like leaves and
a brownish flowering and fruiting cluster.
   CULTURE: Grow Wood Rush in acid, well-drained woodland soil in thin shade.
These are woodland plants.
   HABITAT AND RANGE: Found in woodlands in the eastern half of the continent.
   FLOWER SEASON: Late spring and early summer.
   PROPAGATION: Division of established clumps.
   RELATED SPECIES: Any of the several species of *Luzula* make admirable subjects
for the woodland garden, including *L. bulbosa, L. acuminata,* and *L. multiflora.*
   COMMENTS: *Luzulas* can be used as ground covers or tucked in here and there
among rocks or as filler plants. They are not at all aggressive. They have proved
interesting additions to the woodland garden at Piccadilly Farm. The generic name
Luzula is derived from the Latin *luciola,* or glow worm, alluding to the sparkling of
the dew held by tiny hairs on stems and leaves of the plant.

Carex grayi   Gray's Sedge
Cyperaceae   Sedge Family
   DESCRIPTION: Gray's Sedge is an erect, perennial, grass-like plant with a globose,
pistillate flower cluster.
   CULTURE: Adaptable to most soils, Gray's Sedge seems to prefer moist soil and
light shade.
   HABITAT AND RANGE: Found in moist woods from Vermont to Wisconsin south to
Georgia and Mississippi.
   FLOWER SEASON: Summer.
   PROPAGATION: Division of established clumps.
   RELATED SPECIES: A number of species of *Carex* have garden value and should be
used to a greater extent than they are now. Although the genus is easily recognized, identification of species can be difficult. *Carex* is one of the larger genera of
flowering plants; this adds to the difficulty as does the requirement for the use of
difficult-to-observe technical characters. At Piccadilly Farm, several species have
been effectively used among the rocks surrounding the water garden area with no
concern as to their identity. When interesting and attractive forms are found in the
field, bring them in and use them. Some of the better species for gardens are: *C.
pensylvanica* (Fig. 8-5), with slender leaf blades and fine texture; *C. plantaginea* with
relatively long leaves 0.5–1.0+ in. wide; *C. platyphylla* with shorter leaves 0.6–0.75
in. wide; and *C. laxiflora* a fine-textured, grass-like plant preferring deep shade.
   COMMENTS: The light green leaves and globose heads of Gray's Sedge that
develop during the summer are a fine addition to the garden. Many of the fine-
textured woodland species of *Carex* have characteristics pleasing in the garden.
They can be used to contrast with the bold textures of Hostas or to soften the hard
surfaces of stone work. In most instances a clump or two of *Carex* can be removed
from the woods, providing permission is obtained, without presenting conservation problems.

Cymophyllus fraseri   Fraser's Sedge
Cyperaceae   Sedge Family

DESCRIPTION: Fraser's Sedge is a rhizomatous perennial bearing strap-shaped leaves averaging 1.5 in. by 12 in. long. The flowering stem bears a few sheaths without blades (Fig. 8-6).

CULTURE: Fraser's Sedge prefers a cool, moist, fertile, shaded woodland garden. It is hardy in the Northeast but not recommended for the lower South.

HABITAT AND RANGE: Inhabits fertile, woodland coves in the mountains of Virginia and West Virginia south to Georgia, South Carolina, and Tennessee.

FLOWER SEASON: Spring.

PROPAGATION: Division.

COMMENTS: The coarse, strap-shaped leaves provide an interesting textural feature for the woodland garden (Fig. 8-7).

CHAPTER 9

Hardy Native Ferns and Fern Allies

Because hardy, native ferns grow in such intimate relationships with perennial wild flowers, and are typically used in shade gardens, it is appropriate to devote a synoptic chapter to them. Native ferns are becoming increasingly popular among gardeners, whether used as background plantings, as fillers, as blenders, as ground covers, or as major focal points for the garden. Ferns are wonderful plants; they provide visual buoyancy, they lighten the garden, they offer a wide assortment of foliage of varying shades of green, and they can be of soft and plume-like texture, or of coarse and rugged appearance. Most hardy ferns are easy to grow and some can be used where few other plants thrive. Relatively undemanding, they are perennials that require little attention, and reward the gardener with a variety of beautiful and distinctive leaves. Their woodsy attractiveness is a delight in every garden.

WHAT IS A FERN?

In early geological time when the first *vascular plants* (plants with specialized tissues able to conduct water and nutrients throughout the plant) appeared, some developed large, complex leaves while others did not. The leafy ones are called ferns, the others with small, scale-like leaves are called *fern allies*. The fern allies include the whisk ferns, clubmosses, spikemosses, quill worts and horsetails. The ferns and fern allies both reproduce by dust-like, single-celled *spores,* unlike the conifers and flowering plants which reproduce by seed. The spores are produced in structures called *sporangia* that at first glance may be overlooked. In the case of ferns, the sporangia are usually clustered together into small groups called *sori* located in regular patterns on the undersides of their leaves. In a few fern species, entire leaves or parts of leaves may be modified and covered with sporangia. In some few genera, some leaves may be sterile and produce no sporangia at all.

When spores from the parent plant are released some fall upon bare ground. With sufficient moisture and light, these tiny, one-celled spores start to grow, eventually forming green, heart-shaped *prothallia.* As the prothallia grow, structures are formed that eventually produce eggs and sperms. At maturity, and with the aid of a drop of water forming a path between the male and female organs, sperm cells find their way to the egg cell and fertilize the egg. From the fertilized egg a young fern plant called the *sporophyte* develops. The sporophyte, or spore-bearing plant, eventually develops roots, stems and leaves typical of the mature fern plant and the cycle of spore production begins again. Ferns can be grown from spores, directions are provided in several of the books on ferns cited in the Bibliography. Some commercial nurseries are now producing hardy native ferns grown from spores.

Leaves are the major components of ferns, certainly the part that is most noticeable. The leaves of ferns are often referred to as *fronds.* Young fern fronds start out tightly rolled in a shape like a bishop's crosier or the head of a violin, hence the name *crosier* or *fiddlehead.* As the fronds unroll they mature first at the base and unroll gradually. The fiddleheads differ among genera; some are large and hairy as in Cinnamon Fern, others are like little, green balls. They vary in color; those of

Christmas Fern are silvery white, those of Northern Maiden Hair are reddish brown, and those of Lady Fern yellow-green. The appearance of fern fiddleheads in the spring is always a reminder that winter is over and better days are ahead.

The beauty of ferns rests in their fronds, which may be simple (Walking Fern) or compound (Marginal Wood Fern), evergreen (Christmas Fern) or deciduous (New York Fern). Compound leaves of ferns may be pinnately divided one, two or three times (Fig. 9-1). The Christmas Fern is once-pinnately compound; the leaflets or primary divisions are called *pinnae* (singular pinna). The Marginal Wood Fern is twice-pinnately compound and the Hairy Lip Fern is mostly three-pinnately compound. The ultimate segments or divisions of twice-or three-pinnately compound leaves are called *pinnules*. The petiole portion of a fern frond is termed a *stipe*. The *rachis* is the part of the stipe continuing into the blade and carrying the pinnae or leaflets.

Some species of ferns have decidedly different sterile and fertile leaves. Plants such as the Cinnamon Fern, with brownish, cinnamon-colored, fertile fronds in the spring and green, flattened, sterile fronds, and Sensitive Fern, with broad, sterile fronds and fertile fronds that look like a stick with beads, are said to have *dimorphic* fronds. The thread-like vascular elements in the fronds are called *veins*. They may be *free* if they run directly from the midvein to the margin or *anastomosing* if they form a complex network. Sori may be arranged in geometric patterns, as around the leaf margins in the Marginal Wood Fern, or in dense masses as in the Christmas Fern. The sori of many species are covered by thin protective coverings called *indusia*. In the Christmas Fern the indusia are round; they are kidney-shaped in Marginal Wood Fern and linear in the Spleenworts.

The stems of ferns are a modified form of stem termed a *rhizome*. In ferns the rhizomes are long creeping as in the Sensitive Fern; short creeping as in the Christmas Fern, or ascending as in the Tree Ferns. The Ostrich Fern has long rhizomes with short, ascending stems that produce plume-like fronds forming a vase-like crown. Ferns with long creeping or branching rhizomes, such as Hay Scented Fern, New York Fern, and Sensitive Fern, tend to be more difficult to contain in a small area; ferns such as the Marginal Wood Fern with a single crown of leaves, tend to remain in one place and do not become invasive. Typically, the rhizomes are clothed in an armor of scales, hairs, or the remains of old leaf bases. Rhizomes proceed horizontally, moving along the surface or slightly underground. Roots are produced from the rhizomes and are typically black and fibrous in appearance.

CULTURE OF NATIVE FERNS

Our hardy, native ferns are easy to grow if a few simple gardening rules are followed, and if the conditions of their native habitats are simulated. Basically, one must be concerned with four things: the amount of *light, soil preparation, moisture,* and *maintenance*. Most ferns prefer shade, but not deep, heavy shade. They need light if they are to grow well. Probably dappled shade, where patterns of sunlight move across the plants as the day progresses, is best for ferns. Some ferns such as New York Fern, Sensitive Fern, Ostrich Fern, Bracken Fern, Cinnamon Fern, and Royal Fern will grow in full sun if sufficient moisture is provided. Examine the shade carefully; it may be helpful to limb up trees to allow more light to reach fern plantings. Remember that shade also can be provided by physical structures such

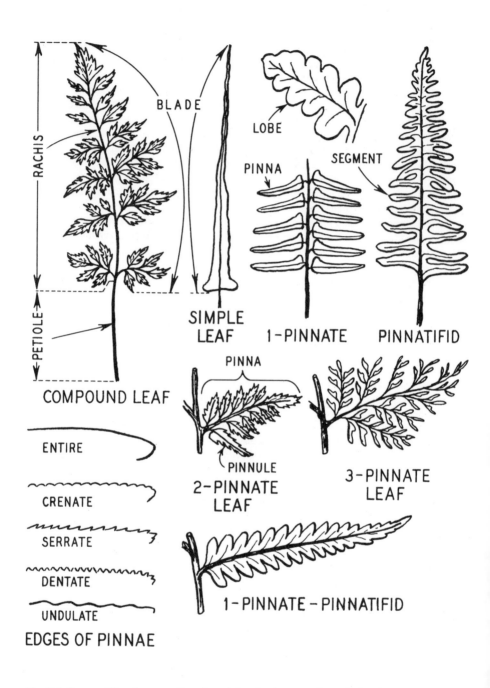

RACHIS

PETIOLE

BLADE

COMPOUND LEAF

SIMPLE
LEAF

LOBE

PINNA

SEGMENT

1-PINNATE

PINNATIFID

ENTIRE

CRENATE

SERRATE

DENTATE

UNDULATE

EDGES OF PINNAE

PINNA

PINNULE

2-PINNATE
LEAF

3-PINNATE
LEAF

1-PINNATE-PINNATIFID

Fig. 9-1. Types of Fern leaves or fronds and details of pinnae. From F. Gordon Foster, *Ferns to Know and Grow,* Timber Press.

as houses, sheds, garages, and walls. Such physical structures also offer protection against the drying effects of wind, which is critical with some fern species.

In general most ferns are not fussy about soil, and grow vigorously when the soil is slightly on the acid side. Limestone-loving ferns may need some ground dolomitic limestone or crushed shells added to the soil. The soil should be dug or tilled to a depth of at least 6–8 in. If sandy, add 3–4 in. of peat moss or ground pine bark and work into the soil. Well-rotted compost is also excellent. If the soil is mostly clay, add coarse builder's sand in addition to the humus. In general, all ferns, except those native to rock crevices or tree limbs, grow best in loose soil with plenty of organic matter. Superphosphate or bone meal should be added to the planting area at the rate of 3–5 lbs. per 100 sq. ft. Additional nitrogen fertilizer is needed only if the ferns tend to appear lighter green in color than normal. The presence of fertile leaves, those bearing sporangia, suggest a strong plant that is happy with its situation. In the commercial production of hardy ferns at Piccadilly Farm, the senior author uses a top dressing of slow release 14-14-14 fertilizer at the rate of 1 tsp. for each gallon container.

When planting ferns, do not allow the roots or plants to become dry. Bare-root plants from mail order nurseries should be unpacked immediately upon arrival. Their roots should be wrapped in wet newspaper and the plants placed in a protected place and kept damp until planted, which should be done as soon as possible. Plant bare-root ferns only in the fall or very early spring. Dig a hole in the planting bed, spread the rhizomes, and plant as any perennial. Ferns with long rhizomes, such as Sensitive Fern, should have the rhizomes placed no deeper than 1 in. below the soil surface. When planting, remove any broken fronds as they will not be repaired.

Container-grown hardy native ferns purchased at garden centers can be planted any time during the growing season. Be sure to plant container-grown plants at the same depth they grew in the container. When planting ferns in cobble or in pockets in rock walls use a soil mixture that is about one-half organic matter. In general, follow the 1-2-3 rule when planting, i.e., small ferns should be planted 1 ft. apart, medium-sized plants 2 ft. apart, and large ferns 3 ft. apart.

Just as natural populations of wild flowers have been carelessly over-exploited, native ferns are commonly dug from the wild and sold directly to gardeners. For this reason, some species are in jeopardy. Purchase native ferns only from nurseries selling nursery propagated plants. Alternatively, ferns may be obtained for the garden through plant rescues, that is salvaging ferns from sites destined for clearing and development. Be sure that written permission is obtained from the owner of the property before attempting to rescue plants. If the salvage is carried out in the summer, be sure to remove some or most of the leaves and water the newly transplanted ferns well until they are established. Transplanted ferns typically send up a few new fronds before frost when handled in this way.

Sufficient moisture is essential for the successful use of ferns in gardens. Ferns should NEVER be allowed to become bone-dry. When planting ferns make sure that resources are available to supply water during droughts. Water deeply several times each week during dry spells. Watering needs to be continued even when they begin to go dormant in the fall as they are making leaf buds for the next season at that time. A good mulch applied at the time of planting helps to conserve moisture as well as retard the growth of weeds. Wood chips purchased from tree pruning companies make excellent mulch for ferns; pine straw, oak leaves, and other organic materials available locally can be used. In the fall, follow the lead of nature and allow tree leaves to remain where they have fallen on the ferns.

Ferns require relatively minimal maintenance. Little in the way of fertilizer is required other than a good mulch of leaves each fall. Limestone-loving ferns need some additional lime from time to time. Pull weeds by hand. Never use hoes, rakes or small tillers around ferns. Fern rhizomes are close to the soil surface and fiddleheads are easily injured. In the spring, prior to the appearance of the fiddleheads, remove dead limbs that have fallen on the ferns over winter; crumble up by hand any erect dead fronds of the deciduous species; add mulch if needed, and with this, the ferns are ready for the new growing season.

SELECTED LIST OF NATIVE FERNS FOR VARIOUS PURPOSES

1. Ferns Easy to Grow and Good for the Beginner:
   Adiantum pedatum, Northern Maiden Hair Fern
   Athyrium filix-femina, Lady Fern
   Dryopteris species
   Matteuccia struthiopteris, Ostrich Fern
   Polystichum acrostichoides, Christmas Fern

2. Ferns for Wet Soil:
   Lorinseria areolata, Small Chain Fern
   Matteuccia struthiopteris, Ostrich Fern
   Osmunda cinnamomea, Cinnamon Fern
   Osmunda regalis, Royal Fern
   Woodwardia virginica, Virginia Chain Fern

3. Ferns for Moist Soil:
   Adiantum pedatum, Northern Maiden Hair Fern
   Athyrium filix-femina, Lady Fern
   Onoclea sensibilis, Sensitive Fern
   Thelypteris hexagonoptera, Broad Beech Fern
   Thelypteris kunthii, Widespread Maiden Fern

4. Ferns for Well-drained Upland Soils:
   Asplenium platyneuron, Ebony Spleenwort
   Dryopteris marginalis, Marginal Wood Fern
   Polystichum acrostichoides, Christmas Fern
   Pteridium aquilinum, Bracken Fern

5. Ferns for Ledges and Crevices of Rock Walls or in Cobble:
   Asplenium platyneuron, Ebony Spleenwort
   Asplenium trichomanes, Maidenhair Spleenwort
   Cheilanthes lanosa, Hairy Lip Fern
   Polypodium virginianum, Rockcap Fern
   Pteris multifida Spider Brake

6. Ferns for Crevices in Limestone or Masonry (Lime-loving):
   Adiantum capillus-veneris, Southern Maiden Hair Fern
   Camptosorus rhizophyllus, Walking Fern
   Pellaea atropurpurea, Purple Cliff Break
   Pteris multifida, Spider Brake

7. Ferns for Ground Covers:
   Athyrium filix-femina, Lady Fern
   Dennstaedtia punctilobula, Hay Scented Fern
   Dryopteris marginalis, Marginal Wood Fern
   Polystichum acrostichoides, Christmas Fern
   Pteridium aquilinum, Bracken Fern
   Thelypteris noveboracensis, New York Fern

USING NATIVE FERNS IN THE GARDEN

Although the fiddleheads of most hardy ferns appear early in the spring, the leaves do not fully mature for nearly six weeks, Thus, it is possible to have many wild flowers and even early blooming non-natives tucked in amongst ferns. Use Virginia Bluebells, Trilliums, Dutchman's Britches, Solomon Seal, Jack-in-the-Pulpit, and Wild Geranium, as well as the exotics among the spring flowering bulbs, such as species Tulips, Narcissus, Crocus, and Dutch Iris. Actually, some ephemeral wild flowers such as Virginia Bluebells must be interplanted with species such as ferns that appear later or their area of the garden will be bare for the remainder of the growing season. With deep watering during droughts, the beautiful foliage of the deciduous species of ferns lasts until frost and those of the evergreen species over winter.

Many native ferns are suitable for a variety of locations and purposes in the garden. Tall species are useful as background plantings, in framing pools, and to form unusually pleasant boundaries dividing one garden segment from another. Small ferns are useful in rock gardens, and large stately specimens in shady areas. The subtle blending shades of green found in ferns harmonize with more colorful flowering plants or soften the bold features of plants such as Hostas. This blending effect of ferns is certainly one of the many reasons they have so much value in the garden.

The ferns described in this chapter provide a wide range of sizes, patterns, shades of green, and habitat requirements. All have proved their worth when placed in the proper environment and properly placed in the garden design.

RECOMMENDED SPECIES OF HARDY NATIVE FERNS

Arranged alphabetically by genus and species as the family classification is relatively unstable and being reorganized.

Adiantum pedatum   Northern Maiden Hair Fern
Adiantaceae   Maiden Hair Family
   DESCRIPTION: The silhouettes of the fronds appear as dainty, fan-shaped arching branches. The fronds are 12–24 in. long with brown stipes and petioles; the oblong sori are borne on the underside of the reflexed margin. The plants are 12–24 in. tall and just as wide (Fig. 9-2).

CULTURE: Provide the Northern Maiden Hair Fern with well-drained, humus soil and sufficient moisture in moderate to deep shade.

HABITAT AND RANGE: Moist, well-drained woodlands from Quebec to Alaska south to Georgia, Louisiana, Oklahoma, and California.

RELATED SPECIES: *Adiantum capillus-veneris,* the Southern Maiden Hair or Venus Hair grows best where limestone has been added to the soil. This southern native is ideally suited for planting in limestone cobble.

COMMENTS: The Northern Maiden Hair Fern, with its graceful and delicate texture, should be included in every woodland garden. It is ideal for combining with coarse textured plants such as Hostas. Remaining attractive from spring until fall, it should be planted in groups spaced 18 in. apart or tucked in here and there for its fine texture and softening effect.

Asplenium platyneuron   Ebony Spleenwort
Aspleniaceae   Spleenwort Family

DESCRIPTION: The sterile fronds are spreading and lie close to the ground, while the fertile ones are erect and bear oblong sori in two rows on the pinnae. The fertile leaves of Ebony Spleenwort are rather slender, tapering at top and bottom, once-pinnate, deep green, 6–18 in. long and 1–2 in. wide. The pinnae are alternate and auricles are present at their bases. Petiole and rachis are dark, glossy brown. The plants are 8–18 in. high and about 6 in. wide.

CULTURE: Plant Ebony Spleenwort in loose, woodsy soil amongst rocks. Once present in the garden, it volunteers frequently, is readily established, and generally maintains itself with little care required..

HABITAT AND RANGE: Dry woods, often on rocks from Quebec to Ontario south to Florida and Texas.

COMMENTS: An excellent, small fern for the rock garden or beside rocks bordering a path. It may be grown either among acid granitic or sandstone rocks or tucked in crevices of limestone rocks.

Asplenium trichomanes   Maidenhair Spleenwort
Aspleniaceae   Spleenwort Family

DESCRIPTION: This is a small, delicate fern about 3–6 in. high with spreading leaves. The evergreen fronds are slender, once-pinnately compound, dark green, about 0.5 in. wide and up to 6 in. long. The roundish to oblong pinnae are opposite to subopposite and bear 2–3 pairs of linear sori on each pinna.

CULTURE: Grow the Maidenhair Spleenwort in humus pockets in limestone or between two limestone rocks, maintaining moisture until the plant is established.

HABITAT AND RANGE: Found on shaded, mostly calcareous rocks in much of eastern North America.

RELATED SPECIES: *Asplenium pinnatifidum,* the Lobed Spleenwort, and *A. montanum,* the Mountain Spleenwort, both grow in crevices in acid rocks. They are more difficult to establish in the garden than *A.trichomanes.*

COMMENTS: A small, neat species for the cool, moist, rock garden.

Athyrium filix-femina (**including var.** *asplenioides*)   Lady Fern
Aspleniaceae   Spleenwort Family

DESCRIPTION: The fronds of the Lady Fern are lanceolate, twice-pinnately compound to thrice-pinnate. The pinnules are lobed or pinnatifid; the fronds 18–36 in.

tall, highly variable in size, and 5–12 in. wide, with colors ranging from green to light yellow. The elongated and slightly curved sori are located midway between the mid-vein and the frond margin (Fig. 9-3).

CULTURE: One of the easiest ferns to grow, providing the plants are not allowed to become dry. Grow in slightly acid, moist to wet soil and furnish water during droughts to maintain the foliage.

HABITAT AND RANGE: Lady Fern is a cosmopolitan species found over much of the eastern two-thirds of North America in moist woods, meadows, and mountain coves, and along streambanks.

RELATED SPECIES: A number of varieties have been recognized by botanists; var. *asplenioides*, the Southern Lady Fern, is the common variety in the Southeast and may be mentioned in regional floras.

COMMENTS: An excellent species for the moist, woodland garden or for naturalizing along stream banks or around shady springs. It produces new fronds continually during the growing season. Its fine texture blends well with many native and exotic shrubs and perennials.

Athyrium pycnocarpon   Glade Fern, Narrow Leaved Athyrium
Aspleniaceae   Spleenwort Family

DESCRIPTION: Fronds of the Glade Fern are of two types; the fertile, bearing sori, are longer and narrower than the sterile; they are lanceolate in shape, once-pinnate, 12–24 in. long and 6 in. wide; the long-tapering pinnae are joined obliquely to the rachis by well defined stalks; the sori are long and straight. Well grown plants reach about 2 ft. in height.

CULTURE: Glade Fern requires cool, rich humus containing ground limestone. The plants should never be allowed to become dry.

HABITAT AND RANGE: Found in cool, moist, woodland situations, often on limestone taluses where the soil is circum-neutral, ranging from Quebec and Ontario south to Georgia and Louisiana.

RELATED SPECIES: The Silvery Glade Fern, *Athrium thelypterioides*, bears pinnae that are deeply pinnatifid. It ranges south to Georgia and is also readily grown in the garden.

COMMENTS: A species supplying interesting and unusual textural combinations for the cool, moist, wild garden. Excellent for naturalizing on talus slopes. When leaves of the Glade Fern first appear, they are a light, brilliant green, later changing to dark green and finally becoming russet prior to frost.

Camptosorous rhizophyllus   Walking Fern
(= *Asplenium rhizophyllum*)
Aspleniaceae   Spleenwort Family

DESCRIPTION: This species has an interesting method of vegetative reproduction; the tips of the long, tapering fronds arch over, touching the rock on which they are growing. There they root, producing new plantlets and giving the visual effect of walking across the rock surface. The fronds are simple, tapering, long-triangular in outline, 4–12 in. long; the fronds usually have rounded lobes at the base. The sori are elongate and arranged in an irregular pattern (Fig. 9-4).

CULTURE: A highly desirable fern for a shaded limestone outcrop. Plant it in a humus pocket in crevices in the limestone or in rock cobble. Establishment is aided by keeping the plants moist.

HABITAT AND RANGE: Look for the Walking Fern growing on the surface of moss-covered, calcareous boulders; it ranges from southeastern Canada southward to Georgia and Oklahoma.

COMMENTS: A unique fern sure to be a conversation plant because of its method of vegetative propagation.

Cheilanthes lanosa   Hairy Lip Fern
Adiantaceae   Maiden Hair Family

DESCRIPTION: The Hairy Lip Fern has dense masses of rhizomes producing twice or thrice pinnately compound, narrowly lanceolate fronds, 6–16 in. long. They typically form clumps a foot or more across and 6–12 in. tall. The stipe and rachis are purplish brown, covered with spreading hairs. Sori are produced along the margins of the frond and are covered by the reflexed margins.

CULTURE: Plant the Hairy Lip Fern among non-calcareous rocks; it can tolerate brief dry periods, once established.

HABITAT AND RANGE: Found on cliffs or rock outcrops, in acid soil from Connecticut to Minnesota south to Georgia and Texas.

RELATED SPECIES: *Cheilanthus tomentosa,* the Wooly Lip Fern and *C. alabamensis,* the Alabama Lip Fern, are rather similar in appearance to *C. lanosa.* Alabama Lip Fern occurs on calcareous rocks and is rather local and rare.

COMMENTS: All three of the Lip Ferns are small, interesting ferns for the rock garden.

Cystopteris protrusa   Brittle or Fragile Bladder Fern
(= *C. fragilis* var. *protrusa*)
Aspleniaceae   Spleenwort Family

DESCRIPTION: Brittle Fern forms low clumps 10–12 in. tall and 2 ft. or more across. The fronds are lanceolate-ovate, twice-pinnately compound, 10 in. long and 3 in. wide with 8–12 pairs of nearly opposite pinnae. The sori are few in number and are positioned over veins.

CULTURE: Brittle Fern is easily grown in slightly acid to circum-neutral soil in moist shade. Supply extra water during the growing season to keep the plants green and encourage the production of new fronds.

HABITAT AND RANGE: Inhabits circum-neutral soil on moist, shady slopes; circumboreal in distribution, extending southward in North America to Georgia and Louisiana.

RELATED SPECIES: The similar appearing *Cystopteris bulbifera,* the Bulblet Bladder Fern forms asexual bulblets along its rachis that fall off and form new plants. It grows best when its rhizomes are inserted into a limestone crevice packed with humus. The fronds of *Cystopteris bulbifera* are narrowly triangular in outline.

COMMENTS: The name Bladder Fern refers to the bladder-like covering of the sori. This species forms fresh appearing, attractive, light green clumps that always attract attention, especially in the spring, at Piccadilly Farm. The characteristic of continual production of fronds during the summer helps to maintain its garden value over a long period.

Dennstaedtia punctilobula   Hay Scented Fern
Dennstaedtiaceae   Hay Scented Family

DESCRIPTION: The fronds of Hay Scented Fern are lanceolate and twice-pinnately compound, the pinnules are lobed, and the fronds yellow-green, 18–30 in. long, and as much as 10 in. wide. The sori are marginal, cup-like structures located in the sinuses of the pinnules (Fig. 9-5).

CULTURE: In some areas Hay Scented Fern can spread aggressively, but in the garden at Piccadilly Farm, it has posed no problems. It grows best in slightly acid, moist, upland, forest soil. Use it as ground cover to form natural-appearing drifts of fine-textured fern foliage. It is best used in larger gardens where it has room to spread.

HABITAT AND RANGE: Look for Hay Scented Fern in upland, open woods and clearings from Newfoundland and Minnesota south to northern Georgia and Alabama westward into Arkansas.

COMMENTS: The fine texture of the fronds of Hay Scented Fern make a pleasing contrast with other coarse-textured species. Use it naturalized in drifts in the wild or native flora garden. The fronds smell like hay hence its common name. Hay Scented Fern is an excellent ground cover.

Dryopteris goldiana   Goldie's Wood Fern, Giant Wood Fern
Aspleniaceae   Spleenwort Family

DESCRIPTION: A large, impressive fern, Goldie's Wood Fern forms clumps typically 3 ft. tall and 18–24 in. across. Its fronds are oblong-triangular, once-pinnatifid, 30–48 in. long by 8–14 in. wide, and leathery in appearance. The sori are light green and positioned near the pinna midrib.

CULTURE: Goldie's Wood Fern requires a cool, moist, shady location in a slightly acid, humus-rich soil. It is not a fern for the deep South, although it grows well and is attractive in the shade garden at Piccadilly Farm located in the Piedmont of northern Georgia. It is, however, at its best further north or in the higher elevations of the Southeast.

HABITAT AND RANGE: Goldie's Wood Fern inhabits moist woodlands in rich slightly acid to circum-neutral soils from New Brunswick to Ontario and Minnesota south to Iowa and the mountains of northern Georgia.

COMMENTS: Use Goldie's Wood Fern as a tall background plant or as a focal point. It is a highly recommended, handsome fern rewarding the gardener with attractive, long-lasting foliage.

Dryopteris marginalis   Marginal Wood Fern, Marginal Shield Fern
Aspleniaceae   Spleenwort Family

DESCRIPTION: The leathery, evergreen fronds of Marginal Wood Fern are lanceolate to ovate-oblong, twice-pinnately compound, 18–24 in. long and 6–10 in. wide. The stipe is covered with prominent, brownish scales. The kidney-shaped sori are positioned near the frond margins, hence the name Marginal Wood Fern. The plants are upright, clump-formers, 20 in. tall (Fig. 9-6).

CULTURE: Grow Marginal Wood Fern in fertile humus in full to partial shade. Provide water during dry periods.

HABITAT AND RANGE: The Marginal Wood Fern grows naturally in woods and on rocky slopes from Nova Scotia to Ontario and Wisconsin south to Oklahoma and into northern Georgia and Alabama.

RELATED SPECIES: *Dryopteris marginalis* forms hybrids with *D. goldiana*. The hybrids have sori positioned half-way between the margins and the midribs of the pinnae. *D. ludoviciana,* the Florida Wood Fern, Southern Wood Fern, or Southern Shield Fern, is a much sought after species for gardens in the Coastal Plain from Texas to North Carolina. The fertile fronds of *D. ludoviciana* bear sori only on their upper half.

COMMENTS: Marginal Wood Fern is one of the better species of native ferns for the garden. It is evergreen, with a nice ferny texture and a pleasing upright habit of growth. It is not at all aggressive, forming clumps that stay put.

Equisetum hyemale
Equisetaceae

Scouring Rush, Horsetail
Horsetail Family

DESCRIPTION: Stems of this fern ally are evergreen, unbranched, jointed, 20–36 in. tall. Brownish sheaths are present at the nodes with a black band above and below the sheath. Spores are borne in a terminal, cone-like structure with a sharp terminal point.

CULTURE: Grow Scouring Rush in moist soil, pH 6–7, in partial shade to almost full sunlight. It should be stressed that, in a favorable situation, this fern ally can become an aggressive, serious pest and practically impossible to contain in a small area. It is best planted in a large, buried nursery container to restrain the rhizomes, thus keeping it under control.

HABITAT AND RANGE: *Equisetum hyemale* occurs naturally in damp places near streams, often on calcareous soil, and is Eurasian and North American in distribution.

RELATED SPECIES: *Equisetum arvense,* the Field Horsetail, has branched sterile stems and unbranched fertile ones. It is common to the North, where it is weedy, but uncommon and rare in the South.

COMMENTS: Scouring Rush stems are unusually handsome, proffering contrast in a Japanese garden or a poolside setting. Use it to make a strong statement as an important focal point. The rough-textured stems accumulate silica and were used by settlers in North America for scouring pots and pans, hence the name.

Lorinseria areolata
(= *Woodwardia areolata*)
Blechnaceae

Netted or Small Chain Fern

Chain Fern Family

DESCRIPTION: Fronds of the Netted Chain Fern are of two types: the fertile frond has very narrow pinnae while the sterile frond is oblong-lanceolate in shape, 12–20 in. tall, and has light, glossy green pinnae which are much wider than those of the fertile fronds. This species forms spreading drifts about 12–18 in. tall. The sori are elongate in a chain-like arrangement on the back of the fertile fronds. The sterile fronds have some resemblance to those of Sensitive Fern, *Onoclea sensibilis* (Fig. 9-8).

CULTURE: Readily grown in acid, wet soil in partial shade to nearly full sunlight. Because of its tendency to spread, give Netted Chain Fern plenty of room.

HABITAT AND RANGE: Found in wooded swamps and openings, in acid soil, from Nova Scotia to Michigan south to Florida and Texas.

RELATED SPECIES: The Netted Chain Fern is often confused with the unrelated Sensitive Fern: the fronds of both are dimorphic (of 2 types) and their sterile fronds somewhat resemble each other.

COMMENTS: The Netted Chain Fern can be used to form natural appearing drifts in wet soil; it spreads rapidly by means of rhizomes once it becomes established, if growing conditions are favorable.

Lycopodium digitatum   Running Ground Pine or Ground Cedar
(= L. flabelliforme)
Lycopodiaceae   Club Moss Family

DESCRIPTION: The stems and foliage of this fern ally resemble that of a low growing cedar. Its rhizomes are as long as 3–6 ft., and the erect stems are 5–10 in. tall and branched to a fan-like configuration. Tiny, awl-shaped, dark green leaves are borne in 4 rows and spores are produced in terminal, cone-like structures usually borne on forked branches.

CULTURE: A plant difficult to transplant; it is best handled by removing an intact "sod" and transferring this into the garden site.

HABITAT AND RANGE: Running Ground Pine is found on dry or slightly moist soils in coniferous or deciduous woodlands from eastern Canada to Minnesota south to Georgia and Alabama. Once rare, it has made a surprising comeback as secondary forests have regenerated from former farmland in eastern North America.

COMMENTS: An attractive and unusual ground cover, but one difficult to establish. It grows rapidly in favorable sites covering large areas. It is best used in the native flora garden. The spores of *Lycopodium* were once used in flash powder for photography and to coat condoms, keeping them from sticking together.

Matteuccia struthiopteris   Ostrich Fern
(= M. pensylvanica)
Aspleniaceae   Spleenwort Family

DESCRIPTION: The Ostrich Fern has fronds of two types: the sterile are large, plume-like, leathery, elliptic-lanceolate and 2–5 ft. tall, broadest above the middle, once-pinnately compound, with the pinnae gradually reduced in length toward the base; the smaller fertile fronds appear in late summer and are 6–24 in. in length and lyre-shaped, with ascending pinnae which tightly enclose the sori, the fertile fronds become brown and woody in the fall (Fig. 9-9).

CULTURE: Grow the Ostrich Fern in cool, wet, marshy soil in partial to full sunlight. This is a fern for the cooler parts of North America and should not be attempted in the Southeast. It can be grown easily in the garden if provided with suitable growing conditions but garden specimens seldom reach the size of plants in their native locations.

HABITAT AND RANGE: Ostrich Fern inhabits swamps and wet woods in Europe and in North America from Newfoundland to Alaska and British Columbia south to Missouri, Ohio, and Virginia.

COMMENTS: A regal species when grown in a suitable habitat and climatic zone. All too often it is placed in landscape designs south of where it can be grown. The young fiddleheads are gathered, cooked, and eaten. They have a taste and texture similar to that of Asparagus.

Onoclea sensibilis   Sensitive Fern
Aspleniaceae   Spleenwort Family

DESCRIPTION: Fronds of the Sensitive Fern are of two types: the sterile frond deltoid-ovate, 12–30 in. long; the fertile, 12–24 in. long with bead-like pinnules which enclose the sori, the pinnules becoming hard and brown in the fall. The sterile fronds tend to resemble the sterile fronds of *Lorinseria areolata.*

CULTURE: Grow the Sensitive Fern in wet to slightly moist, acid soil in light shade or even in part sun if the soil is quite wet. In the southeast, and perhaps elsewhere, the fronds are attacked by chewing insects, causing an unsightly appearance. This species produces long, robust rhizomes and under favorable conditions can be quite aggressive.

HABITAT AND RANGE: Sensitive Fern is found in swamps, wet open woods, and moist meadows, and under bridges from Newfoundland to Minnesota south to Florida and Texas.

COMMENTS: This is a species more suitable for the larger garden where its vigorous rhizomatous growth will not be a problem. The dried fertile fronds with their beads-on-a-stick appearance make ideal material for dried arrangements. The senior author has enjoyed a vase of the dried fertile fronds on his desk for several years.

Osmunda cinnamomea   Cinnamon Fern
Osmundaceae   Royal Fern Family

DESCRIPTION: The Cinnamon Fern has dimorphic fronds, that is, fronds of two types: cinnamon stick-appearing fertile fronds, brownish, without leafy tissue, borne in early spring and soon disappearing; sterile ones yellow-green and leafy, once-pinnately compound, deeply pinnatifid with a dense tuft of rusty hairs beneath the base of each pinna. The sterile frond becomes 24–36 in. long and 4–6 in wide. Under favorable growing conditions the plants stand 30–36 in. tall and make handsome clumps (Fig. 9-11).

CULTURE: Grow Cinnamon Fern in wet, acid soil in partial shade; in full sunlight it needs soil that is continually wet.

HABITAT AND RANGE: The Cinnamon Fern occurs in wet soil of wooded swamps, marshy places and wet savannas of eastern North America south into tropical South America.

RELATED SPECIES: *Osmunda claytoniana,* the Interrupted Fern (Fig. 9-12), has fertile pinnae on the lower half of the otherwise sterile fronds; in other words the fertile pinnae interrupt the sterile leaf, hence the common name. It is good for garden use in the North and at higher elevations in the mountains of the Southeast. This handsome, 24–36 in. species is one of the first to appear in the spring. As the fronds uncurl, the tender, yellow-green pinnae are exposed, resembling the pinnae of Cinnamon Fern, but soon the fertile pinnae appear, surrounded above and below by sterile pinnae, and identification becomes easy. The Royal Fern, *Osmunda regalis* (Fig. 9-13), has fertile pinnae at the top of an otherwise sterile frond. It is an excellent choice for landscaping if provided with wet, acid soil and some shade. The Royal Fern has a much coarser texture than the other two species of *Osmunda;* it forms large clumps 24–36 in. tall.

COMMENTS: All three species are excellent in the garden provided suitable growing conditions are available. They can be grouped to form a background planting or used in the foreground to make a bold statement of plant material.

Pellaea atropurpurea   Purple Cliff Brake
Adiantaceae   Maiden Hair Family

DESCRIPTION: The fronds of Purple Cliff Brake are lanceolate to triangular, once-pinnately compound at the top of the frond, twice pinnately compound below, 6–20 in. long, gray to bluish green. The stipes are brownish purple to black. The sori develop beneath the reflexed edge of the fertile pinnules.

CULTURE: Plant in pockets of humus soil in limestone, in light shade to partial sunlight. The plants grow in surprisingly small fractures and crevices in limestone rocks. Once established, they can tolerate considerable dryness.

HABITAT AND RANGE: The Purple Cliff Brake grows on calcareous rocks in partial to full sunlight from Rhode Island to British Columbia south to Florida and Mexico.

COMMENTS: Valuable for planting in crevices in large boulders or on ledges of calcareous rocks in the rock garden.

Polypodium virginianum   Rockcap Fern, Common Polypody
Polypodiaceae   Polypody Family

DESCRIPTION: Rockcap Fern covers large boulders, hence the common name. It has oblong-lanceolate fronds, deeply pinnatifid, 6–10 in. long and 2 in. wide. The fronds are leathery and evergreen, with round sori lacking indusia. The sori are located nearer the margin than the midvein. The rhizomes grow in a mat partly exposed, and the leaves form a dense yellow-green mass.

CULTURE: Plant the Rockcap Fern in crevices between acid or basic rocks in open shade. Mats of the species can be placed on suitable rock surfaces with a bit of humus and weighted down. Several years are required for permanent establishment. Supply additional moisture in periods of drought to keep the plants in good condition.

HABITAT AND RANGE: Found on rocks and banks, occasionally on trees or circumneutral soil, in North America from Newfoundland to Alaska south to Georgia, Alabama, Arkansas, and California.

RELATED SPECIES: The Resurrection Fern, *Polypodium polypodioides* (Fig. 9-14), is more southern in distribution and prefers tree substrates, although it also grows on rocks. It also can be established on boulders in the garden. In dry weather the fronds turn brown and curl up, but with the return of moisture they become bright green and uncurl into a normal position.

COMMENTS: The generic name *Polypodium* means "many feet" and alludes to the leaf scars that remain on the rhizome where the old leaves have fallen away. Use Rockcap or Resurrection Fern to soften large boulders in the woodland garden.

Polystichum acrostichoides   Christmas Fern
Aspleniaceae   Spleenwort Family

DESCRIPTION: The evergreen fronds of the Christmas Fern are of two types: fertile and sterile. The fertile fiddleheads are among the first to appear in the spring and are covered in silvery scales. Fertile fronds are 12–24 in. long and 3–4 in. wide, linear-lanceolate and leathery, becoming darker green later in the season. The pinnae are auricled; the fertile portions of the fronds are near the tips; these pinnae are contracted and have rounded sori. Smaller, sterile fronds are produced later in the season. The plants tend to be 18–24 in. tall and about 2 ft. across (Fig. 9-15).

CULTURE: One of the easist native ferns to establish in the garden. Readily grown in fertile, well drained, woodland soil in partial to almost full shade. If grown in partial sunlight, the plants should be kept consistently moist. Christmas Fern responds to frequent watering and, as it is a clump former, tends to stay in place.

HABITAT AND RANGE: The Christmas Fern is found in moist to well-drained upland woodland habitats from Nova Scotia to Wisconsin south to Florida and Texas.

COMMENTS: One of the best species of fern for the woodland or native flora garden and one of the easiest to transplant and to establish. Its evergreen habit of growth insures garden interest throughout the year. Use it massed as a groundcover.

Pteridium aquilinum
Dennstaedtiaceae

Bracken Fern
Hay Scented Family

DESCRIPTION: Bracken Fern is a morphologically highly variable species, with long rhizomes and a coarsely textured frond 12–48 in. tall. The fronds are broadly triangular, twice-to thrice-pinnately compound; the sori are partially protected by a recurved margin.

CULTURE: Under favorable growing conditions, Bracken Fern may become invasive. It should be planted where it can be controlled by mowing or cultivation.

HABITAT AND RANGE: Found in well-drained soil of thin woods, almost world-wide in distribution, with a number of regional varieties.

COMMENTS: It is best used as a ground cover at the edge of woodlands or along roadsides; definitely not a species for a small, intensive garden, but better used in naturalistic situations. It has been known to cause livestock poisoning. The fiddleheads are sometimes gathered for human consumption but this practice is associated with a high rate of stomach cancer. It should not be eaten.

Pteris multifida
Adiantaceae

Spider Brake
Maiden Hair Family

DESCRIPTION: Fronds of the Spider Brake are 10–20 in. long with the stipe about ⅓ of this length. The blade is pinnate with 3–7 pairs of pinnae, mostly undivided with the exception of the lowermost pair. The sori are marginal, somewhat hidden by the recurved margin.

CULTURE: Add bits of limestone, concrete or shells to the soil and grow the Spider Brake in partial shade.

HABITAT AND RANGE: An introduced species which has become commonly naturalized along the southeastern Coastal Plain. It is typically found in pockets and crevices in masonry walls.

COMMENTS: This non-native fern was included as it is so widely naturalized along the coast of the Southeast and because it is so useful tucked in here and there on the masonry walled gardens so common to gardening in New Orleans, Mobile, Savannah, and Charleston. Ferns, with their green color, provide a cooling appearance badly needed in hot, sticky climates.

Selaginella apoda
Selaginellaceae

Meadow Spikemoss
Selaginella Family

DESCRIPTION: The Meadow Spikemoss is a fern ally that forms large, creeping, light green, moss-like mats. Its stems have 4 rows of leaves, the lateral oval, the 2 middle rows of leaves narrower, with pointed tips.

CULTURE: Readily grown in fertile, moist garden soil in partial shade.

HABITAT AND RANGE: Meadow Spikemoss is found in moist meadows and along streambanks in partial shade thoughout much of eastern and midwestern North America.

COMMENTS: Use it in the rock garden where there is moist soil and a shading overstory, or between stepping stones in a walk or patio. At Piccadilly Farm, Meadow Spikemoss is very succesful when planted between large sandstone rocks of the terrace below the water garden.

Thelypteris hexagonoptera   Broad Beech Fern, Southern Beech Fern
Thelypteridaceae   Maiden Fern Family

DESCRIPTION: Fronds of the Broad Beech Fern are 12–24 in. long, twice-pinnately compound and broadly triangular. The rachis is winged and the lowermost 2 pinnae point downward in relation to the blade. The sori are positioned near the margins, without indusia (Fig. 9-16).

CULTURE: The Broad Beech Fern requires a fertile, woodsy soil in moist shade. It is a clump-former which spreads at a reasonable rate.

HABITAT AND RANGE: Look for Broad Beech Ferns in moist, fertile, undisturbed woodlands from Maine to Ontario and Minnesota south to Florida and Texas.

COMMENTS: This is a valuable and attractive fern for the garden because it holds its grand green color over the entire growing season. Based upon its performance in the garden at Piccadilly Farm, it is highly recommended and has become one of our favorite ferns.

Thelypteris kunthii   Widespread Maiden Fern
(= T. normalis)
Thelypteridaceae   Maiden Fern Family

DESCRIPTION: Fronds of the Widespread Maiden Fern are 20–40 in. in height, hairy, 6–10 in. wide ,and twice-pinnately compound to pinnatifid. The sori are positioned midway between the midvein and the margin of the leafy segments (Fig. 9-17).

CULTURE: Grow this species in moist, fertile, humus-rich woodland soil to which ground limestone has been added.

HABITAT AND RANGE: It is found in moist, often calcareous, soils along river and stream banks and in swampy woods from Central America north along the Coastal Plain from Texas to South Carolina.

RELATED SPECIES: Other *Thelpteris* species excellent for gardens in the deep South include:

T. torresiana, Mariana Maiden Fern
T. dentata, Downy Maiden Fern
T. hispidula, Variable Maiden Fern
T. ovata, Ovate Maiden Fern
T. palustris, Marsh Maiden Fern

COMMENTS: The Widespread Maiden Fern is a fine choice for southern gardens and deserves to be used widely in landscaping. Although apparently hardy when planted in the woodland garden at Piccadilly Farm in the Piedmont of Georgia, it does not over-winter in containers in the production area of our perennial nursery at the same location. For this reason, plantings of *Thelypteris kunthii* are recommended only for the lower South.

135

Thelypteris noveboracensis   New York Fern
Thelypteridaceae   Maiden Fern Family
DESCRIPTION: The light green fronds have a graceful form tapering gradually toward either end. They are 12–24 in. long, once pinnately compound-pinnatifid; the lower pinnae become shorter and more widely spaced until the tiny basal pinnae are reached.

CULTURE: Grow the New York Fern in fertile soil with abundant humus in partial shade. An aggressive spreader at the northern parts of its range, it is much less aggressive to the south.

HABITAT AND RANGE: Found in woodlands from Newfoundland to Ontario and Minnesota south to Georgia, Mississippi, and Arkansas.

COMMENTS: Use New York Fern where there is no danger of crowding other species. It is an excellent ground cover and can be used to form natural drifts in the woodland garden.

Woodwardia virginica   Virginia Chain Fern
Blechnaceae   Chain Fern Family
DESCRIPTION: Fronds of the Virginia Chain Fern are 18–24 in. tall. The sterile and fertile fronds are alike, once pinnately compound, the pinnae pinnatifid. The veins form a row of areoles arranged in chain-like fashion along the midrib. On the fertile fronds, the sori form elongate mounds parallel to the midrib.

CULTURE: Grow Virginia Chain Fern in wet, marshy soil in full sunlight.

HABITAT AND RANGE: It inhabits the acid soil of swamps, marshes, and roadside ditches from Nova Scotia south to Florida and Texas.

COMMENTS: This is one of the few ferns that grows in full sun, providing the soil is constantly wet. Use the Virginia Chain Fern in a wet spot in the native flora garden. Under favorable conditions it can spread rapidly and should not be used in a restricted area.

CHAPTER 10

Native Herbaceous Groundcovers

This chapter deals with native herbaceous perennials that can be used in the garden as groundcovers. A groundcover is a low-growing plant or grouping of plants used to cover bare soil in a landscape setting. Given enough time, nature will clothe a patch of bare ground with some form of plant life in the course of plant succession. Thus the idea of planting groundcovers is a natural and ecologically sound element of gardening and landscaping.

In the gardening literature, groundcovers are typically described as dense, aggressive, persistent, evergreen plants, under 1 ft. tall and capable of forming dense carpets, discouraging weeds in the process. Groundcovers are also thought of as decorative problem-solvers often flourishing in the shade where few lawn grasses will grow. But groundcovers can be more than just standard, over-used Ivy, Liriope, and Green Pachysandra. Some, like *Mitchella repens*, are valuable for wildlife, or bear decorative blossoms covering the ground in color. In this chapter, as well as in others, many native species of ferns, wild flowers, grasses, and grass-like plants ideally suited for making interesting groundcovers of unique beauty and variety are identified.

A few common misconceptions should be noted. Groundcovers should not be used only to solve garden problems, but also to enhance the landscape. Groundcovers are not trouble or maintenance free. Regardless of the vigor of the groundcover, weed and tree seedlings must be pulled, fallen limbs or leaves removed, and general tidiness maintained seasonally. Simply put, all the elements of a garden and all forms of plantings require effort on the part of the gardener. Groundcovers are not the answer to all maintenance problems.

When using groundcovers, certain practical considerations must be taken into account. First, choose the proper plant for each particular site in the garden. Does the plant need shade, sun, partial shade, moist soil, dry soil, soil high in humus, or ordinary garden soil? Second, because perennial groundcovers remain in place for years, soil preparation must be done as carefully as in a perennial border. Basically, soil needs mechanical preparation, 4–6 in. of organic matter, and 3–5 lbs. each of lime, superphosphate, and 10-10-10 fertilizer for each 100 sq. ft. of planting area. Weeds must be controlled and irrigation supplied in dry weather.

Certain native plants of the eastern half of the continent can be used effectively for groundcovers. They can be planted in the foreground of shrubs, under shrubs, in narrow or odd-shaped areas, or as a substitute for grass. They may be interplanted with bulbs or several species of groundcovers may be intermixed together. Ferns are especially good for this purpose as ferns blend well with many wildflowers. Groundcovers can be used to create textural and color contrasts, and to soften masonry and rock work. Properly selected groundcovers embellish the overall scene of the garden and tie the larger woody plants together. A selection of unusual native species used as groundcovers encourages the appreciation of foliage as leaves are present much longer than ephemeral seasonal blossoms.

Those species best suited for use as groundcovers, but not discussed in previous chapters, are featured here, but many other native plants function well as groundcovers when massed and planted thickly. Some suggestions of species suitable as groundcovers but discussed in previous chapters are listed below:

Ferns:

Adiantum pedatum, Northern Maiden Hair Fern
Athyrium filix-femina, Lady Fern
Dennstaedtia punctilobula, Hay Scented Fern
Dryopteris marginalis, Marginal Wood Fern
Osmunda cinnamomea, Cinnamon Fern
Osmunda regalis, Royal Fern
Polystichum acrostichoides, Christmas Fern
Thelypteris kunthii, Widespread Maiden Fern
Thelypteris noveboracensis, New York Fern

Grasses, Rushes and Sedges:

Carex grayi, Gray's Sedge
Chasmanthium latifolium, Upland Sea Oats
Cymophyllus fraseri, Fraser's Sedge
Luzula echinata, Wood Rush

Shade Plants:

Aquilegia canadensis, Columbine
Coreopsis auriculata, Dwarf Tickseed
Dicentra eximia, Wild Bleeding Heart
Eupatorium coelestinum, Hardy Ageratum
Geranium maculatum, Wild Geranium
Lysimachia ciliata, Fringed Loosestrife
Jeffersonia diphylla, Twin Leaf
Medeola virginiana, Indian Cucumber Root
Phlox divaricata, Blue Phlox
Phlox stolonifera, Creeping Phlox
Sanguinaria canadensis, Bloodroot
Sisyrinchium angustifolium, Blue Eyed Grass
Stylophorum diphyllum, Wood Poppy
Thalictrum thalictroides, Wind Flower
Tradescantia virginica, Spiderwort

Sun Plants:

Amsonia tabernaemontana, Blue Star
Asclepias tuberosa, Butterfly Milkweed
Coreopsis verticillata, Thread-leaved Coreopsis
Lupinus perennis, Eastern Wild Lupine
Oenothera fruticosa, Sundrops
Oenothera speciosa, White Evening Primrose
Phlox subulata, Thrift
Rudbeckia fulgida, Perennial Blackeyed Susan
Stokesia laevis, Stokes' Aster
Verbena canadensis, Rose Verbena
Verbena rigida, Rigid Verbena
Verbena tenuisecta, Roadside Verbena

Asarum shuttleworthii   Shuttleworth's Ginger
(= *Hexastylis shuttleworthii*)
Aristolochiaceae   Birthwort Family
DESCRIPTION: Shuttleworth's Ginger is an evergreen herb rising from long or short rhizomes. The leaves are mostly rounded-cordate, with curious mottling; the old leaves are persistent. The solitary flowers are thick and fleshy, hidden under the foliage.
CULTURE: Grow Shuttleworth's Ginger in moist, fertile, acid soil, pH 5–6, in shady woodland with an abundance of humus. it is rather slow to establish but is one of the more attractive Gingers, making the wait worthwhile. Some natural populations of this species have short rhizomes and tend to form clumps, while others have long creeping rhizomes and tend to spread. Plants of the latter make better groundcovers.
HABITAT AND RANGE: Inhabits rich, moist woodlands from Virginia and West Virginia to Georgia and Alabama.
FLOWER SEASON: Spring flowering but the leaves are evergreen.
PROPAGATION: Division.
RELATED SPECIES: The cultivar 'Callaway' of *Asarum shuttleworthii* selected by Fred Galle has more variegation than is normally found in wild populations (Fig. 10-1). *Asarum canadense*, the Wild Ginger, is a deciduous, rhizomatous, rapid-growing species found mostly on neutral to calcareous soils from eastern Canada south to Georgia and Alabama (Fig. 10-2). With its dark green leaves, it has proved to be an excellent ground cover in the woodland garden at Piccadilly Farm and, although it is deciduous, may be the best *Asarum* for groundcover use. Another species, *A. arifolium*, the Heart Leaf or Wild Ginger, is evergreen and occurs in woods from Virginia and Kentucky south to Florida and Louisiana. *A. virginicum*, the Wild Ginger or Little Brown Jug, has leaves similar in shape to *A. shuttleworthii*, but its flowers are smaller; it inhabits woodlands from Virginia and West Virginia to Georgia. Rootstocks and leaves of all *Asarum* species have a ginger odor. The odd, little flowers are borne at ground level so fertilization is done mostly by beetles, fungus gnats, flesh-flies, and other ground-feeding insects.
COMMENTS: Members of this genus make excellent and unusual groundcovers, sure to attract attention in the shady garden. At the present time botanists use the generic name *Asarum* rather than the more familar *Hexastylis*, for reasons relating to the classification of the group.

Pachysandra procumbens   Allegheny Spurge
Buxaceae   Box Family
DESCRIPTION: Allegheny Spurge is a low perennial with long rhizomes and with toothed leaves crowded near the summit of the somewhat fleshy, erect stems. The fragrant, white flowers are crowded in a spike, the many staminate flowers above, the few pistillate flowers below. Deciduous in the North, evergreen in the South; once the new shoots mature, the leaves and stems of the previous season disappear (Fig. 10-3).
CULTURE: Readily grown in light shade, in fertile, humus-rich soil, pH 6.5–7.
HABITAT AND RANGE: Found locally on circum-neutral to basic soils over calcareous parent material, ranging from eastern Kentucky south to Florida and Louisiana.

FLOWER SEASON: April–May.

PROPAGATION: It can be propagated by softwood cuttings taken in May and treated with a rooting hormone, but the best method is by division of established clumps in August or September. At Piccadilly Farm, divisions are made in September from stock maintained in a shady increase bed. Saleable plants are then available the following season.

RELATED SPECIES: When *Pachysandra* is mentioned, the common, over-used, Asiatic *P. terminalis* comes to mind, but the native *P. procumbens* is much more attractive.

COMMENTS: *Pachysandra procumbens* is an excellent groundcover for shady gardens. It is a most desirable, but under-used, native species.

Linnaea borealis   Twinflower
Caprifoliaceae   Honeysuckle Family
DESCRIPTION: Twinflower is an evergreen perennial with slender, trailing stems; the erect branches bear a few leaves and two pink to white flowers.

CULTURE: Grow in a acid, pH 4–5, cool, damp, shady woodland only in the northern part of the continent.

HABITAT AND RANGE: Native to moist, cool northern woodlands; circumboreal in distribution; in the east ranges south to West Virginia.

FLOWER SEASON: June–August.

PROPAGATION: Division or cuttings.

COMMENTS: A dainty, little groundcover to grow in mossy habitats over rotten stumps and logs. Said to be the favorite flower of Linnaeus.

Antennaria plantaginifolia   Pussy-toes, Everlasting, Ladies Tobacco
Compositae or Asteraceae   Sunflower Family
DESCRIPTION: Pussy-toes are white, woolly herbs, a few inches high, increasing by runners. The plant bears silvery, ovate to elliptic leaves, and erect stalks supporting several, silvery heads of white tubular flowers (Fig. 10-4).

CULTURE: Grow in partly shady to partly sunny sites, in poor, dry, acid, woodland soil. Thrives when neglected.

HABITAT AND RANGE: Naturally found in open woodlands and along woodland ecotones from Quebec to Minnesota south to Florida and Texas.

FLOWER SEASON: Flowers in the spring but the foliage is effective to some extent throughout the year.

PROPAGATION: Division.

COMMENTS: A good groundcover for the edge of the wild woodland garden where it forms flat, silvery patches.

Chrysogonum virginianum   Green and Gold, Golden Star
Compositae or Asteraceae   Sunflower Family
DESCRIPTION: Green and Gold plants are perennial herbs with opposite, ovate, hairy leaves with small heads having 5 yellow, ray flowers.

CULTURE: Green and Gold grows best in light shade, in ordinary, well-drained garden soil, pH 6. Do not over-fertilize, nor water except in times of drought; the plants seem to grow better if neglected rather than pampered.

HABITAT AND RANGE: Found along thin, well-drained, woodland edges from southern Ohio and Pennsylvania to Florida and Mississippi.

FLOWER SEASON: March–June, with scattered flowers throughout the year in the South.

PROPAGATION: Best propagated by division. At Piccadilly Farm, 35 plants grown for 4 months in a prepared, well-drained, shady, increase bed yielded 500 divisions.

RELATED SPECIES: A highly variable species, taxonomically divided into two varieties; the more northern variety is taller and upright, the southern one prostrate and creeping. Among several selections in the trade, the cultivar 'Piccadilly' is an excellent prostrate form (Fig. 10-5).

COMMENTS: One of the best-selling native wildflowers at Piccadilly farm, Green and Gold is a fine groundcover for woodland edges, or lightly shaded gardens. It requires little maintenance.

Cornus canadensis   Bunchberry, Dwarf Cornel
Cornaceae   Dogwood Family

DESCRIPTION: Bunchberry is a low, herbaceous perennial growing from a woody rhizome; it forms large colonies of plants 4–8 in. tall. The erect stems bear a cluster of 4–6 leaves; the small, yellow flowers are in tiny clusters surrounded by 4 white, petal-like bracts similar to those of Flowering Dogwood.

CULTURE: Grow Bunchberry in acid soil, pH 4–5, with ample humus and where falling conifer needles provide mulch. The soil must be kept constantly moist but not water-logged. It should not be attempted in the South.

HABITAT AND RANGE: Found in moist, acid woodlands and bogs across North America and in the east, south to West Virginia.

FLOWER SEASON: June–July.

PROPAGATION: Seeds, division, or by transplanting sods from sites about to be destroyed by development.

COMMENTS: Grows well in cool, damp, northern woodlands, in acid soils where it makes an outstanding groundcover. Definitely not a plant for the sunny southland.

Galax urceolata   Galax, Galaxy, Coltsfoot, Wand Flower
(= G. aphylla)
Diapensiaceae   Diapensia Family

DESCRIPTION: Galax is an evergreen, rhizomatous, perennial herb, with long-petioled, orbicular to broadly ovate leaves. The small, white flowers are borne on spike-like racemes. The leaves become reddish purple with the onset of winter.

CULTURE: This southerner is hardy in New England. Slow to become established, it grows best in acid, pH 4–5, soil to which some sand and humus have been added.

HABITAT AND RANGE: Native to well-drained woodlands from Maryland to Kentucky south to Georgia and Alabama.

FLOWER SEASON: June–July.

PROPAGATION: Division or transplanting of intact sods from sites threatened by development.

COMMENTS: An outstanding, evergreen groundcover around Rhododendrons and Azaleas, which require an acid soil. It was once gathered in large quantities for the florist trade and the leaves used as background greenery in funeral wreaths. Galax, Virginia, is named for this plant.

Shortia galacifolia   Oconee Bells, Shortia, One Flowered Coltsfoot
Diapensiaceae   Diapensia Family
DESCRIPTION: *Shortia galacifolia* is an evergreen, rhizomatous, perennial herb with long-petioled, orbicular to elliptic-orbicular leaves. Erect scapes bear a single, large, white or slightly pinkish flower. The leaves turn bronze in the fall (Fig. 10-6).
CULTURE: Although native to the mountains of the Southeast, Oconee Bells is hardy in New England. For best results, grow it on north-facing slopes in light shade and in a well-drained, acid soil, pH 4.5–6, with an abundance of sand and humus. It is difficult to establish and slow to spread but is well worth having in the garden.
HABITAT AND RANGE: Locally common in only a few locations on fertile, wooded streambanks of the low Appalachian mountains of Georgia, South Carolina, and North Carolina; in nature rare, but commonly cultivated.
FLOWER SEASON: March–April.
PROPAGATION: Division.
COMMENTS: An interesting but slow-growing groundcover with attractive flowers. Most states in its native range list it as an endangered species, with severe penalties if removed from public lands. Originally discovered in 1788 by the French botanist André Michaux in the Carolina mountains, it was named by the American botanists Asa Gray and John Torrey in 1842 from a Michaux specimen found in the Museum of Natural History in Paris. The species, in spite of much searching, was not found again until rediscovered in 1877 in North Carolina by 17-year-old George Hyams. Many of its natural sites have been destroyed by hydroelectric projects, but the survival of this species has been enhanced by its cultivation in countless gardens.

Iris cristata   Dwarf Crested Iris
Iridaceae   Iris Family
DESCRIPTION: Drwaf Crested Iris is perennial from narrow, elongate rhizomes, and has typical, deciduous, Iris foliage; the leaves are 4–8 in. long. Bluish flowers are borne nestled within the foliage (Fig. 10-7).
CULTURE: This dwarf Iris is easily grown in ordinary, well-drained soil, pH 6, in partial shade.
HABITAT AND RANGE: Found in well-drained, rich, woodland soil from Maryland to Oklahoma south to Georgia and Arkansas.
FLOWER SEASON: April–May.
PROPAGATION: By division in early September.
RELATED SPECIES: *Iris verna*, the Violet Iris, with narrow leaves and a yellow to orange band on the sepals and no crest occurs on acid, sandy soils from Pennsylvania and Kentucky south to Georgia and Mississippi. Cultivars of *I. cristata* include: 'Alba', with white flowers; 'Shenandoah Sky', with light blue flowers; and 'Summer Storm', with deep blue flowers.
COMMENTS: Simply marvelous when in flower; the foliage holds up well during much of the summer, making this a good choice for a groundcover.

Maianthemum canadense   Wild or False Lily of the Valley
Liliaceae   Lily Family
DESCRIPTION: A low, perennial herb arising from a slender rhizome. The stems bear 2–3 oval leaves and a short terminal raceme of small, white flowers.
CULTURE: Grow this species in cool, moist, humus rich, woodland soils, pH 5–6. In

the South attempt to grow it only at the higher elevations.

HABITAT AND RANGE: Occurs naturally on moist, woodland soils from Newfoundland and Minnesota along the mountains into north Georgia.

FLOWER SEASON: May–June.

PROPAGATION: Can be grown from seed planted in the fall or it may be transplanted from sites slated for development by removing an intact sod of plants.

COMMENTS: Useful as a readily grown groundcover for the northern shade garden. A plant that does well in heavy shade if given adequate moisture. Under favorable conditions, it spreads to cover fairly large areas.

Trientalis borealis   Star Flower, Chickweed Wintergreen
Primulaceae   Primrose Family

DESCRIPTION: The Star Flower is a perennial arising from a slender rhizome. The erect stems bear a few leaves clustered at the summit of the stem; white, star-like flowers arise on slender pedicels from the leaf axils.

CULTURE: Grow Star Flower in damp, cool, humus-rich soil in shady woodlands. Not a suitable plant for the warmer portions of the Southeast.

HABITAT AND RANGE: Occurs in rich, moist, acid woods and bogs from Newfoundland to Saskatchewan south to Minnesota, Illinois, and Virginia and into the mountains of northern Georgia. The one known station in Georgia makes it one of the rarest plants in the state.

FLOWER SEASON: Spring.

PROPAGATION: Seeds õr by sod from rescue operations.

COMMENTS: A stellar groundcover for cooler climates; it naturalizes and spreads once established.

Anemone quinquefolia   Wood Anemone
Ranunculaceae   Buttercup Family

DESCRIPTION: The Wood Anemone is a delicate, creeping perennial, 3–6 in. tall, bearing whorled leaves with 3–5 leaflets. The leaflets are coarsely or unevenly toothed or lobed. The flowers are white, solitary, and nodding (Fig. 10-8).

CULTURE: Wood Anemone grows well in slightly acid, pH 6, fertile soils in sheltered woodlands where it eventually forms a persistent carpet.

HABITAT AND RANGE: Found in moist woodlands from Quebec to Manitoba south to New Jersey and Iowa, and along the mountains into north Georgia.

FLOWER SEASON: March–June.

PROPAGATION: Seeds or root cuttings.

RELATED SPECIES: *Anemone patens*, the Pasque Flower, occurs in prairie regions. The attractive *A. caroliniana* extends well into the Southeast.

COMMENTS: *Anemone quinquefolia* is a fine species for a woodland groundcover for the upper South and northward. For effect, combine it with mosses.

Hepatica acutiloba   Sharp Lobed Hepatica, Liverleaf, Hepatica
Ranunculaceae   Buttercup Family

DESCRIPTION: Sharp-Lobed Hepatica is a low, herbaceous perennial, with relatively thick, almost evergreen leaves with 3 sharp-pointed lobes. New leaves appear immediately after flowering. The dainty whitish or bluish flowers have 3 conspicuous bracts located behind each flower (Fig. 10-9).

CULTURE: Plant in light shade, in moist, humus-rich soil, pH 6.5–7.

HABITAT AND RANGE: Found on calcareous soils in upland woodlands and along carbonate rock outcrops from Quebec to Minnesota south to Georgia, Alabama, and Mississippi.

FLOWER SEASON: March–April; in the South, blossoms can be found during warmer periods in December.

PROPAGATION: Division or by self-sown seedlings.

RELATED SPECIES: *Hepatica americana,* the Round-leaved Hepatica, or Liverleaf, has round leaf lobes and fewer flowers. It is very similar to the Eurasian *H. nobilis,* in which it is sometimes included. At Piccadilly Farm, *H. americana* seems to perform better than *H. acutiloba.* The exact reason is not known, but the natually acid soil of the garden is suspected.

COMMENTS: Among the earliest spring wild flowers to bloom, flowering at a time when the blossoms are very welcome. A dense planting of this low species makes an interesting groundcover. Plants of *H. acutiloba* grown in acid soil often have blue flowers and seem to grow poorly; addition of dolomitic limestone is essential in such conditions.

Waldsteinia fragarioides — Barren Strawberry
Rosaceae — Rose Family

DESCRIPTION: This is a rhizomatous perennial somewhat resembling a strawberry plant. The basal leaves are composed of 3 leaflets, and the flowering stem bears several small, yellow flowers.

CULTURE: Grow Barren Strawberry in light shade, in moist, acid soil, pH 6.

HABITAT AND RANGE: Native to woodlands from Quebec to Maine, west to Minnesota, and south along the mountains and Piedmont into Georgia and Alabama.

FLOWER SEASON: April–May.

PROPAGATION: Division.

RELATED SPECIES: The rare *Waldsteinia lobata* is similar in appearance.

COMMENTS: This is a fine, low-maintenance groundcover, with unique beauty. Use it in the woodland garden to cover areas around deciduous Azaleas.

Mitchella repens — Partridge Berry, Twin Berry
Rubiaceae — Madder Family

DESCRIPTION: Partridge Berry is a creeping, matted, evergreen herb with small, opposite, rounded leaves. It bears small, whitish, twin flowers and twin, scarlet fruit.

CULTURE: Readily grown in dense to moderate shade, in moist but well-drained soil, with added humus, pH 5–6.5. For best results, the soil moisture should be augmented during droughts.

HABITAT AND RANGE: Found in rich, moist woodlands from Nova Scotia to Minnesota south to Florida and Texas.

FLOWER SEASON: April–July.

PROPAGATION: Cuttings, division or layering.

COMMENTS: A splendid, dainty groundcover for small, shaded gardens. Plant it in the native flora garden among mosses and decaying stumps or logs. It is an important food source for Ruffed Grouse.

Heuchera americana

Saxifragaceae

Common Alum Root, Rock Geranium

Saxifrage Family

DESCRIPTION: Common Alum Root is an attractive, evergreen, herbaceous perennial rising from a stout, thickish rootstock, bearing attractive rosettes of geranium-like leaves. The flowers are small and insignificent and not comparable to those of the commercial hybrid cultivars of *Heuchera*. The blackish rootstock, when broken, exposes a white interior the color of alum, hence the common name.

CULTURE: Plant Common Alum Root in thinly shaded woodland, in well-drained soil, pH 5–6, after adding plenty of sand and humus. Remove the flower stalks once they appear as the plants are grown for their foliage. The appearance of the plants is enhanced by division of the clumps every 3–4 years. The plants tolerate low moisture and poor soil.

HABITAT AND RANGE: Dry woods, especially on rock outcrops, from Connecticut to Ontario and Minnesota south to Georgia and Louisiana.

FLOWER SEASON: April–June; its foliage is handsome throughout the year.

PROPAGATION: Division of established clumps.

RELATED SPECIES: *Heuchera villosa*, the Hairy Alum Root, flowers later in summer and fall; *H. parviflora* also blooms later than *H. americana* and is very attractive. All three species are highly variable and offer splendid possibilities for selection of desirable forms. The genus offers good possibilities for commercial production, yet is often overlooked as a possible groundcover.

COMMENTS: An excellent, low maintenance, evergreen groundcover for the shaded woodland garden. It is under-used.

Mitella diphylla

Saxifragaceae

Mitrewort, Bishop's Cap, Fairy Cup

Saxifrage Family

DESCRIPTION: Mitrewort is a rhizomatous perennial, 6–12 in. tall, with ovate-orbicular basal leaves similar to, but smaller than, those of *Tiarella*. The flowering stem has a pair of smaller, opposite leaves. The flowers are small, dainty, and in a terminal raceme, varying in color from white to green or purple. The flowers are followed by fruit with tiny, shiny, black, exposed seed (Fig. 10-10).

CULTURE: Mitrewort requires shade and moisture. Grow it in fertile soil to which a bit of lime has been addded so that the pH is 6–7. It has proven easy to grow at Piccadilly Farm. Space the plants 8–10 in. apart.

HABITAT AND RANGE: Usually inhabits north-facing, limestone or sandstone bluffs and rocky slopes from Quebec to Minnesota, south to Missouri, Georgia, and North Carolina.

FLOWER SEASON: April–June.

PROPAGATION: Seeds or division.

COMMENTS: An exquisite, dainty groundcover that tends to stay in bounds; a useful plant for the small, shady garden where a simple, soft texture is needed.

Tiarella cordifolia var. cordifolia

Saxifragaceae

Foam Flower, False Mitrewort

Saxifrage Family

DESCRIPTION: Foam Flower is a stoloniferous perennial 6–12 in. tall, with a rosette of broadly lobed leaves resembling *Heuchera* but smaller. The small, whitish flowers, sometimes tinged with pink, are borne on a leafless stem clustered in a showy raceme.

CULTURE: Provide a well-drained soil, pH 5–6.5, rich in organic matter, and extra moisture during droughts. In the South, avoid sunny exposures that cause the leaves to burn later in the season; it tolerates more sun to the North.

HABITAT AND RANGE: Found in rich woodlands from Nova Scotia to Ontario and Wisconsin southward into Georgia and Mississippi.

FLOWER SEASON: March–June.

PROPAGATION: Divisions are the easiest, but Foam Flower can be grown from seed. The variety *cordifolia* produces runners that form new plants which can easily be lifted from around established plants.

RELATED SPECIES: *Tiarella cordifolia* var. *collina* (= *T. wherryi*) is more southern in distribution and lacks stolons, so it is easier to keep in bounds in the small garden (Fig. 10-11). It forms clumps which can easily be pulled apart and divided. Side-by-side trials at Piccadilly Farm have demonstrated that var. *collina* is superior under southern garden conditions. The raceme is larger and more attractive, and the leaves have intriguing purple markings adding interest to the plantings.

COMMENTS: Foam Flower is a handsome, spring-blooming wild flower and an outstanding groundcover, with its evergreen leaves, for the lightly shaded woodland garden. It is one of the best selling native species at Piccadilly Farm and one of our favorites (Fig. 10-12).

CHAPTER 11

Natives for Aquatic and Bog Situations

This chapter is intended to encourage and aid those wishing to extend their interests in native wild flowers to aquatic and wetland species suitable for pond, stream-side, or marshy area plantings. Many of the plants recommended inhabit either true aquatic situations such as ponds or lakes, actually growing in or on the water, or are found emergent at the edge of the water. Others are native to the margins of streams, or may be found in sunny, wet, open places such as marshes or meadows where water stands close to the surface of the soil. Among these ecologically diverse habitats are found some of our most interesting wild flowers in bloom, texture, foliage, and habit of growth; they can add picturesque interest to gardens. Many bloom in the summer after the beauty of the woodland wild flowers has disappeared. They include relatively tiny plants, such as Duckweeds, that float freely on the surface of water, to rooted aquatics such as Water Lilies of open water, or Cattails that form massive clumps along the shoreline. Some aggressive and rugged wetland natives are both decorative and useful in stabilizing banks and ditches, thus preventing erosion.

Water, whether moving or still, is a delightful medium to surround with wild flowers and in which to grow them. A water feature offers great possibilities for creative design as well as a source of continuing interest and satisfaction. A seepage area, pond, or stream is a real asset in a wild flower garden. One lucky enough to have wet soil bordering a stream, lake or man-made pond is indeed fortunate. Many wild species can be used to enhance such environments. All too often, gardeners, when confronted with wet areas, attempt to alter the habitat by drainage or fill, with the purpose of creating lawns or planting shrubs in an attempt to shape a landscape into a scene resembling every other developed landscape. At best, this is a costly procedure resulting in little that might be considered creative, and at worst it may not improve the drainage. Certainly one is well advised to question the wisdom or need for making every landscape resemble or duplicate the design and plant lists of every other landscape. Why not work within the parameters of the existing environment, making use of water to create a landscape of both stability and beauty? Use the assets of the site, such as its natural moisture for a pool or a marshy habitat rather than fighting nature. The creation of a wet habitat also offers unexpected pleasures in the form of the wild species that may appear naturally or be brought in by migrating birds.

Garden designers have long taken into account the value of water in design and the use of plants to enhance such features. But not to be forgotten is the value of water and its associated plant cover to all forms of wildlife. Pools provided with sloping banks allow creatures to get in and out of the water. Aquatic plants provide a place for native animals to seek shelter and hide from predators. Boggy areas are vital homes to many amphibians and birds. Introduced floating-leaved plants shade out algae and submerged aquatics, oxygenate the water, and provide hiding places for small fish in pools. In turn, fish and amphibians reduce the numbers of insects such as mosquitoes by controlling larval populations.

There are many excellent books on water gardening some of which are provided in the bibliography. Information is readily available on design, construction, and maintenance of water features, as are instructions and suggestions for gardening in boggy areas. One or more of these books should be consulted prior to undertaking the implementation of a water garden or developing a naturalistic landscape in a wet place. The information available in these references can be readily related to the native species suggested here and is presented in greater detail than our space allows. A bit of homework often prevents later problems, a fact to which the senior author can attest in light of his experiences with the pools at Piccadilly Farm.

Planting techniques for aquatic and wetland species are basically the same as those used with more typical plants. A few helpful hints include the usual note of caution not to allow the plants to dry out while planting, and to avoid planting too shallowly or too deeply. Aquatics can be planted directly in a thick layer of soil at the bottom of a pond, but they are best planted in containers because many are aggressive and quickly become unmanageable if the rootstocks are not restricted by a container. In addition, removing and shifting the position of the plants is impractical unless they are grown in containers. Specially designed plastic Water Lily baskets with perforated sides are best. If these are unavailable, plastic dish pans or used 3-gal. nursery containers, their sides perforated to allow for gaseous exchange, can substitute. Aquatics should be potted in good, clean, garden soil free from organic matter and low in nutrients, both of which encourage algae. To discourage algae, fertilizer should not be added to garden pools.

Submerged oxygenating plants, such as *Elodea,* should be tied in bundles and anchored into holes in the soil of containers. Planting is best accomplished during late spring through the end of August. A 0.5-in. layer of pea gravel should be added to the surface of all containers used in pools to prevent fish from disturbing the soil and causing the water to become cloudy.

Introduce fish only after the plantings have become established as nibbling of fish retards the growth of plants. It is best to introduce fish the second year. Consider using non-herbivorous fish such as native bream or sunfish instead of the usual carp or goldfish. If the pond is extensive, contact the state or provincial Department of Natural Resources or Game and Fish Department for assistance. In northern climates a snow cover over ice may reduce the available oxygen in the pool, causing problems for fish unless there is water exchange or openings in the ice.

Planting depth of aquatics relates not only to the soil but also to the depth of the water over the crown. *Nymphaea* rhizomes are planted horizontally about 1 in. below the soil surface. *Nuphar* rootstocks are planted vertically. Both require a water cover of 2–3 ft., but when first planted the containers should be raised on bricks to within 6 in. of the water surface. When planting aquatics such as these, remove all the old leaves and any dead or decaying matter.

Free-floating aquatics are valuable in reducing the light available for algal growth and many are attractive. They may take over and prove difficult to control; a word of caution is advised. Some are major pests prohibited in some areas by law. Additional benefits of floating aquatics are their ability to remove nutrients from pond water and to provide cover for small fish. Simply plant these aquatics by dropping them on the surface of the water.

Emergent aquatics inhabit the margins of ponds and slow-moving streams. They are used to soften the edge of ponds and streams with contrasting growth habits and textures. Many native, emergent aquatics provide additional summer color and homes for many forms of wildlife. They should be grown in shallow water and covered by 1–6 in. of water. Many emergent aquatics stray onto the banks so again it is better to confine them in containers to prevent uncontrolled spreading. Some, such as Cattail, take over if not controlled. Cattails also spread readily from seed so cannot be totally restricted by containers.

Moisture-loving plants are used in a marsh or bog garden, an area of permanently moist but not water-logged soil. Such a garden site is prepared by excavating to a depth of 15–18 in. and covering the bottom with pool lining material and refilling with the removed soil. Make slits in the liner to allow seepage during wet weather and top off with water during periods of low rainfall to maintain proper moisture levels. The soil in the bog garden should be improved with organic matter.

While the native plants discussed in this chapter are the basis for pool and waterside or bog gardening there are scores of other species described in other chapters which grow in moist soil. These include several of the ferns: Royal Fern, Small Chain Fern, Cinnamon Fern, Ostrich Fern, Lady Fern, and Sensitive Fern, and flowering plants such as Turtle Head, Cardinal Flower, Blue Lobelia, Gentian, and New York Ironweed.

For purposes of organization, the aquatics described here are arranged by families in the following groups based upon their habit of growth: floating rooted aquatics, submerged rooted aquatics, free-floating aquatics, emergent aquatics, and moisture-loving plants.

FLOATING ROOTED AQUATICS

Some of the most commonly used plants in a garden pool are native, floating, rooted aquatics. A floating, rooted aquatic is a plant whose roots and rhizomes are located in the soil at the bottom of the pond and most of whose leaves and flowers are at, or slightly above, the surface of the water, that is, floating or barely emergent.

The exotic blossoms of *Nymphoides*, Floating Heart, *Nymphaea*, the Water Lily, *Nelumbo*, the Water Lotus, and *Nuphar*, the Yellow Cow Lily, are undisputed contributors to the charm and delight of a water feature. They are relatively easy to grow in a warm, sunny pool if placed at the correct depth. While they may be planted directly in soil in the pool bottom, they are best grown in containers for containment. Some of the more desirable species in this group follow.

Nymphoides aquatica   Floating Heart, Water Fringe, Gentain or Bogbean
                                                    Family

Gentianaceae (placed in the Menyanthaceae in some classifications)

DESCRIPTION: A perennial, aquatic herb with rhizomes giving rise to petiole-like stems each of which bears several petiolate, floating leaves 2–6 in. long. White flowers are borne in the leaf axils late in the season and tuber-like roots, resembling a tiny bunch of bananas, are produced in a cluster below the flowers (Fig. 11-1).

CULTURE: The Floating Heart is undemanding and easily grown.

HABITAT AND RANGE: Found naturally in ponds, lakes, and quiet streams in the Coastal Plain from New Jersey south and west to Texas.

FLOWER SEASON: Summer.

PROPAGATION: Division or seeds.

RELATED SPECIES: *Nymphoides cordata* (Fig. 11-2) is similar to *N. aquatica.* The Yellow Floating Heart, *N. peltata,* has been introduced from Europe and is widely naturalized in North America. It does not produce the cluster of little "bananas" as do the two native species; it is worth growing in a water garden.

COMMENTS: *Nymphoides aquatica* is a dainty, little plant, much like a small water lily with heart-shaped leaves; a plant of special value in a small pool where a smaller, floating leaved aquatic is needed; it produces numerous flowers over a long season.

Nelumbo lutea   Yellow Lotus, American Lotus, Water Chinquapin
Nelumbonaceae   Lotus Family

DESCRIPTION: Yellow Lotus is a rhizomatous aquatic with leaves and flower stalks arising directly from the rhizome. The leaf blades are kidney-shaped; some are floating, others emergent. The flowers are solitary with yellow petals. The light, spongy receptacle becomes enlarged, hard, and flat-topped with circular openings, each containing a round, hard fruit (Fig 11-3).

CULTURE: Plant in large containers in ordinary garden soil in 12–18 in. of water.

HABITAT AND RANGE: Found in ponds, lakes and sluggish streams from New York and Minnesota south to Florida and Texas.

FLOWER SEASON: Summer.

PROPAGATION: Yellow Lotus is easily propagated by division of the rhizomes or by scarifying the seeds and rolling them into balls of clay and planting them in pans of soil covered with water.

RELATED SPECIES: *Nelumbo nucifera,* the Sacred Lotus, has been naturalized locally in North America. It can be recognized by its pink flowers.

COMMENTS: Yellow Lotus was extensively used by the American Indians for food. The starchy rhizomes were cooked and eaten and the seeds were ground for breadstuff. *Nelumbo lutea* is a regal, attractive plant for the water garden. The dried receptacles are used in dried arrangements.

Nuphar advena   Yellow Cow Lily, Spatter Dock, Yellow Pond Lily
Nymphaeaceae   Water Lily Family

DESCRIPTION: The Yellow Cow Lily has long-petioled leaves arising directly from the stout rhizome. The leaves may be submerged, floating, or emergent; they are basally cordate. The yellow flowers are borne on long stalks.

CULTURE: This is an easy plant to grow and tolerates a bit of shade. Grow it in 2 ft. of water.

HABITAT AND RANGE: Native to rivers, ponds, lakes, bayous, estuaries and sluggish streams from Maine to Wisconsin south to Florida and Texas.

FLOWER SEASON: Summer.

PROPAGATION: Division of rhizomes.

COMMENTS: Although the flowers of *Nuphar advena* are not as showy as those of *Nymphaea odorata,* they have an exotic, interesting appearance.

Nymphaea odorata   Fragrant White Water Lily, Pond Lily
Nymphaeaceae   Water Lily Family

DESCRIPTION: The Fragrant White Water Lily is a rhizomatous aquatic bearing long-petioled leaves which arise directly from the rhizome. The white to rarely pinkish flowers are borne singly on long stalks arising from the rhizome. The flowers may be floating or emergent, and most are fragrant (Fig. 11-4).

CULTURE: The rhizomes should be barely covered with soil. Keep the newly potted container within 6–8 in. of the water surface until several new leaves have appeared; at that time move it to deeper water.

HABITAT AND RANGE: Occurs in ponds, sloughs, marshes, and swamps from Newfoundland to Manitoba south to Florida and Texas.

FLOWER SEASON: Summer.

PROPAGATION: Division of rhizomes.

RELATED SPECIES: A species with bright, yellow flowers, *Nymphaea mexicana*, the Yellow Water Lily, occurs along the Gulf Coast into Florida, and has been introduced into coastal North Carolina. The Tuberous Water Lily, *N. tuberosa*, has white flowers, sometimes pink-tinged. It occurs in the upper Mississippi River drainage system.

COMMENTS: Planting in containers restricts leaf growth, adding character to the pool planting. Excessive leaf growth obscures the water, detracting from the pool and planting. Only about one-third of the water surface of a pool should be covered with plants.

Polygonum amphibium — Water Smartweed
Polygonaceae — Smartweed Family

DESCRIPTION: Water Smartweed is characterized by alternate, lanceolate to oblong-ovate leaves with dark markings, and reddish flowers.

CULTURE: The aquatic ecotype from the northern parts of its range is best for garden culture; ecotypes from terrestrial situations are far less desirable. The plants are easily grown in ordinary garden soil; they have an unfortunate tendency to self-sow and to become weedy.

HABITAT AND RANGE: Found in marshy situations throughout much of eastern North America.

FLOWER SEASON: Summer and early fall.

PROPAGATION: Stem cuttings of desirable forms.

COMMENTS: Ecotypes with floating leaves and shoots from Canada and the northern states should be used. Emergent and terrestrial forms tend to be weedy. Smartweeds are important food sources for wild ducks and other aquatic birds, so are used widely in wildlife refuges.

Potamogeton pulcher — Pondweed
Potamogetonaceae — Pondweed Family

DESCRIPTION: An aquatic from a slender, rooted rhizome; the stems arising from the rhizome produce two forms of leaves, one submerged and greatly reduced, the other floating. The submerged leaves are semi-opaque and narrowly lanceolate while the floating leaves are leathery, ovate to oblong-elliptic in shape, 1.5–4.5 in. long.

CULTURE: Plant the shoots in a plastic container covered by 12–18 in. of water. The plants are hardy and undemanding, but may form a dense canopy of leaves shading out submerged plants.

HABITAT AND RANGE: This species of Pondweed is found in swamps, ponds and lakes throughout the eastern half of the continent.

FLOWER SEASON: Summer.

PROPAGATION: Collect some of the shoots and pot in garden soil.

RELATED SPECIES: *Potamogeton* is a large genus consisting largely of weedy plants; several, however, have attractive foliage and make good pool plants if kept under control and not allowed to become weedy.

COMMENTS: Several species are pleasing because the texture of both their floating and submerged leaves offers a interesting contrast to the Water Lily foliage so commonly seen in pools.

FREE-FLOATING AQUATICS

The plants in this group float on the surface of the water and are not normally anchored in soil. They are both interesting and attractive. Free-floating aquatics generally propagate well by themselves and are introduced to the garden pool simply by scattering some of the plants on the water surface. If they begin to form dense carpets, a few sweeps of a net or rake reduces the population.

Pistia stratiotes   Water Lettuce
Araceae   Arum Family
DESCRIPTION: Water Lettuce is a floating, stoloniferous species with rosettes of gray-green, velvety leaves on short stems resembling heads of leafy lettuce (Fig. 11-5).

CULTURE: *Pistia* is hardy only in the lower South along the Gulf Coast. Elsewhere, it must be overwintered inside.

HABITAT AND RANGE: Found in pools and slow-moving streams from Florida to Texas.

SEASON: Summer and fall for foliage; it seldom flowers.

COMMENTS: In nature it is often weedy, forming dense mats and clogging waterways. In garden pools, it is a most attractive and unusual aquatic.

Azolla caroliniana   Mosquito Fern
Azollaceae   Azolla Family
DESCRIPTION: *Azolla caroliniana* is a free-floating water fern with small lacy fronds about 0.25 in. long, pale green in summer but red or brownish toward autumn.

CULTURE: Easily grown by scattering some of the plants on the water surface of the pool; under the proper conditions, propagation is rapid.

HABITAT AND RANGE: The plant is locally common in shallow pools and ditches from New England to the Pacific Coast and southward.

SEASON: Summer and fall; it does not flower as it is a true fern.

COMMENTS: The plants resemble small, floating mosses or liverworts.

Spirodela polyrhiza   Large Duckweed, Duckmeat
Lemnaceae   Duckweed Family
DESCRIPTION: The largest of our floating Duckweeds; the plant bodies or fronds are about 0.25 in. long, nearly as wide as long, and with each frond having two or more roots on the lower surface.

CULTURE: These small, green plants are simply scattered on the water where they multiply rapidly.

HABITAT AND RANGE: Found in quiet pools throughout the eastern half of the continent.

SEASON: Summer and fall; the plants seldom flower.

RELATED SPECIES: Natural populations af *Spirodela ployrhiza* are sometimes present in pure stands, but more often are intermixed with other Duckweeds of the genera *Lemna, Wolffia,* and *Wolffiella,* all nice additions to a naturalistic pool.

COMMENTS: Large Duckweed forms a shiny, green covering over a pond, so limiting the light available for submerged aquatics. When crowded remove some of the plants with a dip net. Large Duckweed is a favorite food of waterfowl. The Duckweeds are the smallest representatives of the flowering plants or angiosperms.

Utricularia inflata
Lentibulariaceae

Inflated Bladderwort
Bladderwort

DESCRIPTION: A free-floating aquatic, the vegetative portion comprised of a stem system, parts of which are leaf-like. Urn-like bladders are produced which entrap and digest tiny aquatic animals. The submerged, lateral, finely divided, leaf-like branches are alternate; a whorl of much larger, inflated, floating branches is borne below the flower stalk; the flowers are yellow.

CULTURE: Inflated Bladderwort is often brought in unintentionally with other aquatics. It is durable and undemanding.

HABITAT AND RANGE: Inhabits ponds and sloughs from New Jersey south to Florida and Texas.

FLOWER SEASON: Spring and summer.

RELATED SPECIES: There are a number of species of this curious, insectivorous genus but the best for water gardening is *Utricularia inflata.*

COMMENTS: This is an interesting botanical curiosity because ot its insectivorous habit and its whorl of floating, inflated branches bearing an emergent cluster of yellow flowers.

Eichhornia crassipes
Pontederiaceae

Water Hyacinth
Pickerelweed Family

DESCRIPTION: Water Hyacinth is a floating, stoloniferous, rosette plant with inflated, spongy petioles and decorative, blue-black roots. The flowers are large, with pale violet corollas having a yellow spot; the flowers are arranged in a spike.

CULTURE: Water Hyacinth is not hardy in the North but it does overwinter in the middle south. In the lower south it can become weedy.

HABITAT AND RANGE: This tropical/subtropical species has become naturalized to North America where it inhabits ponds, canals, rivers, and ditches from Virginia south to Florida and Texas and northward into Missouri.

FLOWER SEASON: Summer.

COMMENTS: An attractive plant but a serious aquatic weed in natural waters as it clogs waterways, preventing boating and reducing fish productivity. Many millions of dollars have been spent attempting to eradicate and control Water Hyacinth in subtropical waters; these attempts have been largely unsuccessful. Because of its beautiful flowers, this introduced plant is suggested here for water gardening in small pools.

Salvinia minima
Salviniaceae

Water Spangles
Water Fern Family

DESCRIPTION: *Salvinia minima* is a small, floating fern with a horizontally growing, much-branched shoot axis. The leaves are in whorls of three at each

153

node; two are horizontal, floating and leaf-like, the third is divided into many fine tips that are root-like and extend down into the water.

CULTURE: Water Spangles forms a floating cover over the pool surface that can reduce light availability to submerged plants. It multiplies freely.

HABITAT AND RANGE: Found in ponds and lakes along the Gulf and Atlantic coasts from Georgia to Texas.

SEASON: Summer and fall; it does not flower as it is a fern.

COMMENTS: The introduced floating fern forms a bright green, botanically interesting cover for the garden pool.

SUBMERGED ROOTED AQUATICS

Although the plants in this group are relatively inconspicuous, they are important plants in the pool for they are oxygenating plants, producing oxygen that is dissolved in the water. Additionally, they provide shelter for various small creatures and nursery accomodations for fish. Their continued nutrient requirements help to retard algal growth. Submerged rooted aquatics are not grown for their flowers, which are typically tiny and not at all showy. For this reason, the category "FLOWER SEASON" is omitted.

For best results, plant as bundles in plastic containers with the clumps anchored in place. Propagate submerged, rooted aquatics by taking cuttings about 12 in. long, tying the cuttings into bundles and inserting the bundles directly into the soil. A wire tie can be used to anchor the bundle of plants. If ice covers the pool for several weeks in winter photosynthesis may be reduced so that the plants can not produce oxygen. If fish are present, the ice cover should be broken and the water agitated to add oxygen and prevent build up of carbon dioxide.

Cabomba caroliniana   Fanwort
Cabombaceae   Water Shield Family
DESCRIPTION: The leaves of Fanwort are submerged except for the alternate, kidney-shaped, reddish brown simple leaves below the inconspicuous flowers. The fully submerged leaves are opposite or whorled, and the fan-shaped blades are composed of numerous, finely, dichotomously divided, linear segments.

CULTURE: Fanwort grows best in water with a pH of 4.5–5.

HABITAT AND RANGE: Found in acid ponds and streams from New Jersey to southern Michigan and Missouri south to Florida and Texas.

COMMENTS: The delicate, fan-shaped leaves and the reddish brown coloration of the plant makes this an appealing species.

Vallisneria americana   Eel Grass, Water Celery, Tape Grass
Hydrocharitaceae   Frog's Bit Family
DESCRIPTION: Eel Grass is a submerged aquatic with ribbon-like leaves of varying width borne on short, vertical stems. The leaves arise from basal clusters and range in length from 1–3 ft., the upper part of the leaf often floating. Numerous staminate flowers are released and float on the surface, some contacting the attached female flowers.

CULTURE: A tolerant, frequently cultivated plant, available from aquarium supply stores. Plant in 18–24 in. of water.

HABITAT AND RANGE: Found in both quiet and swiftly running waters, Nova

Scotia west to the Dakotas, south to Florida and Texas.

RELATED SPECIES: Another Eelgrass, *Zostera marina* has ribbon-like leaves but inhabits marine waters.

COMMENTS: Eel Grass is easy to grow and a good oxygenator. The rhizomes are an important waterfowl food so it has been introduced widely into ponds for this purpose.

Elodea canadensis   Elodea, Waterweed, Ditchmoss
(= Anacharis canadensis)
Hydrocharitaceae   Frog's Bit Family

DESCRIPTION: *Elodea canadensis* is a submerged plant, rooted on the bottom or floating in the water. The narrrow, thin leaves are whorled or rarely opposite. The small, white, pistillate flowers are borne at the surface of the water, the perianth tube simulating a pedicel and elevating the limb to the surface.

CULTURE: Elodea's dense mass of foliage makes it an ideal oxygenator for pools. Plenty of light is needed as well as water that is neutral to slightly alkaline.

HABITAT AND RANGE: Found in ponds, lakes, and streams from Quebec and Saskatchewan south to Virginia and Oklahoma.

RELATED SPECIES: *Egeria densa* is often mistakenly labeled *Elodea densa*. The leaves of the former are about 1 in. long, while those of *Elodea* are about 0.5 in. in length. *Egeria densa* is also an excellent oxygenator and does well in warmer waters of the South. The noxious aquatic weed, *Hydrilla verticillata*, is similar to *Elodea* in leaf size but has teeth on the leaf margins. *Egeria* and *Hydrilla* are both introduced species.

COMMENTS: *Elodea canadensis* is a tolerant, hardy plant for cooler waters.

Najas guadalupensis   Common Water Nymph, Naiad
Najadaceae   Water Nymph Family

DESCRIPTION: Water Nymph is a submerged aquatic with slender, much-branched stems and fibrous roots. The leaves are opposite or crowded so as to appear whorled. The flowers are inconspicuous.

CULTURE: A compliant plant rooted on the bottom or floating; one which does well in bright or subdued light.

HABITAT AND RANGE: Water Nymph inhabits ponds, lakes, and springs throughout much of North America.

COMMENTS: It forms dense, attractive aggregations in the water; it provides fine cover for small fishes.

Ceratophyllum demersum   Coontail, Hornwort
Ceratophyllaceae   Hornwort Family

DESCRIPTION: Coontail has bristly, very brittle, dark green leaves which grow in whorls around the stem. The leaf segments are dichotomously branched. Early in the season the plants grow upright, but later they tend to float at the surface, often intermingled with other aquatics. The flowers are very inconspicuous.

CULTURE: Coontail is suitable for pools receiving plenty of light, where it is easily grown. It tolerates very cool water. The stems can be anchored to the bottom or allowed to float free.

HABITAT AND RANGE: Found in quiet waters of streams, ponds, and lakes throughout North America.

COMMENTS: The dense plumes of very narrow, dark green leaves are pleasing.

The species thrives when a few stems are simply dropped in the pond.

Myriophyllum pinnatum   Water Milfoil
Haloragaceae   Water Milfoil Family
DESCRIPTION: Water Milfoil is a submerged plant except for the upper, flower-bearing portion. The leaves are in whorls of 3–4, pinnately dissected into capillary segments.

CULTURE: This species is easily grown from cuttings stuck into the soil of planting containers. It needs full sunlight.

HABITAT AND RANGE: Water Milfoil is common in ponds, lakes, and swamps from Massachusetts to Kansas south to Georgia and Texas.

RELATED SPECIES: The native species, *Myriophyllum laxum* and *M. heterophyllum*, are both useful in pools. *M. aquaticum*, the Parrot Feather, is frequently naturalized and although attractive, can be weedy. The Eurasian Water Milfoil, *M. spicatum*, is considered a noxious weed.

COMMENTS: The soft, very finely cut foliage of Water Milfoil is appealing, as are the emergent stem tips bearing small inconspicuous flowers.

EMERGENT AQUATICS

The plants in this group typically grow with their crowns under 1–6 in. of water, although they often edge up on drier soil. They are sometimes called "marginals" by some horticultural writers, "emergent aquatics" is a more appropriate botanical description. The plants in this group are easily propagated by division of the clumps, can be grown in ordinary garden soil, and are undemanding in their cultural requirements. Several of the species are aggressive colonizers capable of becoming weedy, so need to be restricted in containers.

The garden value of emergent aquatics is enormous, some providing interesting flowers, others attractive foliage and conspicuous textures. They are useful in furnishing a transition from the water to the land environment and in softening the margins of pool structures for landscaping around the edge of lake front sites. Many emergent aquatics are ideal for bog gardens where the water level is kept at or near the soil surface, or for seepage areas of natural springs.

Alisma subcordata   Water Plantain, Mud Plantain
Alismataceae   Water Plantain Family
DESCRIPTION: Water Plantain may be recognized by its long-petioled, ovate to elliptic leaf blades and numerous small flowers arranged in a panicle. The leaves are basal and form a clump around the erect flowering stem.

CULTURE: Grow Water Plantain in containers covered by 3–4 in. of water.

HABITAT AND RANGE: Found in shallow water of ponds and ditches from Vermont to Minnesota south to Florida and Texas.

FLOWER SEASON: Summer.

COMMENTS: Water Plantain foliage contrasts well with that of other emergent aquatics and its flower cluster is most delicate.

Sagittaria latifolia   Arrowhead, Wapato, Duck Potato
Alismataceae   Water Plantain Family

DESCRIPTION: Arrowhead has long-petioled, arrowhead-shaped, emergent leaves. The flowers have showy, white petals and are arranged in a raceme.

CULTURE: Grow in water 2–3 in. deep or in moist soil at the edge of ponds or lakes. It multiplies and makes large colonies (Fig. 11-6).

HABITAT AND RANGE: Arrowhead is found in wet meadows, marshes, ditches, and pond margins throughout southern Canada south to northern South America.

FLOWER SEASON: Summer and fall.

RELATED SPECIES: *Sagittaria* is a large genus with species distinguished largely by mature fruit characters. Leaf blade shape varies from ribbon-like to broadly arrowhead-shaped. Many of the species have garden value, so when desirable forms are encountered in the wild they can be transplanted to the pool or bog garden.

COMMENTS: The arrowhead-shaped leaves are noteworthy and add interest to a pool or bog. The plant is an important waterfowl and snapping turtle food.

Orontium aquaticum   Golden Club, Never Wet
Araceae   Arum Family

DESCRIPTION: Golden Club is strongly rhizomatous, with simple, long-petioled, dark green, oblong-elliptic, often floating, basal leaves. The club-shaped, golden yellow spadix is lax or ascending on a green scape (Fig. 11-7).

CULTURE: Golden Club requires deep, acid, loamy soil and full sunlight for best development. Plant in 6–12 in. of water.

HABITAT AND RANGE: Found in shallow water of pools, streams and swamps mainly in the Coastal Plain from Massachusetts south to Florida, Mississippi and Kentucky (Fig. 11-8).

FLOWER SEASON: March–April; foliage all season.

COMMENTS: The bright yellow spadix contrasts with the velvety green of the leaves. Its habit of flowering early in spring is an advantage in a pool garden as so many other aquatics flower in the summer. If the leaves are placed under water, water immediately rolls off them when they float to the surface, thus the common name, Never Wet. The green fruits and roots are said to have been used for food by American Indians.

Peltandra virginica   Arrow Arum, Green Arum
Araceae   Arum Family

DESCRIPTION: Arrow Arum is perennial from thick, fibrous roots, with long-petioled, arrow-shaped, pinnately-veined, basal leaves. A slender, greenish spathe is borne on a long scape. The fruits are greenish to bronze.

CULTURE: Arrow Arum prefers truly shallow water in full sunlight or very light shade.

HABITAT AND RANGE: An inhabitant of swamps, marshes, ditches and lake shores from Quebec to Michigan south to Florida and Texas.

FLOWER SEASON: Flowers May–June, foliage summer and fall.

RELATED SPECIES: *Peltandra sagittaefolia,* the Spoon Flower or White Arum (Fig. 11-9), inhabits the Coastal Plain from North Carolina to Mississippi. It has a white margin on its spathe and red fruit. It is the more attractive of the two species but much less commonly available in the trade.

COMMENTS: *Peltandra* is not aggressive, which is a distinct advantage in a small pool or bog area.

Eleocharis equisetoides
Cyperaceae

Spike Rush
Sedge Family

DESCRIPTION: Spike Rush has erect, stout, green stems with a brownish basal sheath. The stems are conspicuously septate, giving an Equisetum-like appearance. The small, cone-like cluster of brownish flowers and fruits is solitary and terminal.

CULTURE: Grow Spike Rush in 3–6 in. of water and keep it confined in a container, as it can spread.

HABITAT AND RANGE: Spike Rush occurs in ditches and ponds, and on the margins of lakes from Massachusetts to Wisconsin south to Florida and Texas.

SEASON: Summer and fall; grown for the foliage,not the flowers.

COMMENTS: The unusual, septate stems topped by the small brownish reproductive structures provide exceptional visual interest.

Dulichium arundinaceum
Cyperaceae

Three Way Sedge
Sedge Family

DESCRIPTION: Three Way Sedge is a tall, perennial sedge with hollow, rounded, jointed stems and numerous short leaf blades borne on three sides of the stem, hence the common name. The brownish reproductive structures are borne in conspicuous racemes.

CULTURE: Grow Three Way Sedge in 1–3 in. of water in containers to prevent its spread.

HABITAT AND RANGE: Inhabits stream edges, lakes, swamps, and bogs throughout much of temperate North America.

SEASON: Summer and fall.

COMMENTS: The stem, leaves, and spikelets are all handsome and unusual; it makes a striking statement in the pool or bog garden.

Equisetum fluviatile
Equisetaceae

Water Horsetail
Horsetail Family

DESCRIPTION: Water Horsetail is perennial from a rhizome; it has green, jointed and grooved aerial stems. The stems are hollow, without true leaves but with a toothed sheath surrounding each joint and resembling whorled scales. Reproduction is by spores from a terminal cone-like structure.

CULTURE: Water Horsetail is not difficult to grow. Use garden soil and grow in a container in 1–2 in. of water. It is a northern species and should not be attempted in the deep South.

HABITAT AND RANGE: Inhabits shallow water of ponds, ditches, and meadows and has a circumboreal distribution; in North America it reaches south to Pennsylvania, Minnesota and Oregon.

RELATED SPECIES: *Equisetum hyemale*, the Scouring Rush, and *E. arvense*, the Field Horsetail, often grow in a variety of damp sites and can be used in a bog garden. It should be noted that *Equisetum* almost inevitably becomes weedy if not contained.

COMMENTS: The jointed, erect, green stems are exotic in appearance and add fascination to the wet garden.

158

Zizania aquatica   Wild Rice
Gramineae or Poaceae   Grass Family
   DESCRIPTION: Wild Rice is a tall, robust grass, perennial in the South but annual
in the North. The large panicle has pendulous lower branches bearing staminate
flowers and stiffly ascending upper branches bearing pistillate flowers (Fig. 11-10).
   CULTURE: Grow Wild Rice in a container as a perennial in the South and as an
annual in the North. Prerequisites to its establishment outside its native habitats
are deep, soft mud and slowly circulating water.
   HABITAT AND RANGE: Wild Rice grows in marshes and along marshy shores and
stream borders from Quebec and Nova Scotia west to Manitoba and south to
Florida and Louisiana.
   FLOWER SEASON: Late summer and early fall.
   COMMENTS: The flower clusters are large and handsome, making the plant
worthy of cultivation. The seeds are much used by waterfowl, marsh, and shore
birds, as well as by many songbirds, and, of course, by humans.

Iris versicolor   Blue Flag, Wild Iris
Iridaceae   Iris Family
   DESCRIPTION: Blue Flag is a rhizomatous perennial with sword-like pointed
leaves and large, showy, violet to blue-violet or reddish purple flowers.
   CULTURE: The aquatic species of *Iris* grow best with their rhizomes just covered
with water.
   HABITAT AND RANGE: Blue Flag is found in marshes and swamps and along shores
from Newfoundland to Manitoba south to Virgina and Minnesota.
   FLOWER SEASON: May–July.
   RELATED SPECIES: Any local species of aquatic *Iris* can be used in the pool or bog
garden, at the margins of ponds or along slow water courses. These include the
following native species:
Iris fulva, Red Flag. Flowers copper colored to reddish brown (Fig. 11-11).
Iris tridentata, Bay Blue Flag. Flowers violet.
Iris brevicaulis, Lamance Blue Flag. Flowers light violet to lavender.
Iris hexagona, Anglepod Blue Flag. Flowers deep violet with whitish edges.
Iris virginica, Southern Blue Flag. Flowers light violet to lavender or pinkish
   lavender (Fig. 11-12).
Iris shrevei, Shreve's Iris. Flowers violet or blue-violet to reddish purple.
Hybrids of *I. fulva* and *I. hexagona* form the basis of the plants known in horticul-
ture as the Louisiana Irises. Natural hybrids of these two species are common in
Louisiana. *I. pseudacorus,* Yellow Flag (Fig. 11-13), is native to Eurasia and has
naturalized extensively in North America. Although a non-native, it is indeed
showy and excellent when used in water garden landscapes.
   COMMENTS: The flowers of *Iris* are certainly an important garden consideration,
but are present for only a relatively short periods. The erect, sword-like *Iris* foliage
providing textural contrast throughout the growing season is the true reason for
using *Iris* in the water garden.

Crinum americanum   Swamp Lily, String Lily
Liliaceae (including the Amaryllidaceae)   Lily Family
   DESCRIPTION: *Crinum americanum* is perennial from a large, succulent bulb. The
strap-like leaves are surrounded at the base by tubular sheaths forming a stalk-like

structure. The flowers, which are arranged in an umbel terminating a scape, are delicately fragrant, white or white tinged with pink; the filaments are a striking purplish pink (Fig. 11-14).

CULTURE: Readily grown from seed, the bulbs should be planted in 2–6 in. of water.

HABITAT AND RANGE: Found in the shallow waters of bayous, swamps, marshes, and streams of the Coastal Plain from Georgia to Texas.

FLOWER SEASON: July.

COMMENTS: A most striking plant when in flower; the senior author still recalls, 25 years later, the excitment of visiting a bayou near Biloxi, MS containing thousands of *Crinum americanum* in full bloom. It is under-utilized in gardens.

Thalia dealbata — Powdery Thalia
Marantaceae — Arrowroot Family

DESCRIPTION: *Thalia dealbata* is a robust perennial, 3–6 ft. tall, from a thick rhizome and has large, ovate-lanceolate, long-petioled leaves covered with a white, powdery coating that envelops all parts of the plant. The blue and purple flowers are arranged closely-crowded in an open panicle (Fig. 11-15).

CULTURE: Easily grown with the rhizome covered by 1–6 in. of water. It self-sows.

HABITAT AND RANGE: Found in cypress swamps, ditches, ponds, and marshes of the Coastal Plain from South Carolina to Texas northward into Oklahoma and Missouri.

FLOWER SEASON: May–July.

RELATED SPECIES: *Thalia geniculata* of Florida and the West Indies is 6–10 ft. tall, its flowers are well spaced apart.

COMMENTS: *Thalia dealbata* is often grown as an ornamental plant in outdoor pools as far inland as St. Louis. The Birmingham Botanical Garden once had a lovely colony in a small stream. Seeds washing downstream germinated and established new colonies. This temperate representative of the tropical Marantaceae family is hardier than one might imagine. It is useful in providing a decided tropical effect in the water garden.

Marsilea vestita — Water Clover
(= M. mucronata)
Marsileaceae — Water Clover Family

DESCRIPTION: The leaves of this unusual fern are long-petiolate, with 4 leaflets resembling a 4-leaved clover (Fig. 11-16).

CULTURE: Grow in small pots with the top of the pot barely under the surface of the water.

HABITAT AND RANGE: Water Clover inhabits mud and shallow water of lakes and ponds from Minnesota south to Texas and Florida.

SEASON: Summer, grown for the foliage.

COMMENTS: The attractive dark green, 4-leaflet, clover-like leaves are an interesting conversation plant for the small pool.

Pontederia cordata (including *P. lancifolia*) — Pickerel Weed, Tuckahoe
Pontederiaceae — Pickerel Weed Family

DESCRIPTION: This is a colonizing aquatic herb with erect, broadly cordate, or lanceolate leaves. The flowers are borne in a congested, spike-like panicle on a stalk bearing one leaf and a bladeless sheath (Fig. 11-17).

CULTURE: Pickerel Weed is one of the best and easiest aquatics to grow in shallow water. Although it is seldom invasive, it is best grown in large containers under about 4–6 in. of water.

HABITAT AND RANGE: It is native to marshes, ditches and streams in shallow water from Prince Edward Island and Minnesota south to Florida and Texas.

FLOWER SEASON: Summer and early autumn.

COMMENTS: The blue flowers are produced over a long period, and its glossy, broadly cordate leaves, tilted at an angle, create unusual textures when grown in masses.

Caltha palustris   Cowslip, Marsh Marigold, Kingcup
Ranunculaceae   Buttercup Family

DESCRIPTION: Cowslips are low, perennial herbs of wet places having alternate, petiolate, entire, or toothed leaves and axillary or terminal, sunny, yellow flowers.

CULTURE: Cowslip is readily grown in shallow water or in the wet soil of bog gardens. It is a northern species not suitable for southern gardens. Always grow in clumps or masses where it can be seen from a distance.

HABITAT AND RANGE: Cowslips are found in wet woods, meadows, and swamps and in the shallow water of ponds. The species is circumboreal in distribution and in North America ventures south to Virginia, North Carolina, Tennessee, and Iowa.

FLOWER SEASON: April–June.

COMMENTS: Cowslip is a splendid plant, flowering early and freely in shallow water or marshy soil.

Sparganium americanum   Bur Reed
Sparganiaceae   Bur Reed Family

DESCRIPTION: Bur Reed is an upright, emergent aquatic with long linear leaves that are triangular at the base. The inflorescence is branched, with round, spiky groups of flowers; the plants form colonies by means of shallow rhizomes (Fig. 11-18).

CULTURE: Easily grown in ordinary garden soil covered by 1–2 in. of water. If not confined by a container, it can become rampant.

HABITAT AND RANGE: Bur Reed is native to wet shores, ponds, swamps, and streams in shallow water from Quebec to Minnesota south to Florida and Texas.

SEASON: Summer and fall.

COMMENTS: The round clusters of flowers and fruit, combined with its long, linear leaves, give Bur Reed an unique appearance.

Typha angustifolia   Narrow Leaf Cattail
Typhaceae   Cattail Family

DESCRIPTION: Cattails are perennials from creeping rootstocks with long, narrow leaves that are convex on the back. The flowers are tightly packed into brown, hotdog-like clusters.

CULTURE: Container planting is necessary to curb the invasive tendencies of this species and encourage early production of flowering stems. Plant in 4–6 in. of water.

HABITAT AND RANGE: The Narrow Leaf Cattail grows in marshes throughout the eastern half of the continent but is more common near the coast.

FLOWER SEASON: Summer and fall.

RELATED SPECIES: *Typha latifolia*, the Common Cattail (Fig. 11-19), and *T. domingensis* are both robust, so not recommended for water gardening.

COMMENTS: *Typha angustifolia* reaches 6 ft. in height and is the most graceful of the native Cattails. It should be used sparingly in larger pools. All Cattails self-sow and can become weedy.

MOISTURE LOVING PLANTS

The species in this section, while enjoying abundant moisture, are more terrestrial than those in preceding groups. A botanist might label them wetland plants. Some require full sunlight, others thrive in the shade. All are perennials and typically propagated by division. They are intended for use in bog gardens or in naturally wet seepage areas, meadows, or similar situations.

Myosotis laxa   Forget-me-not
Boraginaceae   Borage Family

DESCRIPTION: Forget-me-not is a delicate, short-lived perennial with light green, oblong leaves. The stems are 4–18 in. long, often floating out from the shore over the water; the pale blue flowers have yellow eyes.

CULTURE: Readily grown in wet soil in the Northeast where it can be aggressive, taking over an entire bog garden. Not recommended for southern gardens.

HABITAT AND RANGE: Occurs naturally in wet soils and shallow waters from Newfoundland and Ontario south to the mountains of North Carolina and Tennessee.

FLOWER SEASON: May–September.

COMMENTS: Use in drifts in wet soil or along creek banks. It is not known how Forget-me-nots obtained their name but one legend suggests that these were the last words of a gallant gentleman who drowned while crossing a stream to gather a bouquet of these sky-blue flowers for his lady love.

Carex glaucescens   Glaucous Carex
Cyperaceae   Sedge Family

DESCRIPTION: *Carex glaucescens* is an erect, stout, waxy-blue, clump-forming perennial, 2–4 ft. tall. The spikes of the pistillate flowers are 1–2 in. long, gracefully drooping.

CULTURE: Grow this sedge in acid, wet soil in full sun.

HABITAT AND RANGE: Native to swamps and pond margins chiefly of the Coastal Plain from Maryland to Texas and inland to central Tennessee.

FLOWER SEASON: Summer and fall.

COMMENTS: *Carex glaucescens* contributes an appealing texture to the bog garden and, unlike so many over-used exotic species, provides something different.

Dichromena latifolia   Giant Sedge, Giant White Topped Sedge
Cyperaceae   Sedge Family

DESCRIPTION: Giant Sedge is a rhizomatous perennial bearing solitary stems with narrow, grass-like blades. The stem is terminated by a cluster of spikelets; the principal bracts subtending the spikelets are leaf-like and conspicously white, with green tips. Viewed from afar, the plants appear to be some sort of lily.

CULTURE: Grow in acid, wet bogs in full sunlight.

HABITAT AND RANGE: Giant Sedge inhabits sandy-peaty bog soils of the Coastal Plain from Virginia to Texas.

SEASON: Summer.

RELATED SPECIES: *Dichromena colorata* is similar but not as showy as *D. latifolia.*

COMMENTS: This is a striking species for the acid bog garden. Most members of the Cyperaceae family are wind pollinated, but the evolutionary trend to wind pollination has been reversed in *Dichromena* as it is insect pollinated. The drooping, pure white bracts assist in attracting a large number of insect pollinators.

Scirpus cyperinus — Bullrush
Cyperaceae — Sedge Family

DESCRIPTION: Bullrush is a coarse, perennial, clump-forming herb, 3–6 ft. tall, with an erect stem that is leafy up to the flower cluster. The flower cluster is made up of drooping branches, 6 in. long, supporting numerous brown spikelets (Fig. 11-20).

CULTURE: A tolerant species as long as it is grown in moist to wet soil in full sun.

HABITAT AND RANGE: The Bullrush is common in wet soil of marshes, swamps, and pond margins from Newfoundland to Saskatchewan south to Florida and Texas.

FLOWER SEASON: Summer and fall.

COMMENTS: The brownish clusters of spikelets make this an interesting and attractive plant for the edge of ponds or for the bog garden.

Eriocaulon compressum — Pipewort
Eriocaulaceae — Pipewort Family

DESCRIPTION: Pipewort is a rosette-forming herb reproducing by offshoots or leafy stolons. The 8–18 in. tall. flower stalks are terminated by chalk-white, globose heads resembling ladies' hat pins.

CULTURE: Grow Pipewort in bogs in wet, acid sand to which peat moss has been added.

HABITAT AND RANGE: The Pipewort can be found in wet, sandy-peaty, acid soils of the Coastal Plain from New Jersey to Texas.

FLOWER SEASON: The flowers are produced in the spring with the heads remaining throughout the summer.

RELATED SPECIES: *Eriocaulon decangulare* flowers in the summer and fall, resembling *E. compressum* but more robust. Several other species of *Eriocaulon* occur in the Southeast but these two are the showiest.

COMMENTS: This conspicuous Pipewort clothes wet pinelands in a white carpet where it is abundant.

Leersia oryzoides — Rice Cut Grass
Gramineae or Poaceae — Grass Family

DESCRIPTION: Rice Cut Grass is a rhizomatous, perennial grass, 2–4 ft. tall, with flat, light green leaves. Its spikelets are borne on short pedicels in small, spike-like racemes. The rough edges of the leaf blades can cut or tear if handled incautiously.

CULTURE: Rice Cut Grass is tolerant if grown in full sun to light shade in wet soil.

It is a vigorous grower, so must be allowed adequate room.

HABITAT AND RANGE: Common in wet places along ponds and streams in much of eastern North America.

FLOWER SEASON: Summer and fall.

RELATED SPECIES: *Leersia hexandra*, *L. lenticularis* and *L. virginica* are similar in appearance and habit of growth to *L. oryzoides*.

COMMENTS: The panicles of the spikelets are pleasing and the foliage is in strong contrast to other bog plants.

Juncus effusus — Soft Rush
Juncaceae — Rush Family

DESCRIPTION: *Juncus effusus* has soft stems arising from scaly rhizomes. The plants form large, bright green tussocks of stems 2–3 ft. high. The leaves are brownish, basally sheathing the stems. The main inflorescence bract is erect, extending much beyond the lateral, brownish fruiting cluster (Fig. 11-21).

CULTURE: Easily grown in any moist soil in full sunlight to partial shade. They can be propagated by division or by direct seeding.

HABITAT AND RANGE: The Soft Rush is common throughout eastern North America, growing in wet soil about waters.

FLOWER SEASON: Flowers in spring but the fruit remains over the summer.

COMMENTS: The species of *Juncus* are difficult to identify. They can be collected from the wild, posing no conservation problems. Select interesting species and add them to the bog garden. The green stems provide unusual textures. They can be planted in sunny flood plains within developed areas. The plants hold the soil in place, provide an attractive scene, and at the same time allow natural flooding to occur with no damage to the developed landscape.

Helonias bullata — Swamp Pink
Liliaceae — Lily Family

DESCRIPTION: The Swamp Pink is perennial from a short rhizome, with a cluster of long, basal leaves and a hollow scape, 1–3 ft. tall, bearing a dense, terminal, spike-like raceme of pink flowers.

CULTURE: Grow Swamp Pink in strongly acid, pH 4.5–5, humus-rich bogs.

HABITAT AND RANGE: Found in swamps and bogs of the Coastal Plain from New York into Virginia, and along the mountains into northern Georgia.

FLOWER SEASON: April–May.

COMMENTS: A splendid plant for the small bog garden with strikingly handsome, pink flowers in the spring. Best grown in the North; use it only at high elevations in the South.

Decodon verticillatus — Water Willow, Swamp Loosestrife
Lythraceae — Loosestrife Family

DESCRIPTION: Easily recognized, the Water Willow is a shrubby perennial, with long, arching, leafy stems, often rooting at the tips. Its lance-shaped leaves are opposite or in whorls of 3–4. The bell-shaped, pink-purple flowers are in dense clusters in the upper leaf axils.

CULTURE: The Water Willow is easy to grow in moist soil at the edge of ponds and streams. The self-rooting tips of the branches can be removed and transplanted to the bog garden or to the edge of a pond or stream.

HABITAT AND RANGE: Found inhabiting swamps, swamp clearings, and pond edges from Nova Scotia to Ontario and Minnesota south to Florida and Texas.

SEASON: July–September.

RELATED SPECIES: *Lythrum salicaria*, Purple Loosestrife, is a member of the Lythraceae family. This introduced species with tall, magenta-colored spikes has become a noxious weed along stream banks and around ponds in the North, choking out many interesting native species. Purple Loosestrife is so aggressive that it should never be planted.

COMMENTS: The appealing flowers and the handsome arching branches make *Decodon verticillatus* a stunning addition to any wet bog garden or water-side situation. It is a large plant so not suitable for the small garden.

Hibiscus coccineus	Wild Red Mallow
Malvaceae	Mallow Family

DESCRIPTION: *Hibiscus coccineus* is a glabrous mallow, with deeply palmately divided leaves, about 4–7 ft. tall. The flowers are deep scarlet and over 6 in. broad.

CULTURE: Easily grown from seeds collected in the wild; the plants need wet soil and full sun to thrive.

HABITAT AND RANGE: An inhabitant of swamps, marshes and ditches, sometimes in standing water, of the Coastal Plain of Georgia, Alabama and Florida.

FLOWER SEASON: July–September.

RELATED SPECIES: The native species of *Hibiscus* have garden value; those suitable for marshy places include:

H. militaris, Smooth Marsh Mallow. Flowers pinkish with purple centers.

H. lasiocarpus, Woolly Mallow. Flowers white or pink, with dark centers.

H. grandiflorus, Large Flowered Mallow. Flowers white, with pink, purple, or red centers.

H. moscheutos, Rose Mallow. Flowers creamy white with dark centers (Fig. 11-22).

H. palustris, Rose Mallow. Flowers pink to white with dark centers.

COMMENTS: The clumps of *Hibiscus* start to grow late in the season, flowering over a long period in late summer. The plants make sizable clumps and are long-lived. Many nurseries are now offering small plants of several of the species listed here.

Rhexia virginica	Meadow Beauty
Melastomataceae	Melastome Family

DESCRIPTION: Meadow Beauty rises from spongy, tuber-like rootstocks forming a plant about 2 ft. high. The stems are erect, rigid, 4-angled, and usually winged. The flowers have 4 large, rose-red petals that typically fall at mid-day. The filaments of the stamens are bent like an elbow and the ripened ovary is vase-shaped.

CULTURE: Divisions are readily transplanted into a sunny bog with a wet, acid, sandy-peaty soil; seed can be scattered in the bog garden as the plants are not aggressive.

HABITAT AND RANGE: Found on the shores of ponds, bogs and wet ditches from Nova Scotia to Wisconsin south to Florida and Texas.

FLOWER SEASON: Summer.

RELATED SPECIES: There are several other species of *Rhexia* in eastern North America but none as striking as *R. virginica*.

COMMENTS: A valuable addition to the small bog garden, providing a bright display of rose-red flowers over a long period in mid-summer.

Spiranthes cernua var. *odorata* — Fragrant Ladies' Tresses
Orchidaceae — Orchid Family

DESCRIPTION: This stoloniferous plant consists of a single stem, 1 ft. tall, with a basal cluster of narrow, grass-like leaves. The stem holds a dense, strongly spiraled cluster of usually fragrant, small, white flowers.

CULTURE: Transplant Fragrant Ladies' Tresses into very wet, muddy soil in partial shade. It forms stoloniferous colonies under favorable conditions.

HABITAT AND RANGE: Found in wooded swamps of the southeastern Coastal Plain and inland in the Tennessee Valley region.

FLOWER SEASON: August–October.

COMMENTS: This is an inviting plant for the bog garden. The generic name is derived from the spiral arrangement of the flowers.

Lysimachia terrestris — Swamp Candles
Primulaceae — Primrose Family

DESCRIPTION: Swamp Candles is an erect plant, 2–3 ft. tall. It has narrow, opposite leaves and long spires of small, yellow petals, the 5 petals marked with purple lines (Fig. 11-23).

CULTURE: Readily transplanted to wet, moderately acid soil in full sun. It has a tendency to spread aggressively and form large colonies.

HABITAT AND RANGE: Found in swamps and wet soil at the edge of ponds from Newfoundland west to Manitoba south along the mountains to Tennessee and North Carolina.

FLOWER SEASON: June–August.

COMMENTS: When planted in masses, *Lysimachia terrestris* produces an array of yellow candle-like flower clusters in sunny wetlands. This is a plant of cooler regions, not one for the South.

Ranunculus septentrionalis — Swamp Buttercup
Ranunculaceae — Crowfoot Family

DESCRIPTION: Swamp Buttercup becomes stoloniferous after flowering; the first stems are erect, the later ones repent. Its leaf blades have three leaflets, each leaflet 3-lobed. The deep yellow flowers are 1 in. across.

CULTURE: Swamp Buttercup self-sows and increases by its stolons. Grow it in masses in lightly shaded wet woodlands or in wet meadows. It is tolerant of most situations as long as moisture is available.

HABITAT AND RANGE: Found in wet woodlands from Newfoundland to North Dakota south to Florida and Texas.

FLOWER SEASON: March–June.

COMMENTS: Swamp Buttercup tends to be weedy but can be useful when confined to low, wet sites in a naturalistic planting. A good species for a wet floodplain.

Sarracenia flava — Trumpet-leaf, Trumpets
Sarraceniaceae — Pitcher Plant Family

DESCRIPTION: *Sarracenia flava* is an insectivorous, perennial herb, with slender, hollow, erect, pitcher-shaped leaves and large, nodding flowers. The pitchers are yellowish green to purple, filled with water and decaying insects; the petals are yellow to greenish.

CULTURE: Grow *Sarracenia flava* in full sunlight, in a wet, acid bog. Growth is encouraged by a late winter burn as its native habitat is one of frequent fires. To conserve the species, collect the seeds in September, mix them with moist peat moss, and store for 2 months at 40°F prior to planting in a peat-lite soil mixture in a warm greenhouse; the seeds germinate readily in this way. Seedlings are transplanted from the seed flats to the bog after a couple of years. Work of the senior author in the reestablishment of the endangered *Sarracenia oreophila*, the Green Pitcher Plant, in northern Alabama has shown that fall is the best season for transplanting in the Southeast.

HABITAT AND RANGE: An inhabitant of sandy, acid bogs and pine flatwoods of the Coastal Plain from southeastern Virginia to southeastern Mississippi.

FLOWER SEASON: April.

RELATED SPECIES: All species of *Sarracenia* add interest to the sunny bog garden, including:

S. purpurea, Pitcher Plant. Leaves in a low, evergreen, basal rosette, green variegated with purple; a northern species, all others listed here are southeastern (Fig. 11-24).

S. psittacina, Parrot Pitcher Plant. Leaves in a low, evergreen, basal rosette, variegated with white spots and purple veins.

S. leucophylla, White Trumpet. Leaves erect, the upper part expanded, white, and reticulate with purple.

S. minor, Hooded Pitcher Plant. Leaves erect, variegated near the top with green and purple veins and white or yellow blotches; a prominent hood over the opening of the pitcher (Fig. 11-25).

S. rubra, Sweet Pitcher Plant. Leaves erect, green with red veinings.

COMMENTS: Hybrids are easily made among the species, resulting in many interesting combinations of colors and types of pitchers. They can be grown out-of-doors successfully north of their natural range. Pitcher plants are insectivorous and desirable for this habit and for their unusual flowers and leaves. *Sarracenia oreophila* is on the Federal List of Endangered Species and should not be molested.

Saururus cernuus   Lizard's Tail
Saururaceae   Lizard's Tail Family

DESCRIPTION: Lizard's Tail is an erect perennial from a rhizome and bears broadly to narrowly heart-shaped leaves on an 18–24-in. stem. Its showy, white flowes are borne tightly clustered together on long, nodding spikes (Fig. 11-26).

CULTURE: Readily grown in light shade in wet soil where it forms large colonies. It should be confined in a container to prevent it from spreading.

HABITAT AND RANGE: Lizard's Tail is a plant of shallow water or quite wet soils from New England to Minnesota south to Florida and Texas.

FLOWER SEASON: Summer.

COMMENTS: The nodding, white spikes are eye-catching and Lizard's Tail has the advantage of being shade tolerant.

167

Parnassia asarifolia   Grass of Parnassus
Saxifragaceae   Saxifrage Family

DESCRIPTION: Grass of Parnassus has a basal cluster of evergreen leaves with kidney-shaped blades.The solitary, white flowers are on stems 6–12 in. tall each bearing a single leaf; the petals are delicately veined with bluish green (Fig. 11-27).

CULTURE: *Parnassia asarifolia* must be grown in permanently wet, acid soil of seepage areas or springs, or along small water courses in light or partial shade.

HABITAT AND RANGE: Found about spring heads or along small stream branches from Virginia and West Virginia to Georgia, Tennessee, and Alabama.

FLOWER SEASON: August–October.

RELATED SPECIES: *Parnassia glauca* is northern in distribution and has subcordate to obtuse leaf bases; it must be grown on neutral to basic, wet soils in full sun.

COMMENTS: Grass of Parnassus flowers late in the season when most other species have already bloomed, thus adding late season interest. Plant it where the flow of a cool spring enters the bog garden; its clean, white flowers and glossy leaves thus brighten an otherwise dim spot.

Mimulus alatus   Monkey Flower
Scrophulariaceae   Figwort Family

DESCRIPTION: *Mimulus alatus* has stems 2–3 ft. tall, with thin-winged angles. The opposite, toothed leaves are petioled. It bears solitary, violet-blue flowers on short stalks in the axils of the upper leaves. The two-lipped corolla resembles a monkey's face, hence the common name.

CULTURE: Grow in slightly acid, pH 6–6.5, moist soil in full sun or very light shade.

HABITAT AND RANGE: Native in wet woods and along creek banks and lake shores from Connecticut and Ontario to Michigan south to Florida and Texas.

FLOWER SEASON: June–October.

RELATED SPECIES: *Mimulus ringens* is very similar but has sessile leaves.

COMMENTS: Monkey Flower is recommended for stream-side or bog-side plantings in the wild garden.

Xyris caroliniana   Yellow-eyed Grass
Xyridaceae   Yellow-eyed Grass Family

DESCRIPTION: A perennial herb, with basal, grass-like leaves and a leafless scape 2–3 ft. tall bearing a cone-like spike with yellow flowers rising from between the scales. The yellow flowers appear in the afternoon.

CULTURE: Grow Yellow-eyed Grass in an acid, pH 4.5–5, sandy bog in full sun.

HABITAT AND RANGE: Found on wet sands of the Coastal Plain from New Jersey to Texas.

FLOWER SEASON: Summer.

RELATED SPECIES: The species of *Xyris* are difficult to distinguish; however, any of the larger ones are worthwile in a sunny bog garden including: *X. ambigua, X. difformis, X. fimbriata. X. iridifolia, X. platylepis,* and *X. torta.*

COMMENTS: The distinctive, cone-like spikes with beautiful, yellow flowers make *Xyris* a pleasing species for the bog garden.

Glossary

Acuminate: tapering gradually to a prolonged point.

Acute: ending in a distinct point, but not extended.

Adventitious: term applied to a bud developing elsewhere than at a node of a stem or root.

Alternate leaf arrangement: having one leaf at each node.

Annual: a plant that lives for one growing season, then dies.

Anther: the part of the stamen where pollen is produced.

Asexual propagation: increasing plants without sexual union of gametes; includes producing additional plants by grafts, cuttings, division, tissue culture, etc.

Aquatic plants: plants which grow in or on the water or are emergent along the shoreline.

Auriculate: having ear-like appendages or lobes.

Axil: the upper angle formed between the main stem and any plant part that arises from the stem.

Axillary: situated in the axil.

Basal: leaves located at ground level.

Berry: a soft and fleshy fruit, e.g., tomato, grape.

Biennial: a plant requiring two growing seasons to complete the life cycle of two years' duration.

Binomial system of nomenclature: the system used to name plants whereby the botanical name consists of two words, the generic name and the specific epithet. See scientific name.

Biternately compound: a leaf twice-compound and divided into 3 parts each time.

Blade: the expanded, flattened part of a leaf.

Bract: a reduced or highly modified leaf often found around flower clusters or subtending a flower.

Bud: an immature stem tip; an embryonic shoot.

Bulb: a short basal underground stem surrounded by thick, fleshy leaves, e.g., an onion.

Calcareous rocks: rocks containing some calcium carbonate.

Calyx: all of the sepals; the calyx occupies the outermost position on the flower (outside the petals) and is usually green.

Capsule: a fruit from a compound ovary that splits when mature.

Caudex: the hard, overwintering base of an herbaceous perennial.

Circumboreal: found at high latitudes around the world.

Climax: the stable community which is the end product of plant succession; a plant community capable of regenerating and maintaining itself.

Cold frame: an outdoor box covered with glass and heated by the sun in winter; often covered with lath or shade cloth in summer; used for plant propagation.

Collected: as used in this book, plants gathered from natural populations in the wild for sale or use in a garden. See nursery propagated.

Competition: the interaction of adjacent plants for available light, moisture, and nutrients.

Compound leaf: a leaf whose blade is divided into smaller, blade-like parts called leaflets.

Conservation: the perpetuation and enhancement of our native flora by wise management of critical habitats, including essential stages of plant succession from bare soil to climax wilderness.

Cordate: heart-shaped with a broad notch.

Corm: a short, upright, hard or fleshy bulb-like stem; usually covered with thin, papery, dry leaves.

Corolla: the inner whorl of the perianth located inside the calyx next to the stamens; the collection of petals.

Cultivar: distinct plant forms produced in cultivation by hybridization, selection or other processes; not to be confused with the taxonomic category of variety; derived from the words cultivated and variety.

Cuneate: wedge-shaped, tapering toward the point of attachment.

Cuttings: propagation of plants by inducing new growth from pieces of roots or shoots.

Decurrent: a term applied to a leaf when part of the leaf extends in a ridge down the stem below the node.

Dichotomous: branching by repeated forking in pairs.

Dimorphic: of two forms; applied to those ferns in which the sterile and fertile fronds differ in appearance.

Direct seeded flowers: a planting by direct seeding to produce a scene with a preponderance of colorful blossoms; not a meadow or prairie in the true sense.

Disk flower: one of many central flowers in the head of a member of the Compositae (Asteraceae), composed of 5 petals united into a tube.

Division: propagation of herbaceous perennials by cutting, separating, and planting portions to increase their numbers.

Dolomitic limestone: a carbonate rock composed predominately of dolomite; a term usually restricted to any limestone containing 15% or more magnesium; when used for soil applications the rock is ground.

Dolostone: a sedimentary rock composed of fragmented, concretionary, or precipitated dolomite; calcium magnesium carbonate.

Double digging: an English method of deep digging to a depth of 18–30 in. of soil; often used in perennial culture.

Doubly serrate: with small serrations on the larger serrations; refers to leaf margins.

Drift: a naturalistic aggregation or colony of a species typically dense near the center and thinning toward the edges.

Ecotype: a genetically adapted ecological race of a species.

Edaphic conditions: describing the features of the soil.

Elliptical: having the shape of a flattened circle.

Endemic: a species found only in a restricted geographic area or ecological habitat.

Evergreen: a plant with leaves remaining green over winter.

Exotic: a species which has been brought into an area; a non-native.

Family: taxonomically, an aggregation of related genera providing a biologically meaningful unit.

Filament: part of the stamen; the stalk-like structure supporting the anthers.

Flora: the plant life of a region; or an identification manual of plants of a given area;

a check list of plants of a region.

Flower: a highly modified shoot with specialized appendages typically including sepals, petals, stamens and pistil.

Frond: the leaf of ferns; the plant body of duckweeds.

Fruit: matured ovary or ovaries containing seed.

Garden value: the overall value of a plant in a garden setting, including its floral display, leaves, form, fall color and stem characteristics.

Genus: taxonomically, an inclusive category whose species have more characteristics in common with each other than with species of other genera of the same family; an aggregation of closely related species.

Glabrous: without pubescence (hairs) of any kind; smooth.

Glade: a treeless area in a normally wooded forest zone, usually with very thin soil over rock; e.g., the cedar glades of central Tennessee.

Glaucous: having a waxy appearance; coated with wax.

Grasses: members of the Gramineae (Poaceae) with highly reduced floral structures appearing as tiny bracts and having "grains" as fruit.

Groundcover: a grouping of low-growing plants used to cover bare ground in a landscape setting.

Hardpan: a layer of hard, often impermeable, compacted, or cemented soil that develops below the normal tillage zone in a garden or cultivated field.

Hastate: arrowhead-shaped.

Head: a dense cluster of stalkless flowers, e.g., a sunflower; members of the Compositae (Asteraceae) have flowers arranged in heads.

Herbaceous: not woody; dying to the ground at the end of the growing season.

Herbaceous perennial: a non-woody plant which typically lives for several years but dies back to the ground each fall and reappears the following spring from overwintering buds on rhizomes or rootstocks; in horticulture, usually called a perennial.

Herbicide: a chemical used to kill or prevent the growth of plants.

Humus: partially decomposed organic material, e.g., peat moss.

Inflorescence: the arrangement of flowers on the stalk; a flower cluster.

Internode: that part of the stem between two successive nodes.

Invasive: aggressively weedy; a plant spreading into other plants.

Island beds: perennial beds surrounded by mowed lawn grass; beds that can be viewed from all sides.

Lanceolate: lance-shaped, tapering from a broad base to the apex.

Leaves: generally broad, flattened, and photosynthetic structures, borne at the nodes of a stem, each consisting of a blade, petiole, and often a stipule.

Leaflets: the parts of a compound leaf.

Linear: long and narrow, with parallel sides.

Loam: soil with good structural properties consisting of more or less equal parts of clay and sand.

Lobed: a leaf blade divided into parts with rounded sinuses extending one-third to one half the distance between margin and leaf blade.

Meadow: land predominately in grass but with some herbaceous, perennial, wild flowers.

Micorrhizal fungus: a fungus intimately associated with the roots of a higher plant.

Microhabitats: small areas which differ in temperature, light, moisture, or other environmental factors from those typical in the general area or within a garden.

Native: as used in this book, a species growing naturally in eastern North America prior to the arrival of European settlers.

Naturalized: a non-native species introduced to an area which has become established and reproduces in the wild, e.g., *Daucus carota*.

Node: the area of a stem where a leaf and bud are borne.

Nomenclature: the system by which names are assigned to plants.

Noxious weed: plants legally determined to threaten human health or agricultural operations.

Nursery propagated: plants multiplied in a nursery and not collected from wild habitats. Use of nursery propagated plants conserves natural populations.

Nutrients: basic chemical elements required by plants for proper growth and development.

Offset: small plantlets formed around the rootstock of an herbaceous perennial.

Opposite leaf arrangement: having two leaves, one on either side of the stem, at each node.

Orbicular: flat with a circular outline.

Ovary: the usually enlarged, basal part of the pistil where the ovules are borne; the ovary develops into the fruit.

Ovate: egg-shaped, with the broadest part toward the base.

Palmately divided: a leaf with its divisions diverging from one common point like fingers from the palm of the hand.

Palmate venation: the main veins of a leaf radiate from the point where they join the petiole.

Parallel venation: primary veins of a leaf blade occur side by side without intersecting; typical of many, but not all, monocotyledons.

Panicle: a highly branched flower cluster.

Pedicel: the stalk of an individual flower in a flower cluster.

Peduncle: the stalk supporting the entire flower cluster or a solitary flower.

Peltate: attachment of the petiole to the lower surface of the blade rather than the margin.

Perennial: as used in horticulture, a herbaceous, flowering plant which dies back in winter but continues to live for several seasons.

Perennial border: a traditional planting of perennials in a long, narrow bed against a background of hedge, woods, wall, or walkway.

Perfoliate: opposite leaves with bases united around the stem so the stem appears to pass through the leaves.

Perianth: collective term for the floral envelope, i.e., the calyx and corolla.

Petals: individual parts of a corolla, usually giving the flower its color and form.

Petiole: the supporting stalk of a leaf.

Pinnae, (singular, pinna): the leaflets or primary divisions, of a pinnately compound fern frond.

Pinnate venation: a leaf blade having one central vein with lateral veins arising along its length and at angles from it.

Pinnatifid: cleft or divided in a pinnate manner.

Pinnules: the ultimate segments or divisions of a twice-or thrice- pinnately compound fern frond.

Pistil: the innermost part of a flower, usually divided into stigma, style and ovary; the female organ of a flower.

Pistillate: having pistils but no stamens.

Plant community: an association or group of species within a particular habitat, e.g., a beech/maple forest.

Prairie: an area dominated by grasses and deep-rooted, perennial wild flowers.

Propagule: a portion of a plant that may be used to increase or propagate the plant.

Pubescent: covered with short, soft hairs.

Raceme: a flower cluster with a single axis, the flowers on pedicels.

Ray flower: a flower of the Compositae (Asteraceae) with a strap-shaped, elongated corolla of united petals; often located at the margin of a head.

Receptacle: the portion of the stem bearing the flower parts.

Reniform: kidney-shaped.

Restoration: reestablishment of plant communities typical of a regional landscape and flora.

Rhizome: a horizontal underground stem bearing nodes and buds.

Rock garden: a garden developed in and upon a natural or artificial rock outcrop.

Roots: descending axis of the plant without nodes or internodes or regularly spaced buds and leaves, usually underground, branching irregularly; may produce adventitious buds, e.g., sweet potato.

Rootstock: the underground portion of a plant; often referring to a caudex or a rhizome.

Rosette: a cluster of spreading or radiating basal leaves.

Runner: a horizontal, above-ground stem, usually rooting and producing plants at the nodes, e. g., strawberry; see stolon.

Rushes: grass-like plants of the Juncaceae, having round stems and numerous, fine seeds in a capsule.

Scabrous: rough to the touch.

Scape: a leafless, flowering stem.

Scarification: a mechanical or chemical treatment to break down or soften a hard seed coat to promote germination.

Scientific name: plant name consisting of a generic name followed by a specific epithet. e.g., *Mertensia virginica*. The generic name is capitalized; the specific epithet is in lower case. The scientific name is italicized.

Sedges: grass-like plants, members of the family Cyperaceae, typically with stems triangular in cross-section (three-angled) and lens-shaped or triangular nutlets as fruit.

Seed: a mature ovule containing an embryo.

Self-sow: the dropping of seeds by parent plants to give rise to progeny.

Sepals: individual components of the calyx; the outermost whorl of the flower, often green but may be colored and petaloid.

Septate: divided by partitions.

Sexual propagation: production of offspring by the union of gametes; production of additional plants by means of seed.

Serrate: having marginal teeth on a leaf, usually pointed toward the apex.

Sessile: a leaf without a petiole.

Simple leaf: a leaf with an undivided blade.

Slow release fertilizer: a chemical fertilizer designed to slowly release nutrients over time in contrast to standard commercial fertilizers which release nutrients relatively rapidly.

Sod: transplanting an intact section of soil and plant. Used for species that are difficult to transplant.

173

Soil pH: a scale of 0–14 used to describe soil acidity or alkalinity; seven is neutral, below seven is acid, and above, alkaline. The scale is logarithmic, so a pH of 6 is 10 times more acid, and a pH of 5 is 100 times more acid than a pH of 7.

Sori (singular, sorus): clusters of sporangia often appearing as a series of regularly spaced dots on the back of fern fronds.

Species name: see scientific name.

Spadix: a thick or fleshy, spike-like flower cluster with very small flowers often densely massed together and enclosed in a spathe.

Spathe: an enlarged bract enclosing a flower cluster, e.g., Jack-in-the-Pulpit.

Species: taxonomically, a group of plants fundamentally alike; ideally a species should be separated by distinct morphological differences from other closely related species.

Spike: a flower cluster with a single axis and sessile flowers (without pedicels).

Spikelet: a unit of a grass flower cluster consisting of two glumes and one or more flowers; a unit of the flower cluster of sedges.

Sporangia (singular, sporangium): the structure in which spores are produced.

Spores: single-celled reproductive structures of the ferns and fern allies.

Sporophyte: the spore-producing stage of a fern plant.

Stamen: the pollen-producing part of a flower, located just inside the corolla and typically composed of an anther and filament; the male organ of a flower.

Staminate: having stamens but no pistil.

Stems: the main axis of plants, having regularly spaced nodes and internodes. Many stems are highly specialized, particularly those underground which function as storage or overwintering mechanisms.

Stigma: that portion of the pistil receptive to pollen grains.

Stolon: a horizontal stem rooting at the nodes; a runner.

Stratification: seed storage in moist conditions at refrigerator temperatures or in alternating warm/moist and cool/moist conditions to promote germination.

Style: part of the pistil; the elongated stalk connecting the stigma and ovary.

Succession: an orderly progression of plant communities leading to a climax community.

Talus: a pile of rock fragments forming a slope at the foot of a steeper declivity.

Thyrse: a compound, compact panicle.

Trifoliate: a compound leaf with three leaflets.

Tuber: an enlarged, fleshy tip of an underground stem, e.g., Irish potato.

Tunicated: composed of concentric coats, e.g., onion bulb.

Umbel: a flower cluster of few to many flowers on pedicels of nearly equal length arising from the top of a peduncle.

Vascular plants: plants with specialized tissues that conduct water and nutrients.

Venation: the positioning of veins (vascular bundles) in a leaf blade.

Weed: an undesirable plant; a plant growing in the wrong place.

Wetland plants: plants growing in marshes, bogs, or other situations where water stands at or close to the surface.

Whorled: having three or more leaves or flowers at one node.

Wild flower: as used in this book, a native, herbaceous, perennial flowering plant.

Winter annual: a plant that germinates in the fall, overwinters, flowers and produces seed the following year, then dies.

Woodland garden: a garden developed in a shady, woodsy setting.

Commercial Sources
of Native Herbaceous Seeds and Plants*

Applewood Seed Company, 5380 Vivian Street, Arvada, CO 80002. [seed]
Bamert Seed Co., Rt. 3, Box 192, Muleshoe, TX 79347. [seed]
Beersheba Wildflower Gardens, Beersheba Springs, TN 37305. [plants]
Boehlke's Woodland Gardens, West 140 North 10829 Country Aire Road, Germantown, WI 53022. [plants]
Botanic Garden Seed Co., Inc., 9 Wyckoff Street, Brooklyn, NY 11201. [seed]
Bullbay Creek Farm, Rt. 2, Box 381, Tallahassee, FL 32301. [plants]
Burpee Seeds, 300 Park Ave. Warminster, PA 18991. [seed]
Clyde Robin Seed Co., P.O. Box 2855, Castro Yalley, CA 94546. [seed]
Cory's Wildflower Gardens, 1461 Valley Drive, Chillicothe, OH 45601. [plants]
Crownsville Nursery, 1241 Generals Highway, Crownsville, MD 21032. [plants]
Daystar, Rt. 2, Box 250, Litchfield, ME 04350. [plants]
Eco-Gardens, P.O. Box 1227, Decatur, GA 30031. [plants]
Environmental Seed producers, P.O. Box 5904, El Monte, CA 91734. [seed]
Fancy Fronds, 1911 4th Ave., W., Seattle, WA 98119. [plants]
Fern Hill Farm, Rt. 3, Box 305, Greenville, AL 36037. [plants]
Garden Place, P.O. Box 388, 6780 Heisley Road, Mentor, OH 44061. [plants]
Gardens of the Blue Ridge, U.S. Highway 221 North, Pineola, NC 28622. [plants]
Glasshouse Works, 10 Church St., Stewart, OH 45778. [plants]
Harris Moran Seed Co., 3670 Buffalo Rd., Rochester, NY 14624. [seed]
Henderson's Botanical Gardens, Rt. 6, Greensburg, IN 47240. [plants]
Hungry Plants, 1216 Cooper Drive, Raleigh, NC 27607. [plants]
Illini Gardens, P.O. Box 125, Oakford, IL 62673. [plants]
Izard Ozark Native Seeds, P.O. Box 454, Mountain View, AR 72560. [seed]
Juniper Edge, Box 223, Harpswell Road, S. Harpswell, ME 04079 [plants]
Lilypons Water Gardens, 6800 Lilypons Rd., P.O. Box 10, Lilypons, MD 21717. [plants]
Lofts, Inc., Chimney Rock Road, Bound Brook, NJ 08805. [seed]
Louisiana Nursery, Rt. 7, Box 43, Opelousas, LA 70570. [plants]
Lounsberry Gardens, P.O. Box 135, Oakford, IL 62673. [plants]
Maver Nursery, Rt. 2, Box 265B, Ashville, NC 28805. [seed]
Midwest Wildflowers, P.O. Box 64, Rockton, IL 61072. [seed]
Moon Mountain Wildflowers, P.O. Box 34, Morro Bay, CA 93442. [seed]
Native Gardens, Columbine Farm, Rt. 1, Box 494, Greenback, TN 37742. [plants]
Native Plants, Inc., P.O. Box 177, Leigh, UT 84043. [seed]
Native Seeds, Inc., 114590 Triadelphia Mill Rd., Dayton, MD 21036. [seed]
Natural Gardens, 113 Jasper Lane, Oak Ridge, TN 37830. [plants]
Natural Habitat Nursery, 4818 Terminal Road, McFarland, WI 53558. [seed]
Orchard Gardens, 6700 Splithand Rd., Grand Rapids, MN 55744. [plants]
Owl Ridge Alpines, 5421 Whipple Lake Road, Clarkston, MI 48016. [plants]

*Nurseries frequently charge for price lists of seeds and plants.

L. L. Olds Seed Co., 2901 Packers Ave., P.O. Box 7790, Madison, WI 53707. [seed]

Park Seeds, Highway 254 N., Greenwood, SC 29647. [seed]

Passiflora, Rt. 1, Box 190A, Germantown, NC 27019. [seed, plants]

Piccadilly Farm,. 1917 Whipporwill Rd., Bishop, GA 30621. [plants]

Prairie Moon Nursery, Rt. 3, Box 163, Winona, MN 55987. [seed, plants]

Prairie Nursery, Rt. 1, Box 365, Westfield, WI 53564. [seed, plants]

Prairie Restorations, Inc., P.O. Box 327, Princeton, MN 55371. [seed, plants]

Prairie Ridge Nursery, 9738 Overland Rd., Mt. Horeb, WI 53572. [seed, plants]

Prairie Seed Source, P.O. Box 83, North Lake, WI 53064. [seed]

Primrose Path, Rt. 1, Box 78, Scottdale, PA 15683. [plants]

Putney Nursery, Putney, VT. 05346. [plants]

Rockscapes, Silver Birch Lane, Lincoln, MA 01773. [plants]

S & R Seed Co., Box 86, Cass Lake, MN 56633. [seed]

S & S Seeds, P.O. Box 1275, Carpenteria, CA 93013. [seed]

Stock Seed Farms, Inc., R Rt. 1, Box 112, Murdock, NE 68407. [seeds]

Sunlight Gardens, Inc., Rt. 3, Box 286B, Loudon, TN 37774. [plants]

Sunshine Seed Co. R Rt. 2, Box 176, Wyoming, IL 61491. [seed]

Varga's Nursery, 2631 Pickertown Rd., Warrington, PA 18976. [plants]

Vermont Wildflower Farm, Rt. 7, Box 5, Charlotte, VT 05445. [seed]

Vick's Wildgardens, Conshohocken State Rd., Box 115, Gladwyne, PA 19035. [plants]

André Viette Farm and Nursery, Rt. 1, Box 16, Fishersville, VA 22939. [plants]

We-Do Nurseries, Rt. 5, Box 724, Marion, NC 29801. [plants]

Wehr Nature Center, 9701 W. College Ave., Franklin, WI 53132. [seed]

Weston Nurseries, East Main St., Hopkinton, MA 01748. [plants]

Wicklein's Aquatic Farm and Nursery, 1820 Cromwell Bridge Rd., Baltimore, MD 21234. [plants]

Wildginger Woodlands, P.O. Box 1091, Webster,NY 14580. [plants]

Wildseed, Inc., 16810 Barker Springs, Suite 21B, Houston, TX 77084. [seed]

Windrift Prairie Shop, Rt. 2, Oregon, IL 61061. [seed]

Woodland Acres Nursery, Rt. 2, Crivitz, WI 54114. [plants]

Woodlanders, Inc., 1128 Colleton Ave., Aiken, SC 29801. [plants]

Woodstock Wildflower Nursery, Roseland Park Road, Woodstock, CT 06281. [plants]

Woodstream Nursery, Box 510, Jackson, NJ 08527.

Bibliography

Aiken, G. D. 1968. *Pioneering with Wildflowers*. Prentice-Hall, Englewood Cliffs, NJ.

Art, H. W. 1968. *A Garden of Wildflowers*. Gardenway Publishing. Pownal, VT.

Austin, R. L. 1968. *Wild Gardening*. Simon & Schuster, Inc., New York, NY.

Bailey, L. H. 1935. *The Standard Cyclopedia of Horticulture*. 3 Vols. Macmillan, New York, NY.

Baines, C. 1985. *How to Make a Wildlife Garden*. Elm Tree Books, London.

Birdseye, C. & E. G. Birdseye. 1951. *Growing Woodland Plants*. Oxford University Press, New York, NY.

Bradshaw, A. D., D. A. Goode, & E. Thorp. (Eds). 1986. *Ecology and Design in Landscape*. Blackwell Scientific Publications, Palo Alto, CA.

Brooklyn Botanic Garden. 1982. *Propagation*: Handbook No. 24. Brooklyn, NY.

Brown, E. 1986. *Landscaping with Perennials*. Timber Press, Portland, OR.

Browse, P. M. 1979. *Plant Propagation*. Simon & Schuster, Inc., New York, NY.

Bruce, H. 1976. *How to Grow Wildflowers and Wild Shrubs and Trees in Your Own Garden*. Van Nostrand/Reinhold, New York, NY.

Burke, K. (ed). 1982. *All About Ground Covers*. Ortho Books, San Francisco, CA. [Excellent basic reference on ground covers.]

Burke, K. (ed). *Shade Gardening*. Ortho Books, San Francisco, CA. [A good summary for the beginning gardener.]

Cobb, B. 1963. *A Field Guide to the Ferns*. Houghton Mifflin Co., Boston, MA.

Crockett, J. U. & O. E. Allen. 1977. *Wildflower Gardening*. Time-Life Books, Alexandria, VA. [Excellent general information.]

Cumming, R. W. & R. E. Lee. 1960. *Contemporary Perennials*. Macmillan, New York, NY.

Curtis, J. T. & H. C. Greene. 1953. The Re-establishment of Prairie in the University of Wisconsin of Arboretum. *Wildflower*. 29:77–78.

Davis, R. H. 1988. The Ferns of F. Gorden Foster. *Horticulture* LXVI(9):14–21.

Dean, B. E., A. Mason, & J. L. Thomas. 1973. *Wild Flowers of Alabama and Adjoining States*. University of Alabama Press, Tuscaloosa, AL.

DeWolf, G. (ed). 1987. *Taylor's Guide to Ground Covers, Vines and Grasses*. Houghton Mifflin, Boston, MA.

Diekelmann, J. & R. Schuster. 1982. *Natural Landscaping*. McGraw-Hill Book Co., New York, NY.

Durand, H. 1923. *Wildflowers and Ferns: In Their Homes and In Our Gardens*. Putnams, New York, NY. [A classic in gardening with wildflowers.]

Eyles, D. E. & J. L. Robertson, Jr. 1976. *A Guide and Key to the Aquatic Plants of the Southeastern United States*. U.S.P.H. Service. P.H. Bulletin 286.

Fassett, N. C. 1940. *A Manual of Aquatic Plants*. McGraw-Hill Book Co., New York, NY.

Foley, D. J. 1961. *Ground Covers*. Chilton Co., Philadelphia, PA.

Foote, L. E. & S. B. Jones. 1989. *Native Shrubs and Woody Vines of the Southeast*. Timber Press, Portland, OR. [Information on landscape use of woody natives for gardens.]

Foster, F. G. 1984. *Ferns to Know and Grow*. Timber Press, Portland, OR. [An excellent book by an author who made ferns his life-time avocation.]

Gilman, A. 1988. Hardy Ferns. *Horticulture* LXVI(10):22–28.

Gleason, H. A. 1952. *New Britton and Brown Illustrated Flora of the Northeastern United States and Adjacent Canada*. New York Botanical Garden, Bronx, NY. [Illustrations and excellent keys.]

Gleason, H. A. & A. Cronquist. 1963. *Manual of Vascular Plants of Northeastern United States and Adjacent Canada*. Van Nostrand/Reinhold Co., New York, NY. [Excellent keys.]

Godfrey, R. K. & J. W. Wooten. 1979. *Aquatic and Wetland Plants of Southeastern United States. Monocotyledons*. University of Georgia Press, Athens, GA.

Godfrey, R. K. & J. W. Wooten. 1981. *Aquatic and Wetland Plants of Southeastern United States. Dicotyledons*. University of Georgia Press, Athens, GA.

Gottehrer, D. 1982. *Natural Landscaping*. McGraw-Hill Book Co., New York, NY.

Gould, T. 1988. Prairie Reborn. *American Nurseryman* 168(5):36–48.

Gupton, O. W and F. C. Swope. 1979. *Wildflowers of the Shenandoah Valley and Blue Ridge Mountains*. University Press of Virginia, Charlottesville, VA.

Harper, P. & F. McGourty. 1985. *Perennials*. H P Books, Tucson, AZ. [Excellent information on growing perennials.]

Hartman, H. T. & D. E. Kester. 1983. *Plant Propagation* 4th ed., Prentice-Hall, Englewood Cliffs, NJ.

Heritage, W. 1973. *Water Gardening*. Hamlyn, London.

Hessey, J. 1964. *Wildflowers to Know and Grow*. Van Nostrand, Princeton, NJ.

Hill, L. & N. Hill. 1988. *Successful Perennial Gardening*. Gardenway Publishing, Pownal, VT.

Hipps, C. B. 1988. Purple Coneflower. *Horticulture* LXVI(8):46–49.

Hoepfner, E. 1987. Meadows. *Harrowsmith* 2(9):80–89.

Horticultural Associates. 1984. *Top-rated Ground Covers*. Golden Press, New York, NY.

Hull, H. S. 1952. *Wild Flowers for Your Garden*. N Barrows & Co., New York, NY.

Hull, H. S. (ed). 1982. *Handbook on Gardening with Wildflowers*. Brooklyn Botanic Garden, Brooklyn, NY. 18(1).

Jones, S. B. & A. E. Luchsinger. 1986. *Plant Systematics*. 2nd ed., McGraw-Hill Book Co., New York, NY. [Information on the classification of plants.]

Justice, W. S. & C. R. Bell. 1968. *Wild Flowers of North Carolina*. University of North Carolina Press, Chapel Hill, NC.

Kaye, R. 1973. *Modern Water Gardening*. Faber and Faber, London.

Kenfield, W. G. 1970. *The Wild Gardener in the Wild Landscape*. Hafner, New York, NY.

Klinas, J. E. & J. A. Cunningham. 1974. *Wildflowers of Eastern North America*. Knopf, New York, NY.

Kruckeberg, A. R. 1982. *Gardening with Native Plants of the Pacific Northwest*. University of Washington Press, Seattle, WA. [Contains good information that can be applied in the eastern United States.]

Loewer, H. P. 1977. *Growing and Decorating with Grasses*. Walker and Co., New York, NY.

Loewer, H. P. 1988. Searching for Wild Flowers. *Amer. Horticulturist*. 67(2):10:13. [Information on several wild flower nurseries].

Luer, C. A. 1975. *The Native Orchids of the United States and Canada excluding Florida*. New York Botanical Garden, Bronx, NY.

McHarg, I. 1971. *Design with Nature*. Natural History Press, Garden City, NY.

McHoy, P. 1986. *Water Gardening*. Blandford Press, Poole, England.

McKinley, M. 1983. *How to Attract Birds*. Ortho Books, San Francisco, CA.

Martin, A. C., H. S. Zim, & A. L. Nelson. 1951. *American Wildlife and Plants*. Dover, New York, NY. [Information on species useful to wildlife.]

Martin, L. C. 1986. *The Wildflower Meadow Book*. East Woods Press, Fast & McMillan Publishers, Charlotte, NC.

Mickel, J. T. 1979. *How to Know the Ferns and Ferns Allies*. Wm. C Brown Co. Publishers, Dubuque, IA. [For identification.]

Miles, B. 1976. *Wildflower Perennials for Your Garden*. Hawthorn Books, New York, NY. [Contains much useful information.]

Montgomery, F. H. 1977. *Seeds and Fruits of Plants of Eastern Canada and Northeastern United States*. U Toronto Press, Toronto, ONT.

Mooney, H. A. & J. A. Drake (Eds.) 1986. *Ecology of Biological Invasions of North America and Hawaii*. Springer-Verlag, New York, NY.

Morrison, D. G. 1975. Restoring the Native Midwestern Landscape. *Landscape Architecture* 65:398–403.

Morrison, D. G. 1979. The Prairie Invades the Backyard. *Landscape Architecture* 69:141–145.

Morrison, D. G. 1988. Designing with Native Plants: Potentials and Challenges. *Wildflower* 1(1):13–18.

Muenscher, W. C. 1944. *Aquatic Plants of the United States*. Comstock Publishing Co., Ithaca, NY.

Mühlberg, H. 1982. *The Complete Guide to Water Plants*. EP Publishing Ltd., London.

Naveh, Z. & A. Lieberman. 1984. *Landscape Ecology, Theory and Application*. Springer-Verlag, New York, NY.

New England Wild Flower Society. 1986. *Cultivation Guide*. Framingham, MA.

New England Wild Flower Society. 1986. *Propagation of Wildflowers*. Framingham, MA.

New England Wild Flower Society. 1987. *Nursery Sources, Native Plants and Wildflowers*. Framingham, MA.

Niering, W. A. & N. C. Olmstead. 1979. *The Audubon Society Field Guide to North American Wildflowers, Eastern Region*. Knopf, New York, NY.

North Carolina Wildflower Preservation Society. 1977. *North Carolina Native Plant Propagation Handbook*. Chapel Hill, NC.

Northington, D. 1988. Wildflower Focus. *Wildflower* 1(1):4–5.

Penn, C. 1982. *Landscaping with Native Plants*. John Blair, Winston-Salem, NC.

Perl, P. 1977. *Ferns*. Time-Life Books, Alexandria, VA.

Perry, F. 1962. *Water Gardens*. Penguin Books, Baltimore, MD.

Perry, F. 1981. *The Water Garden*. Van Nostrand/Reinhold, New York, NY.

Peterson, R. T. & M. McKenny. 1968. *A Field Guide to Wildflowers of Northeastern and Northcentral North America*. Houghton Mifflin, Boston, MA.

Phillips, H. R. 1985. *Growing and Propagating Wild Flowers*. University of North Carolina Press, Chapel Hill, NC.

Radford, A. E., H. E. Ahles & C. R. Bell. 1968. *Manual of the Vascular Flora of the Carolinas*. University of North Carolina Press, Chapel Hill, NC.

Ramsey, G. W. 1988. A comparison of vegetative characteristics of several genera with those of the genus *Cimicifuga* (Ranunculaceae). *Sida* 13:57–63. [Aid in identification of *Actaea*, *Aruncus*, and *Astilbe*.]

179

Rickett, H. W. 1966–1975. *Wild Flowers of the United States*. 6 Vols. McGraw-Hill Book Co., New York, NY [Undoubtedly the best of the wild flower books; not suitable for use in the field due to the size of the volumes.]

Roberts, E. A. & E. Rehmann. 1929. *American Plants for American Gardens*. Macmillan, New York, NY. [A classic in the use of native plants.]

Robinson, P. 1987. *Pool and Waterside Gardening*. Timber Press, Portland, OR. [Probably the best on water gardening.]

Rock, H. W. 1975. *Prairie Propagation Handbook*. Boerner Botanical Gardens, Hales Corners, WI.

Sawyers, C. E. (ed.) *Gardening with Wildflowers & Native Plants*. Brooklyn Botanic Garden Record, Handbook 119(1).

Schenk, G. 1984. *The Complete Shade Gardener*. Houghton Mifflin Co., Boston, MA. [Perhaps the best book on shade gardening.]

Small, H. V. 1966. *Michigan Wildflowers*. Rev. Ed. Cranbrook Institute Science Bulletin, No. 42.

Smyser, C. 1981. *Nature's Design*. Rodale Press, Emmaus, PA.

Snyder, L. H. & J. G. Bruce. 1986. *Field Guide to the Ferns and Other Pteridophytes of Georgia*. University of Georgia Press, Athens, GA.

Soil Conservation Service, *National List of Scientific Plant Names*. 1982. 2 Vols. Washington, DC.

Sperka, M. 1973. *Growing Wildflowers*. Harper & Row Publishers, New York, NY.

Steffek, E. F. 1983. *The New Wild Flowers and How to Grow Them*. Timber Press, Portland, OR.

Stevenson, V. 1985. *The Wild Garden: Making Natural Gardens Using Wild and Native Plants*. Penguin, New York, NY.

Steyermark, J. A. 1963. *Flora of Missouri*. Iowa State University Press, Ames, IA. [Illustrations and distribution maps.]

Sullivan, G. A. & R. H. Dailey. 1981. *Resources on Wildflower Propagation*. National Council of State Garden Clubs. Missouri Botanical Garden, St. Louis, MO.

Swindells, P. 1984. *The Overlook Water Gardener's Handbook*. Overlook Press, Woodstock, NY.

Taylor, K. S. & S. F. Hamblin. 1976. *Handbook of Wildflower Cultivation*. Collier Books, New York, NY. [One of the better books on gardening with wild flowers.]

Tekulsky, M. 1985. *The Butterfly Garden*. Harvard Common Press, Boston, MA.

Tenenbum, F. 1973. *Gardening with Wildflowers*. Ballatine Books, New York, NY.

Thomas, G. S. 1989. *Perennial Garden Plants*. Timber Press, Portland, OR.

Wharton, M. E. & R. W. Barbour. 1971. *A Guide to the Wildflowers and Ferns of Kentucky*. University Press of Kentucky, Lexington, KY.

Wherry, E. T. 1955. The Genus *Phlox*. Morris Arboretum Monographs III, Philadelphia, PA.

Wherry, E. T. 1964. *The Southen Fern Guide*. Doubleday, Garden City, NY. [Line drawings and descriptions.]

Wherry, E. T. 1968. *The Fern Guide*. Doubleday & Co., NY. [Discusses 135 species; all illustrated. Northeastern & midland U.S. & adjacent Canada.]

Wilson, W. H. W. 1984. *Landscaping with Wildflowers and Native Plants*. Ortho Books, San Francisco, CA.

Wisley Handbook. 1985. *Ground Cover Plants*. Royal Horticultural Society, Wisley, England.

Common Name Index

186

Scientific Name Index

Zizia
  aptera 77
  aurea 77, 108
  trifoliata 77
Zostera marina 155

Subject Index

Allelopathy, definition 35
Annual, definition 10
Aquatic plants 147–162, Figs. 2-8, 11-1 to
  11-27
Asexual propagation, definition 37

Biennial, definition 10
Bog plants 162–168, Figs. 11-18 to 11-27

Chemical fertilizer 30
Classification of plants 13
Cold frame 44–45, Fig. 4-4
Color combinations 19–20
Common names, *see* Nomenclature
Competition, definition 34
Container gardening 28
Conservation
  definition 11
  practice of 36
Cultivar, definition 13
Cuttings, *see* propagation

Division, *see* propagation
Double digging 26

Ecotype, definition 34
Endemic plant, definition 9
Exotic, definition 9

Family, definition 14
Fern
  cultivation 121–124
  definition 120
  design 125
  morphology 120–121, Fig. 9-1
  photographs Figs. 9-2 to 9-17
Fertilizer 29–30
Flora, definition 9

Garden
  beginning 16, 24–25
  design 22–23
  irrigation 32–33
  mulching 31
  planning 17–23
  planting 30–31
  shade 21–22
  weeding 32
  wildflower, definition 10
  woodland 21–22
Gardening, organic 29–30
Genus (genera), definition 14
Grass family 112–117
Grasses
  design 111
  photographs Figs. 7-10, 7-11, 7-17, 8-1 to
    8-4
Groundcovers
  cultivation 137–138
  definition 137

Herbaceous, definition 10
Herbaceous perennial, definition 10
Herbicide 32
Humus 25
Hybrid, definition 14

Indigenous plant, definition 9
International Code of Botanical Nomencla-
  ture 12
International Code of Nomenclature for
  Cultivated Plants 13
Introduced species, definition 9
Irrigation 32–33

Light requirements 33, 48–49, 78

194